THE
HEALTH
FOOD
SHOPPER'S
GUIDE

THE HEALTH FOOD SHOPPER'S GUIDE

HARALD JAY TAUB

A DELL TRADE PAPERBACK

A DELL TRADE PAPERBACK BOOK

Published by
Dell Publishing Co., Inc.
1 Dag Hammarskjold Plaza
New York, New York 10017

Dell ® TM 681510, Dell Publishing Co., Inc.
Printed in the United States of America
First printing—September 1982

Library of Congress Cataloging in Publication Data

Taub, Harald J.
    The health food shopper's guide.

    1 Food, Natural.   2. Dietary supplements.   3. Herbal
cosmetics.   4. Exercise—Equipment and supplies.
I. Title.
TX741.T38   613.2   82-2528
ISBN 0-440-53349-X   AACR2

About the Author
Harald Jay Taub, before he retired, was Executive Editor
of *Prevention* magazine. Currently he is the editor of
the newsletter of the Institute of Nutritional Research
in Woodland Hills, California.

CONTENTS

INTRODUCTION:
THE HEALTH
FOOD
LABYRINTH

Well over three billion dollars a year is spent on the products of the health food industry by Americans seeking better health. Faced with choosing from among thousands of products, most health food customers are bewildered and seek advice from store personnel who don't know any more than they do. If you have ever had to buy tires for your car, think of how confused you were in trying to determine the best quality and price among just a few brands and types. Then consider that there are more kinds of vitamin E alone than there are of automobile tires, that vitamin E is only one of thousands of products, and that the descriptive terminology is every bit as mystifying and impossible to understand as that of the tire industry, and you begin to grasp just how tough it is to buy health food products intelligently.

Why should this be? Is obfuscation deliberately employed by the health food industry? It is, as much as in any other business. Health food is a business and its business ethics are no worse, yet certainly no better, than those of any other business. Just as meat packers classify inferior beef as "Grade A" and innocuous hard candies are sold at double the price as "cough drops," so the makers of health foods will use words like "natural" and "organic" to give an aura of quality and an unreasonably high mark-up to inferior products.

A specific, definable meaning of those marketing terms is as elusive as "first line" applied to tires.

Yet there are many fine health food products that give the consumer exactly what he thinks he is buying. The real problem is to be able to distinguish, and that is what this book should make possible, for the first time, for every devotee of health foods to do.

Nor is the quality maze the only one through which the consumer must pick his way. There can be enormous differences in price for the same product, depending upon where it is bought. For one good example, a bottle of pineapple juice combined with coconut milk is priced at $1.49 in health food stores, while the identical bottle sells for 89¢ in supermarkets. Why should there be such a difference? Is the health food merchant a gouger? On the contrary, he is often far from prosperous and sometimes finds it a struggle to pay the rent each month. He is often the victim of the distribution methods of his industry.

If we go back some thirty or forty years, we find that health food was then a very small business hardly worth noticing in the roster of American industry. Typically, an aging couple concerned about their own health would decide to open a little store that would give them a small semiretirement income. If they felt that vitamins and vegetable juices had benefited them, they would often decide that health food was a nice kind of business to go into. Having no idea how to go about it, they would respond to a magazine ad offering the advice and services of a distributor. The distributor would then ship them some $15,000 worth of varied health food products—enough to stock the shelves of a small store—and they were in business.

They knew little about health food and nothing about business and were completely dependent on the distributor's salesmen to tell them when to restock with how much and what new products to buy. And for this they paid a price. A full 25 percent of the price they paid for each vitamin bottle and every other product was the distributor's profit, in distinction to the other food industries, where a distributor rarely makes more than 5 percent on any item. Paying a high wholesale price, Mom and Pop naturally had to charge a high retail price, which was all right as long as they had no competition.

Today, however, public demand for health food products has increased so greatly that some are found in every supermarket and drugstore. But the supermarket gets them from a different distributor at a lower price and also takes a lower mark-up itself to encourage volume sales. Hence, if you can get the identical item in a supermarket, it is going to be cheaper. Today, Mom and Pop have mostly vanished from the health food business, having sold their stores to one of the many growing chain store operations or having been forced out of business by competition. But the old pricing practices persist. A multitude of small companies and individuals, breaking into the business, have no way to sell their products except through distributors who force prices up. Some companies are large enough to have their own sales forces and wholesale at lower prices—if they choose to do so. Discount retail chains have come into being, buying house brands directly from the few manufacturing laboratories that supply most of the products to most of the industry, regardless of the brand name. Direct mail operators advertise absurdly low prices on desirable products.

Can you take advantage of the discount prices that are becoming more available every day, or should you suspect that the merchandise is of lower quality? You have never, until now, had any way to make such a decision with any certainty that you were correct. The appropriate listing in the material following will give you enough information so that you can purchase health food shrewdly.

A major source of confusion is the abundance of periodicals and lecturers dealing with nutrition and health as their subject matter and sometimes misinforming great numbers of people, either deliberately or simply because they are misinformed themselves. Take the problem of the person who decides that he ought to add some supplemental magnesium to his diet. He is quite likely right.

Magnesium is an essential nutrient entering into many vital enzyme systems, yet easily destroyed by cooking and food processing. So what kind of magnesium supplement should a person take? The chief form of magnesium available as a health food is dolomite. It is nothing but limestone, crushed and formed into tablets. It was first advocated by the late J. I. Rodale, publisher of a mass circulation health magazine, as one of his periodic nutritional "discoveries." Rodale, whose profitable advertising pages were bought by a few direct mail advertisers completely dependent on the editorial power of his magazine for their business, felt an obligation to stimulate business for his captive advertisers by discovering new health products they could introduce and sell. He had read some old French books, circa 1900, that blamed prostate problems on a magnesium deficiency in the French food supply and described purportedly successful treatment of the prostate with magnesium sulfate. Rodale decided to "discover" magnesium, but could not advocate magnesium sulfate because it is a pharmaceutical product and besides, he had a strong prejudice against sulfur. He decided on dolomitic limestone, or what is now known as dolomite.

Unfortunately, the human stomach is not well adapted to the digestion of stone. People who tried dolomite and had enough morbid curiosity to examine their feces began finding whole undigested tablets of dolomite in their stool. Rodale would not acknowledge any error and persisted in his advocacy, and today every major manufacturer and distributor of food supplements numbers dolomite among his wares.

There is another health magazine that, notoriously, is so eager to sell advertising pages that it will publish just about anything an advertiser wishes, including articles written by the advertiser. In this magazine, a manufacturer of veterinary products who wanted to break into the health food business began touting one of his own products, magnesium chelated, or molecularly attached, to an amino acid, an elemental form of protein. This product, he claimed, is actually absorbed and utilized, unlike dolomite. A good public demand was soon whipped up, whereupon other manufacturers brought out their own forms of protein-chelated magnesium using different amino acids.

Today, if you go to buy some supplemental magnesium, you will find a wide variety of products to choose from, but how are you going to make your choice? You'll look up the magnesium listing that follows, of course.

Magnesium is one of the least confusing of health food products. Everyone agrees that it is good for you, and all you have to do is find a form of it that your body will actually use as it uses the magnesium in your food. With many others, though, the pundits of nutrition are in wild disagreement. For one good example, there is an enzyme known as superoxide dismutase, that has lately come into vogue. There are those who claim that it has indispensable life-saving properties, while others say that it induces the formation in the body of a poisonous material that could shatter your health. There are people with good scientific credentials on both sides of the debate, and which are you going to believe?

Here the author cannot claim any superscientific knowledge that will end the raging debates about dozens of health food products. All that can honestly be done is to make you aware of the pros and cons regarding any particular product so that you can make your own decisions more intelligently.

When it comes to potencies, we stand on firmer ground. There are, of course, potency wars among the makers of health food products, just as there are among the makers of pharmaceutical products like cold remedies and sleeping pills. It is all too easy to persuade people that if a little of anything is good, more must be better. If someone successfully sells a selenium supplement of 50 micrograms, someone else is sure to bring out another containing 100 micrograms. Is it really twice as good for you, or are you running a risk of overdosing yourself? You'd better know the answer to this one, because selenium and a number of other health food products, just like drugs, can become dangerous if used to excess. Is a 500 milligram tablet of vitamin C five times as good as a 100 milligram tablet? Do you really need an iron supplement and how big should it be? For questions such as these, there is solid information, and the answers can be given to you with assurance.

One very special characteristic of the health food industry is that, from manufacturer to retailer, the people who sell the products seldom give any indication of what purpose they are supposed to serve. This is because the industry is regulated by the Food and Drug Administration (FDA) and that agency has set up some very strict rules. If a vitamin company, in its advertising or on its product labels, were to say that vitamin C is good for the common cold, there is little doubt that the FDA would seize all that company's bottles of vitamin C and condemn them as mislabeled. In the old days such seizures occurred thousands of times, until all concerned learned their lesson.

Today, with only a very few exceptions, health food products bear only innocuous labels to which the FDA cannot possibly take exception. Neither the maker nor the retailer will make any statement about a 1,000 milligram tablet of vitamin C except that its purpose is to prevent a vitamin C deficiency. Actually, of course, 50 milligrams would be enough for that purpose and it is understood by everybody that when people buy 1,000 milligram tablets of vitamin C, it is to use it as a drug in the treatment of the common cold and other diseases. There is a legend, which may or may not be true, that an herb called goldenseal makes it impossible for the police to determine by a urinalysis that a person has been smoking marijuana. Probably a major portion of the goldenseal sold in health food stores is sold for this purpose, yet as far as the packer and retailer are concerned, its only purpose is for use as a herbal tea that contains no caffeine.

In practice, the strictness of the FDA's regulations has promoted as many abuses as it has curbed. People have learned to rely on publications and lecturers for information about what health food supplements and health foods are good for. Many of the informants are ill-informed themselves and many more are poor writers eager to make a buck and perfectly willing to exaggerate and sensation-alize in order to do so. Much of the information comes from fad-dists and would-be prophets who have strong convictions, but sometimes without any rational evidence for them.

If health food companies were able to make claims for which they can find some scientific backing, even though such claims might not be considered proven by the strict standards of the FDA, the result might well be far less mumbo-jumbo and expectation of miracles by the gullible. The millions of men who have taken vi-tamin E in the effort to heighten their sexual powers might never have been led into such folly if it had been possible to make claims for what some laboratory scientists have come to believe vitamin E will actually do.

Be that as it may, the fact is that many of the buying public use vitamin and mineral supplements and other health food prod-ucts as drugs to treat their diseases. It is time there was a systematic separation of the facts that confirm possible therapeutic values in these products from the wild fancies that run rampant among the millions of health food buyers.

To sum up, you can't just walk into a health food store and get only what you really want at a reasonable price, unless you have a guide. Here it is.

SECTION 1:
VITAMINS AND MINERALS

VITAMINS

VITAMIN A

During World War II, the British used a new device named radar
to detect German planes during night raids. Trying to keep radar
a secret, they circulated the story that their pilots and antiaircraft
gunners were spotting German planes with extraordinary night vision, developed by taking large quantities of vitamin A. That story
was completely and designedly false, but it gained wide currency
and persists to this day. When most people think of vitamin A,
they think of it only as an improver of night vision, which is true
only if your system is deficient in the vitamin. It does enter into
the visual organs that adapt the eye to changes of light, but there
is no way that any amount of vitamin A can improve your night
vision beyond its normal range.

What this vitamin will do is far more important to all of us. It
is integral to the structure of mucous membranes throughout the
body, and it is needed for those membranes to remain soft and
moist and capable of functioning in a healthy way. This affects
most of the body from the nose, mouth, and lungs to the digestive
tract and the genital organs. For functions varying from the ability
of the nose and lungs to expel invading bacteria and pollutants of

all kinds to the ability of the vagina to lubricate and cleanse itself, an adequate amount of vitamin A is required. The vitamin plays an important role in the body's absorption and use of proteins and also in the maintenance of healthy, attractive skin. Contrary to popular belief, however, taken dietarily it does not treat or cure acne. Recently there has appeared impressive scientific evidence that vitamin A has a protective effect against cancer of the mucous tissues of the lungs and the digestive tract.

Here it must quickly be pointed out that the dosage of vitamin A required for strong and definite anticancer activity would be highly toxic for many people. The National Cancer Institute is working hard to produce a synthetic form of vitamin A that will possess the anticancer activity but not the toxicity. But it has not yet been accomplished and with any form of vitamin A that is now available for purchase, very large daily doses threaten hearing loss, blindness, demineralization and weakening of the bones, severe headaches, and loss of hair.

Vitamin A is available in the following types and potencies:

CAROTENE. This is the yellow pigment that colors carrots, butter, squash, etc. It is not actually vitamin A, but is the provitamin that is converted in the liver into true vitamin A. There are some nutritional investigators who believe that a high dietary intake of nitrates, present in plant foods grown with high nitrate fertilizers, reduces the capacity of the liver to convert carotene into vitamin A. The amount of vitamin A that can be derived from any given quantity of carotene is indefinite, because it depends on the efficiency of conversion. Thus, for most people, it is less desirable as a vitamin A supplement. However, it conforms to the strictest vegetarian principles and is therefore preferred by many vegetarians.

CARROT OIL. This, again, is a plant product preferred by strict vegetarians. There are those who believe that the natural and best way to absorb vitamin A is in an oil medium. Carrot oil gives vegetarians the opportunity to take their vitamin A as an oil, but again, it is truly provitamin A and the amount of the vitamin obtained will vary from one person to another.

COD-LIVER OIL. This is one of the oldest of food supplements, and it is still used and trusted by millions. It is a good source of preformed vitamin A that can be absorbed intact into the blood-stream and function immediately, without requiring any transformation within the body. Compared to other fish-liver oils that are commonly used for vitamin A supplementation, cod-liver oil is of relatively low potency. It is therefore sometimes preferred for children, where overdosage is a danger. Children hate it. It has a strong fishy flavor and is easily regurgitated. It is not often packed in capsules because you really have to take it by the spoonful to obtain a significant amount of the vitamin. It also contains vitamin D and sometimes vitamin E.

HALIBUT-LIVER OIL. The liver of the halibut is far richer in vitamin A than that of the cod. The big advantage here is that the oil can be packed in very small capsules that can be swallowed easily by anybody without tasting the stuff. It is a good vitamin A supplement, but has become quite expensive. Many brands have consequently switched to cheaper fish-liver oils that are every bit as good, but simply cost less.

SHARK-LIVER OIL. As a source of preformed vitamin A, shark-liver oil is fully equal to halibut. It might even be considered superior in one respect. Most vitamin A is deactivated and rendered useless by exposure to ultraviolet light. About 35 percent of the shark-liver oil, however, is light stable and will not be harmed by ultraviolet. That superiority is more theoretical than actual, though, since all fish-liver oils are routinely packed in dark bottles to protect them from ultraviolet. Shark-liver oil costs less to produce and should sell for less in the store. If so, this is the one to buy. If it costs as much as halibut-liver oil, somebody is trying to rip you off.

MIXED FISH-LIVER OILS. Many people just don't like sharks and will neither swallow shark-liver oil nor eat a shark steak. To make a fish-liver oil vitamin A supplement that would be cheaper to produce, yet overcome the prejudice against sharks, many brands of mixed fish-liver oils have appeared on the market. They contain shark, halibut, and cod oil, but these are stated in small print and it is the "mixed" that the buyer sees. In terms of quality and potency, it is neither better nor worse than the single fish-liver oils. If it's cheaper, buy it.

VITAMIN A IN VEGETABLE OIL. This product is designed to appeal to those with a vegetarian prejudice against fish-liver oil who still want the preformed vitamin in preference to carotene, and prefer to take the vitamin dissolved in oil because they consider it more natural. Although it is not often stated on the label, it is usually laboratory-synthesized crystals of vitamin A that are then dissolved in vegetable oil. The activity and effects seem just about the same as those of natural vitamin A, but since there are many purchasers who believe that natural vitamins are superior to synthetics, it is cheating not to tell them what they are buying. This type of vitamin A costs less to produce than any fish-liver oil and should be sold for less.

WATER-DISPERSIBLE (OR MISCIBLE) VITAMIN A. There are a number of people whose digestive systems cannot handle oils and who therefore experience problems with oil-based vitamin A. For such people, a laboratory technique has been developed to extract the vitamin from its natural oil base and then mix it into materials that dissolve in water. It is sold as dry tablets. Salespeople sometimes claim that this type of vitamin A offers a special advantage because water is absorbed faster from the digestive tract than is oil. The reverse may be truer. The vitamin is not actually dissolved in water, though its separated crystals and prisms can be dispersed in water. It is entirely possible that in some cases the water is absorbed into the system, leaving the vitamin formations behind, in which case they might never be absorbed at all, but ultimately excreted instead. If it makes a difference to you, the water-dispersible vitamin could be either natural or synthetic. If it is identified as vitamin A palmitate, it is derived from natural fish-liver oil. However, by the time it gets to you in a water-dispersible tablet, it has undergone so much processing that it can hardly be called natural anymore, in spite of its origin. Any other identifying scientific name would indicate that the vitamin is laboratory synthesized.

Vitamin A is sold in the following potencies:

2,000 International Units (IU). This dosage is intended for very small children, who can rarely be gotten to take anything of the sort without a struggle. It is not very popular nor is it widely sold.

5,000 IU. This is a low potency intended for use by children under twelve and the elderly, both of which groups are quite vulnerable to vitamin A toxicity. It is enough to insure against deficiency with virtually no danger attached.

10,000 IU. This potency is the one most widely bought and used by adults in normal health. If there are no unusual requirements because of illness and no abnormal metabolic demands, 10,000 units should provide excellent day-to-day maintenance of a good store of vitamin A that is still not so much as to threaten any unpleasant consequences.

20,000 IU. This is the point at which the daily use of vitamin A for good nutrition and the protection of health begins to change into use of the vitamin as a drug for therapeutic purposes. Not that it is necessarily wrong to use it in that way. If you are a smoker, if you easily contract colds, flu, or bronchitis, if your eyes have difficulty in adapting to changes of light, and so on, this higher daily dose of vitamin A might well be beneficial. Twenty thousand units is not considered a toxic dose, though a few unusual people might experience the symptoms of toxicity at this level. For practically all of us, it is perfectly safe, though for many it is more than is actually required and therefore a waste of money.

25,000 IU. This is the highest potency of vitamin A that is now permitted to be sold. It will not do any harm to most people, though it should never be given to children or to those past sixty. There are quite a few people who not only want this high a dose of vitamin A, but will take anywhere from two to four capsules a day. Why? For the most part, because various publications whose primary mission is to promote sales for their advertisers tell their readers that they need enormous quantities and that there is no danger of toxicity in natural vitamin A. That is obviously false. If you take in more vitamin A, natural or synthetic, than you require, your liver will store the surplus. When the stored surplus grows big enough, the liver is damaged. A great deal of vitamin A may well be called for to treat some health problems, but if you plan to take any more than 25,000 units a day, it is seriously suggested that you do it under medical supervision.

THE B-COMPLEX VITAMINS

The numerous vitamins of the B complex are grouped together because they tend to occur together in foods and to work together in human metabolism. Most of them function within our bodies as enzymes or coenzymes in carbohydrate metabolism. That simply means that they must be present in the body for the transformation to take place that converts starches and sugars into energy. Since the chief and nearly the sole food of the brain is the form of sugar known as glucose, which is the end product of carbohydrate metabolism, it is apparent that the B-complex vitamins are essential to proper functioning of the brain. They are equally essential to the nervous system generally.

Does this mean that an increased consumption of the B-complex vitamins will lead to an improvement in the mental faculties? Most nutritionists do not think so, though there are reputable investigators who believe exactly that. We all understand, of course, that Shakespeare wrote his tragedies and Newton formulated calculus without ever taking a vitamin supplement. Yet it can also be argued that both of these superior intellects were nourished on coarse, whole-grain breads and yeasty beer, that their diets lacked the huge quantities of sugar (a great consumer of B vitamins) that we use today, and that generally their B vitamin status was higher than ours.

During the past twenty years, a group of psychiatrists has been employing what is called megavitamin therapy, involving the administration of enormous doses of selected B vitamins and vitamin C, in the treatment of schizophrenia and similar problems of the mentality and nervous system. Their basic concept is that in some cases these mental disturbances represent a metabolic failure in the use of the vitamin leading to a kind of pellagra, a vitamin deficiency disease that results in insanity. Because of the intensive publicity that has been given to megavitamin therapy, many people have come to feel that they require large daily supplements of the B-complex vitamins. In response to the demand, the potencies available have been growing year by year and there is no end in sight.

Although the B-complex vitamins are usually consumed as a group, each of them is also sold as an isolated vitamin supplement. They are therefore individually listed below.

VITAMIN B_1. Known also as thiamine, this vitamin is essential for healthy nerves. The deficiency disease, beriberi, which is characterized by inflammation and degeneration of the nerves, is induced by a lack of vitamin B_1 and is cured by this vitamin. It does not take very much of the vitamin to make the difference. Perhaps 2 milligrams a day, easily obtained from food, is all that is needed to prevent beriberi.

Thiamine also enters importantly into body functions having nothing to do with beriberi, however. It has been found to be directly connected to the muscle tone of the digestive system, through which an adequate supply of vitamin B_1 aids both digestion and elimination. It is necessary for normal growth and appetite, and for these reasons it is often an ingredient of tonics. The presence or absence of this vitamin can have a decided effect on digestion, particularly of carbohydrates, but also, to a lesser extent, of fats and proteins. And of course, it is essential for healthy nerves.

In a healthy person, 2 milligrams a day should be more than enough to fulfill all the metabolic roles of vitamin B_1. Even at this low requirement, however, supplementation is often of value. Food content of the vitamin is easily destroyed by cooking. The refining of wheat strips away the thiamine content. In fact, it is easy to eat a diet that is practically devoid of vitamin B_1 and you can become deficient in this vitamin if you work at it. One of the best ways to induce a deficiency is to be a heavy user of alcohol, which destroys thiamine at a rapid rate.

Most vitamin B_1, even though it may be called "natural" or "organic," is actually laboratory synthesized. If it is offered in any multivitamin or other kind of dry tablet, it is certainly synthetic. About the only way to get truly natural vitamin B_1, if that is what you want, is to take supplements of a nutritional yeast or desiccated liver, both of which have a naturally high content of the vitamin. And even the yeast is questionable, since it has become a common practice to feed synthetic B vitamins to the growing yeast cultures in order to raise their vitamin potency. Whether the resulting high-potency yeast offers natural or synthetic vitamins is debatable.

Vitamin B_1 is sold in a variety of potencies:

25 milligram and 50 milligram tablets. These are pushed by the salespeople of stores as insurance against depletion. The argument goes that since vitamin B_1 is soluble in water, it is quickly filtered out of the bloodstream by the kidneys and excreted. It is true enough, as far as it goes, but of only limited validity. The fact is that this vitamin is used at the cellular level by the body. The cells rapidly extract as much as they require from the blood. That the surplus is excreted is no loss since the body cannot use it anyway. There is no need for vitamin B_1 to circulate continuously in the bloodstream.

100 milligram, 250 milligram, and 500 milligram tablets. These potencies are also available. There is no danger in their use, but they are an utter waste of money unless they have been recommended by a physician for some therapeutic purpose. Such high potencies might be used in the treatment of alcoholism or as an adjunct to megavitamin therapy. They serve no purpose other than such special therapeutic ones.

VITAMIN B_2. Vitamin B_2, known as riboflavin, is the vitamin in which you are least likely to be deficient. Cooking does not destroy it nor will it dissolve away in water. A remarkably stable vitamin, it occurs naturally in milk, eggs, poultry, fish, and leafy green vegetables, among others. These foods easily supply the 2 milligrams a day or so that represent a normal metabolic requirement.

In the modern Western world deficiencies of vitamin B_2 occur only as a result of particular diseases, notably thyroid insufficiency or inability to absorb the vitamin B_2 that is normally present in the diet. Riboflavin deficiencies do also occur rather widely among children of the poor who do not get enough milk to drink.

The most common signs of vitamin B_2 deficiency are a swollen tongue, tending to be purplish in color, and inflammation of the cornea of the eye. Other than to correct a deficiency, there is really no particular reason why you should require a vitamin B_2 supplement. They are available, however, in potencies up to 100 milligrams. Save your money.

VITAMIN B_3. This vitamin has a multiple identity. Originally known as nicotinic acid, it had its name changed to niacin, which is the identical material. In a slightly different chemical form, it is niacinamide, and this also has an accepted second name, which is nicotinamide. The two chemicals and the four names by which they are known are all vitamin B_3. Let us deal with them as niacin and niacinamide, the names by which they are most commonly called.

Either one can prevent or cure pellagra, a deficiency disease that stems essentially from a lack of tryptophan, a constituent of protein in the diet. It is not easy to eliminate tryptophan from the diet, but if you eat no grain but corn and no meat, milk, or eggs, it can be done. Within the body, tryptophan is converted into niacin. But if you eat no tryptophan and have no other source of niacin, you will develop pellagra, a condition characterized by diarrhea, dermatitis, and especially by dementia. To this day there are those who claim that many of the inmates of mental institutions are actually suffering from pellagra, not because their diets are so poor, but because they are metabolically unable to absorb or synthesize vitamin B_3. In fact, the celebrated megavitamin therapy employed by a substantial group of physicians and psychiatrists has at its core the concept that schizophrenia and some other diseases are subtle forms of pellagra requiring for treatment huge doses of vitamin B_3.

There is no doubt that vitamin B_3 does have important effects on the brain. It is a coenzyme that enters importantly into control of the amount of glucose in the blood, glucose being the basic food of the brain. Too much glucose supplied to the brain induces sluggishness, apathy, and even coma, as in diabetes. Too little results in depression and irrational emotional states. So maintenance of proper levels of glucose in the blood is obviously of prime importance to the mentality.

Another factor in body chemistry that affects the mind is the amount of histamine in the blood. Recall how drowsy you become when you treat a cold with an antihistamine, and you can appreciate that too little histamine in the blood can be as uncomfortable as too much and can have a distorting effect on mentality. Where such a condition is chronic, vitamin B_3 can improve it. This is believed to be a part of its role in the treatment of mental disease.

The vitamin also affects other brain chemicals. For all these roles, it is equally effective whether it is niacin or niacinamide. There are, however, other functions that are fulfilled by niacin in which niacinamide does not participate. When cholesterol levels in the blood are excessively high, niacin is the treatment of choice of many physicians. For several months, at least, niacin will exert a continuous cholesterol-lowering effect, and it seems to do this at least as well as any other drug employed, without inducing any serious or harmful side effects. Niacinamide will not obtain the same results. Niacin also improves the flow of the blood by widening the passages of the blood vessels. This can be important, especially to the elderly who often develop problems related to an insufficient supply of blood to the extremities. Defects in hearing and vision, cold hands and feet, leg cramps, and even senility have all been related to an insufficient supply of blood to the extremities. Niacin does improve that supply.

However, by that very property of opening up the blood vessels, niacin does have one effect that for some people is decidedly unpleasant. It will sometimes induce a flushing that involves a temporary reddening of the face, neck, and back. It also creates a sensation of warmth that for some people can be a very uncomfortable burning sensation, as well as itching and prickling. This does not happen to everyone nor is it always uncomfortable. Some people experience the flush as a pleasant sensation of warmth, and others don't feel it at all. It must be considered, however, when you decide whether to obtain your vitamin B_3 as niacin or as niacinamide.

Because B_3 plays a key role in the increasingly popular megavitamin therapies, it is available in very high potencies indeed, and even what might be called low potencies by contrast are pretty high. Even a 50 milligram tablet is hard to find because the consumer demand is for tablets of at least 100 milligrams and frequently much more. A couple of years ago, the highest potency obtainable in a single tablet was 500 milligrams. At this writing it is 1,500 milligrams and the end is not yet in sight. In the case of vitamin B_3, though, there is frequently good reason for taking such high potencies because they may well serve a constructive purpose provided you use the correct form of the vitamin.

Do not bother asking whether the supplement you buy is natural or synthetic. In the high potencies being offered today, there is no natural source. It is all synthesized in a pharmaceutical laboratory and seems to be quite as effective and useful as the vitamin you obtain from milk, eggs, or nutritional yeast.

50 milligram tablets. In this potency, the tablet may be either niacin or niacinamide without any difference whatsoever in its activity or in the function it performs within the body. It is a good protective dosage of vitamin B$_3$ that will help the body maintain proper levels of glucose in the bloodstream and continuation of normal mental functioning.

100 milligram tablets. Perhaps the most desirable and effective use of vitamin B$_3$ in this potency is the relief of the pain of osteoarthritis. For this purpose niacinamide is far more effective than niacin and if you are buying vitamin B$_3$ to treat your arthritis pains, you should make sure that niacinamide is what you are getting. Some doctors consider it as effective as cortisone, or nearly so, yet without any of the very unpleasant side effects of the steroid hormone. You can take 100 milligram tablets as often as you like, and they will not do you any harm.

250 milligram tablets. At this potency level and above, be very careful and make certain that you are getting only niacin and never niacinamide. The good reasons are that an excess of niacinamide can cause liver damage whereas niacin cannot, and that the effects for which you would want high potencies of vitamin B$_3$ are produced only by niacin. The 250 milligram tablet is very popular. It is taken three times daily with meals, for a total of 750 milligrams a day. At this level of intake, the vitamin will have a definite effect on the size of the internal passages (lumen) of blood vessels, dilating them so that they will transport more blood with less pressure. There is also frequently a reduction in the amount of cholesterol in the bloodstream that is induced by niacin at levels of 750 milligrams a day or more.

For those with blood pressure problems, an intake of niacin at this level makes good sense. Since we all tend to have problems with our blood pressure as we get older, that makes the 250 milligram tablet a good choice for many of us. In many people this potency *will* tend to produce flushing symptoms during the first month or so of use. The skin turns red, particularly in the blush area, and there is a sensation of warmth that can become intense enough to be very uncomfortable. If you get flushing symptoms and they bother you, try taking your niacin in the middle of a meal to reduce or eliminate the flushing. Do not let a sales clerk in a store persuade you to substitute niacinamide, which does not cause flushing—it will not dilate your blood vessels, either.

500 milligrams or more. At such high potencies, you are really taking your vitamin B_3 in medical doses. It may not do you any harm, but there is no reason for such a high intake unless it has been recommended to you for a specific medical problem by the health professional who is caring for you. Such problems could relate to blood pressure and the condition of the arteries, mental aberrations, and some other serious illnesses on which vitamin B_3 has been shown to have a biochemical effect. With serious problems of this nature, however, self-treatment is usually useless and sometimes dangerous.

At potencies of 500, 1,000 or 1,500 milligrams, or anything higher, more is definitely not better unless a doctor has found it so in you after careful testing. If you are just guessing about your own condition, at the very least the 500–1,500 milligram tablet is a waste of money. As a carefully supervised psychiatric therapy, doses of 3,000 milligrams a day and more have been found of decided value in some cases.

VITAMIN B_6. This vitamin, commonly referred to as pyridoxine, might be any one of five different chemical compounds, all of which resemble one another and all of which have identical biochemical effects within the human body. Any one of these compounds can be and is identified as vitamin B_6 and there is no reason to believe that any one of them is in any way preferable to the others.

Vitamin B_6 might well be referred to as the female vitamin. Although it is essential to both sexes, of course, some of this vitamin's most important and desired effects are uniquely female. When a pregnant woman suffers from eclampsia, a particularly painful kind of cramps that some women experience while carrying, it is often vitamin B_6 that gets rid of the eclampsia and makes the pregnancy more tolerable. Menstrual cramps, prolonged and difficult menstruation, and premenstrual tension and waterlogging of the tissues all have been found to respond in many cases to an increase of vitamin B_6 in the diet. It has also been found that women using contraceptive pills tend to become deficient in vitamin B_6 and should routinely increase their daily intake of pyridoxine as long as they continue using the contraceptive.

The functions of the vitamin are not confined to female problems, however. Basically, it is a coenzyme that enters into many enzyme systems of the body, all of them concerned with the body's handling and use of proteins. Through its influence on proteins and metabolism, pyridoxine enters into such diverse bodily functions as the synthesis of hemoglobin, the oxygen-carrying material of the red blood cells, and the manufacture of important brain chemicals such as serotonin and dopamine. Thus the vitamin is of enormous importance and a deficiency is something to be feared.

Because pyridoxine interacts with vitamin B_3 and thus enters into megavitamin therapy, many people have come to believe that large quantities of vitamin B_6 offer special advantages. Not so. Even as it is used with the ultrahigh potencies employed by the megavitamin therapists, there is rarely any employment or recommendation of anything more than 100 milligrams a day to interact with three or more grams of niacin. Aside from such treatment of aberrations in brain chemistry, the maximum requirement for pyridoxine would be 50 milligrams a day, used by some doctors in the treatment of female problems. For the maintenance of health, one would not require more than 5 milligrams a day. Yet the vitamin is sold in potencies ranging from 25 milligrams per tablet all the way up to the utterly ridiculous potency of 1,500 milligrams. Like most vitamins, B_6 is simply excreted if it enters the body in amounts greater than can be used. An excess will not do you any physical harm. It is an utter waste of money, however, to use anything more than 50 milligrams or so that will keep a woman more comfortable during pregnancy and her menstrual periods.

VITAMIN B_{12}. Currently, the use of this vitamin has become a fad and it is being recommended for just about any unlikely illness you can imagine. One influential lay nutritionist says that direct applications of vitamin B_{12} will heal cold sores. It is being used for insomnia, as an aid to weight reduction, and a treatment for senility. There is no good reason to suppose the vitamin is of the slightest use with these problems. It is simply a fad like the use of penicillin twenty years ago.

Fundamentally, vitamin B_{12} in incredibly small quantities functions within the bone marrow in the production of red blood cells. A deficiency will cause pernicious anemia but since our actual requirement is only about 1 microgram (a thousandth of a milligram) a day and the liver is able to store up to a three-year supply, pernicious anemia is very unlikely to actually occur. It does occasionally strike a strict vegetarian because the food sources of vitamin B_{12} are exclusively animal. The vegetarian who permits himself dairy products and eggs is in no danger. The only other cause of pernicious anemia is a lack of another vitamin, folic acid, that facilitates the absorption of vitamin B_{12}, or occasionally a failure of the digestive system. Pernicious anemia hardly occurs anymore in the United States and Canada and for practical purposes represents no reason at all for supplementation with vitamin B_{12}.

The vitamin has, however, been found of some value in a number of nervous problems related to those particular nerves that have a myelin sheath. Myelin is a combination of fat and protein that coats some of the important nerves of the body and must itself be maintained in healthy condition for the nerves to function properly. Apparently vitamin B_{12} is essential to myelin and through it affects a good part of the nervous system. Inasmuch as any lapse or failure of a nerve can cause a health problem, it is apparent that such diverse problems as mental confusion and loss of hearing or vision, muscular weakness, and loss of coordination can all, realistically, stem from a failure of vitamin B_{12} absorption, which in turn leads to a weakness in the myelin. As a result, we have had reports that vitamin B_{12} has successfully treated almost every affliction of the human body. It would seem, however, that what the vitamin actually treats is the myelin sheath of the nerves and that it can help other illnesses only when they are caused by nervous weakness.

When vitamin B_{12} is used therapeutically, it is administered by injection. Getting it from tablets or capsules will only increase the reserve in your liver but will not increase the amount circulating in the blood.

Although supplements of vitamin B_{12} are available, there is little reason to suppose they are of any value to anyone. As much as you can obtain from your food or from a multivitamin is as much as your body is going to utilize.

VITAMIN B_{15}. This is not a vitamin at all. It is a compound, calcium pangamate, that was isolated in the course of research on Laetrile and that was taken up by the Russians. It cannot be classified as a vitamin because there is no disease or health problem whatsoever that is caused by a lack of calcium pangamate in the diet. It does seem to be of some value to the health of many. Since the U.S. Food and Drug Administration does not accept it as a vitamin or permit it to be sold as one, it is sold under a variety of trade names that contain No. 15 or in other ways suggest that the consumer is buying vitamin B_{15}.

In the Russian medical literature this product is credited with improving the breathing of asthmatics and others with breathing problems, with improving the oxygenation of tissues, and thus increasing energy and reducing fatigue. The medical studies on which these conclusions are based would seem to be valid enough for the Russian product. However, it is not being imported into the United States. What is available in the health food stores is a variety of products that American manufacturers consider reasonable replicas of the Russian products although they themselves vary considerably one from another. Thus, even if we accept the Russian medical studies and their conclusions as to the health values of vitamin B_{15}, they do not tell us anything about what we can expect from what we are actually able to buy here in the U.S. There is no government standard of identity, which means that if I wanted to mix aspirin with confectioner's sugar and call it vitamin B_{15}, there would be nothing to stop me.

If you could get the genuine Russian calcium pangamate, or vitamin B_{15}, it might well offer health benefits. What you can buy in the United States might be the same product, it might be something else that is just as good, or it might be worthless. There is no way that anyone can tell.

VITAMIN B_{17}. This is merely an alternative name that is sometimes used for the supposed cancer remedy, Laetrile. The claim of the advocates of Laetrile is that this material, present naturally within the pits of apricots and peaches and perhaps of other fruits as well, is actually an essential nutrient, without which people contract cancer and die. Qualified scientific investigations to date have found Laetrile ineffective as a treatment for cancer, although there are thousands of individuals who will swear that Laetrile has saved their lives or the lives of friends or relatives. We do not propose to discuss cancer remedies as such. We can only say that if you wish to obtain Laetrile or vitamin B_{17}, it is done most easily in Mexico and it is not much more difficult in the state of Nevada. Legally, it is not obtainable anywhere without the prescription of a physician. There is a contraband traffic of which we have no specific knowledge.

BIOTIN. There are no supplements of pure biotin available in your health food store for two very good reasons: it is, gram for gram, the most expensive vitamin that a manufacturer might have to buy; and no one has yet come up with anything resembling evidence that a supplement of biotin would be of any particular use to anyone. The fact is that we obtain most of the biotin in our systems from bacteria that we carry within the gut. Such bacteria synthesize the vitamin and make it freely available to us. We also obtain small quantities of it from the food that we eat. It is of benefit to our nerves and it is extremely unlikely you will ever be deficient in biotin. About the only ways in which you could develop a biotin deficiency would be if an antibiotic killed all the biotin-producing bacteria in your system or if you had a passion for raw eggs. Neutralized by cooking, a material in raw egg white called avidin does destroy biotin.

One way of recognizing the better multivitamin supplements is that they do contain a few micrograms of the expensive biotin. If you think you need some, one of these multivitamin supplements will certainly supply enough.

CHOLINE. Little is written about choline and many vitamin enthusiasts have never even heard the name. Yet this member of the B-complex group of vitamins is of enormous importance. It is directly concerned with the transmission of nerve impulses. Our nerves are electrical conductors, carrying incredibly weak electric impulses between the brain and the rest of the body. Unlike a wiring system, the nerves are not continuous in structure but consist of small lengths of tissue with gaps between them, called synapses. In order to carry an impulse along a nerve we must keep bridging synapses, which we do with a material called acetylcholine, and then destroying those bridges with an enzyme known as cholinesterase.

As you have certainly guessed, choline is the vital element in this process.

If there is a shortage of choline, the transmission becomes erratic, too weak at one moment, too strong the next. There are physicians of good background and reputation who believe that hyperkinesia in children, recognized by inability to concentrate and excessive physical activity, is caused by aberrations in the production of acetylcholine and its neutralizing enzyme. Those who believe that food dyes and preservatives cause the problem, for instance, feel that these food chemicals destroy choline within the body.

It would seem, then, that one ought to be able to solve this and many other problems of nervous conduction by the very simple method of adding a supplement of choline to the diet. There have been magazine and newspaper articles that carried this clear implication and the manufacturers of vitamin products have responded with readily available supplements of choline in potencies ranging anywhere from 25 milligrams to 150 milligrams per tablet. There is only one thing wrong with such supplements. Except to an extremely limited extent, the human body will not absorb them. It would be fine if we could increase our supply of choline simply by taking a tablet with lunch. Alas, it doesn't work that way. If your doctor thinks that your supply of choline should have a radical increase, he will give it to you with an intravenous injection. There is no way that you will ever get it from food or from food supplements.

You may need it. You may well benefit by it. But you will never be able to buy it in a store or fortify your reserve the easy way.

FOLIC ACID. This lesser known but highly important vitamin of the B-complex group is one of the few vitamins in which deficiency is actually common. We do not need much of it. For a healthy adult the daily requirement is actually less than a half a milligram. Yet the vitamin is so vulnerable to losses by cooking, exposure to sunlight, and the processing of food, that informed estimates calculate that as much as half the population may be deficient in folic acid.

The two areas affected by such a deficiency are the body's ability to form new red blood cells and the functioning of the brain and nervous system. Folic acid facilitates the absorption and activity of vitamin B_{12} and a lack of folic acid is often the true cause of a B_{12} deficiency. Therefore the treatment of pernicious anemia requires B_{12} and folic acid together, and while folic acid alone is often enough to bring about a remission, it is the B_{12} that is needed to actually change and improve the blood-forming cells of the bone marrow.

A lack of folic acid can also manifest itself in a wide variety of mental and emotional disturbances. Manic-depressive episodes have been attributed to insufficient supplies of this vitamin and have been successfully treated with the vitamin. Least obviously, but perhaps most important, folic acid is essential to the process by which the nucleic acids, DNA and RNA, reproduce themselves and the patterns they carry, which govern exactly how each cell is to grow, function, and ultimately die. When the instructions carried in the nucleic acids start to blur or distort after many reproductions, cellular changes are induced that become degenerative disease or symptoms of general aging. Such changes are subtle. It would be difficult to pin them down as effects of a deficiency of folic acid. Yet there they are and surely it cannot hurt to make certain you have enough folic acid in your daily diet to stall off these changes as long as possible.

Folic acid supplements are available individually or, frequently, in combination with vitamin B_{12}. Either is an acceptable way to supplement the diet. The folic acid potencies range from 100 micrograms to 500. Unless you have a special purpose in mind, 400 micrograms a day would seem to be just about the most desirable level of supplementation.

INOSITOL. This member of the B-complex vitamin group is one about which little is actually known. Its biochemical activity has not been well studied and while there is a fair amount of theorizing about the vitamin, there is little hard fact. It is usually thought of in combination with choline. Both are lipotropic, which is to say that they have an effect on fats and oils. Both have been found to reduce cholesterol concentrations in the bloodstream, and the vitamins are used primarily for that purpose, which is why they are often combined in a single supplement. The effect on blood lipids is not a strong one. There are other ways, including niacin, that are more effective. If your problem is cholesterol reduction, inositol, with or without choline, is far from being your best choice.

A more valuable role for inositol, though not adequately studied as yet, is its effect as a tranquilizer. Psychiatrists who have used it claim it is every bit as good as Valium or any other standard pharmaceutical tranquilizer for calming the nerves and alleviating anxiety. Taken before bedtime it seems to be an effective sleep inducer. Generally, it is said to have a benign effect on nervous systems jangled by anxiety or too easily overstimulated.

Inositol as a supplement can be purchased in potencies of 250, 500, and 650 milligrams. Since its purposes are limited, you can easily tell with a little experimentation whether you are getting the desired effect. Start with the lowest potency, if that doesn't help, move up a step. There is no particular danger in overdosing, but neither is there anything desirable about it. The best policy is to find the lowest dosage that will do the job you want done.

NIACIN. See VITAMIN B₃ above.

NIACINAMIDE. See VITAMIN B₃ above.

PANTOTHENIC ACID. This vitamin is certainly essential. It is a constituent of coenzyme A which is fundamental in the production of energy. Without coenzyme A we could not live, and without pantothenic acid we would not synthesize coenzyme A. However, you are already getting as much pantothenic acid as you require. The vitamin is produced in just about all living cells. It is quite stable and we obtain it from all our foods. When scientists want to discover the effects of a deficiency of this vitamin, they find it nearly impossible, even under controlled laboratory conditions, to induce such a deficiency in their test animals. So all we can really say is that you need it, but you already have it. To buy more would be pointless. If you happen to see it on a store shelf, stay away from it. It won't do a thing for you.

PARA-AMINOBENZOIC ACID (PABA). This vitamin is just about the best sunscreen known and one that can be used without ill effects. It is therefore a common ingredient of sunburn preventives, and that is just about the only practical use to which anyone has yet put PABA. For a while it had an unjustified reputation for restoring gray hair to its youthful color, but while it did this neat trick for rats it never did manage to do it for human beings. Since a deficiency would be hard to find, you really have no need whatsoever for PABA as a food supplement.

PYRIDOXINE. See VITAMIN B₆ above.

RIBOFLAVIN. See VITAMIN B₂ above.

THIAMINE. See VITAMIN B_3 above.

B-COMPLEX VITAMIN COMBINATIONS. The potency wars for the consumer dollar have nowhere led to fiercer battles than in the marketing of the B-complex vitamins. Somehow the vitamin buyer has let himself be persuaded that if it's bigger, it must be better. This has led to vitamin B potencies that are astronomically high in terms of the actual needs of a person, and which, instead of shrinking to reasonable dimensions, keep growing larger every day. In the not very distant past, a normal B-complex supplement contained, per tablet, perhaps one milligram of vitamin B_1, two of riboflavin, and not more than 10 or 15 milligrams of vitamin B_3. Today it takes some searching to find a tablet containing less than 25 milligrams of each of these vitamins. Will it be of any greater benefit to you? Hardly. It is manufactured because the average customer will pay a much higher price for it and think he is getting a bargain.

What do you actually need in the way of a B-complex supplement? Not very much. As described above, there can be very good reasons why you would want or even require high-potency supplementation in one or two of the numerous B vitamins. Since it is well established scientifically that the vitamins of the B-complex group interact biochemically and reinforce one another's therapeutic value, it makes good sense when you take any one of the B vitamins to also take a reasonably small quantity of B-complex vitamins that will interact with it. That is about the only actual value that a B-complex supplement offers you. You are not suffering from any B-complex deficiency. No one ever has. Each of the B vitamins has its own biochemical roles and health values, but the body can use only a limited amount and will simply excrete the rest. It should be apparent that high-potency B-complex supplements give you nothing for the extra cost except extra wastage.

Let's compare it to driving a car. Your car needs oil, gasoline, tires, water in the cooling system, etc. Each works better when you have the others as well. But if you buy 50 gallons of gasoline at one time and fifty tires and 50 quarts of oil, there is still no way that your car can use any of it beyond its capacity.

Slow or sustained or delayed release. It is readily admitted that whatever your body does not use from your B-complex tablet is going to be excreted. That simple fact, however, has been turned into a sales argument. Since the B vitamins are water-soluble, it goes, the water that contains them is filtered out of the bloodstream by the kidneys and excreted in the urine. Therefore, in order to keep the B vitamins circulating in the bloodstream and supplying your needs all day long, you must either keep taking tablets four or five times a day or else take one of the slow-release preparations that slow up the rate at which the vitamins are actually digested and assimilated into the blood. It sounds quite reasonable if you don't have any knowledge of what actually goes on.

In actuality, B vitamins when in good supply will be incorporated into the cells and tissues in sufficient quantity for at least twenty-four hours of activity and perhaps two or three times that much. A surplus remaining in the bloodstream will be stored in the liver for future use and it is only beyond that banking of reserves that B vitamins pass into the urine and are excreted. This means, simply, that there is no reason to take a B-complex supplement more than once a day and that slow release serves no purpose whatsoever. As a matter of fact, it may well have a negative effect. The slow release is accomplished by coating each tablet with some material that will not break down in the stomach and will not yield to the stomach acids. But the stomach acidity is the normal digestive medium for the B vitamins to accomplish the necessary transformations and be assimilated into the blood through the stomach wall. If digestion is delayed until the tablet reaches the duodenum, it is then surrounded by an alkaline medium that is fine for dissolving the slow-release coating, but not so fine for digesting B vitamins. Taken in slow-release tablets, most of your B-vitamin supplement never gets into your bloodstream because it is not digested.

The conclusion: slow-release coatings on your B-vitamin supplements cost you more money and give you less. Avoid them.

TYPES OF B-VITAMIN SUPPLEMENTS.

Brewer's yeast. The yeast is a bacterial organism that is of great value to man in a number of ways. In a process known as fermentation, yeasts transform sugar into alcohol and thus turn grape juice into wine. The particular strain of yeast that is used in brewing beer, which transforms grain sugars into alcohol, is known as brewer's yeast. Because it is a high-protein material, waste brewer's yeast has been used as a cheap animal feed in laboratories, and it is through this use that it was discovered that brewer's yeast contains relatively rich supplies of every single one of the B-complex vitamins. It also contains certain special minerals that are of particular value in the human diet, a form of protein that may be of particular significance to humans, and generally seems almost to have been designed to supply man with a superfood. That it is also unpleasantly bitter to the taste and a copious former of gas in the digestive tract explains why brewer's yeast is not used as human food but is largely irrelevant to this discussion.

Brewer's yeast was the original choice of those progenitors of today's health food devotees who felt that man should improve his nutrition by supplementing his diet with natural foods naturally high in vitamins and minerals. The original supplements of brewer's yeast in tablets or capsules provided such potencies as 1 milligram of thiamine and 2 milligrams of riboflavin per tablet. Then it was discovered that if the brewer's yeast was cultured specifically to be a source of B-complex vitamins, you could simply feed more of any particular vitamin to the yeast and wind up with a yeast that had a higher content of that vitamin. It is now possible to get brewer's yeast supplements that will furnish up to 10 milligrams of vitamin B_1 and proportionately more of the other B-complex vitamins.

Needless to say, the B vitamins in such brewer's yeast supplements, are, in fact, the synthetic B vitamins that were fed to the yeast cultures, and there is no meaningful distinction between "natural" and "synthetic."

What brewer's yeast does offer the consumer in B-complex vitamins is a more realistic range of potencies and low cost. It is a good buy.

Desiccated liver. The liver, in humans and many other mammals, is a natural storehouse for the entire B complex of vitamins. Thus, frequently including beef or calf liver in the diet would be one good way of insuring that the diet is high in B vitamins. Liver has other nutritional virtues as well, and it has seemed desirable to many to include some liver in the diet every day. That was far more feasible in the old days when practically no one ate liver and butchers used to give it to their customers as food for their cats. In any case—no one, not even the cat—eats whole liver daily, even though there are many people who believe that it is advantageous to do so. What they do is take desiccated liver, which is simply raw liver dehydrated to perhaps one fourth of its original weight, then pulverized, with the resulting powder made into tablets or sold in jars.

Desiccated liver is a reliable source of all the vitamins of the B complex. Since the potency depends on such variables as the diet of the parent steer, the actual quantity of vitamins will vary from one tablet to another and it is impossible to make an assay that will stand up under inspection. Consequently, no claim for B vitamin potencies is ever made on a desiccated liver label. Nor would the potencies ever be high if someone did make an assay. Yet the vitamins are there, and for many people they are quite as much B complex as is needed. Desiccated liver is not quite as potent or calculable a source of B-complex vitamins as brewer's yeast. It remains a good source.

Nutritional yeast. Because brewer's yeast has a bitter flavor that makes it unpleasant to many people, and also because it is a copious producer of gas in the digestive tract, enterprising vitamin companies have sought and have found several other strains of yeast that offer the same nutritional characteristics as brewer's yeast but are pleasanter to take. They are seldom identified by name (which would be meaningless to most people anyway), but all are identified as nutritional yeast and are just about the same in worthiness. After all, as vitamin packaging has developed, the nutritional value of yeast depends less on what it contains naturally than it does on what you put into it.

Nutritional yeast, like brewer's yeast, can be cultured to contain anywhere from 1 to 10 milligrams of thiamine per 500 milligram tablet, and so on through the entire range of B vitamins. It can also be endowed with minerals that are considered desirable, like selenium and chromium, and thus is quite the equal of brewer's yeast in every respect. It is not exactly pleasant to the taste, but it is more so than brewer's yeast, and for that reason probably represents a more desirable type of yeast to buy. The price should be just about the same as that of brewer's yeast.

Liquid B vitamins. There are some people who find it difficult or impossible to swallow tablets and prefer to take any medicines or supplements in liquid form. This represents no particular problem with the B vitamins, since they are all soluble in water. For those who prefer to take supplemental B vitamins this way, it is available.

Rice bran. The B vitamins were first discovered by investigations of the deficiency diseases caused in people who lived largely on polished rice. It was shown that the rice bran polished away contained the thiamine and riboflavin that people required. Because many are familiar with this history, rice bran has come to have a largely unjustified reputation as a source of B vitamins. It is sold without any claims on the label, which is as it should be since there is really nothing you can claim for it. There is nothing especially wrong with it, but do not mistake it for a provider of high vitamin content. It is not. It is probably more valuable nutritionally as bran than as a source of B vitamins.

Torula yeast. This particular variety of yeast is very attractive to processors because it has a talent for living and growing on waste materials that would kill most anything else. It is therefore the cheapest yeast to produce. For a long while it was raised on the sulfite liquor that is a waste by-product of paper manufacturing. More recently an oil company developed a strain that can be cultured in the wastes of oil refining. It is our own feeling, which we cannot substantiate with hard evidence, that products derived from fossil fuels should not be put into the human stomach. Torula yeast cultured on oil by-products falls within that category. Dozens of times food additives derived from coal tar, coal, or oil, have been developed for use in foods, certified to be "safe," and have ultimately turned out to cause such ills as cancer and birth deformities. Although torula yeast seems to be nutritionally the same as any other nutritional yeast, we advise against using it. There are plenty of other nutritional yeasts that do not raise the same safety questions.

Wheat germ. Wheat germ, the interior portion of the wheat berry that would actually sprout and grow if it were used for seed, has a relatively high content of vitamin E and also contains some of the B vitamins. Since the milling of wheat will generally eliminate the wheat germ in order to get rid of its oily vitamin E content, that material is available at very low cost for use as a food supplement. It has been touted as a source of vitamin E and also for its B vitamin content. This is neither complete nor very large, but wheat germ does make a perfectly acceptable food to add to your diet in order to improve your general nutrition. Toasted, it even tastes good.

"Balanced" B complex. Somehow there has grown a myth that could hardly be more erroneous, that a B-complex tablet containing equal weights of each of the numerous vitamins is therefore "balanced" and offers better interaction between the various vitamins contained in the tablet. It is obviously false. From what we have written above, it should be apparent that 50 milligrams of vitamin B_3 might easily be less than you require for your particular purpose, while 50 milligrams of thiamine (vitamin B_1) is an enormous dosage, far, far beyond anybody's realistic possibility of using and benefiting by the vitamin.

The situation is a strange one. There are thousands of physicians, chiropractors, dentists, and nutritionists who use and recommend the products of health food manufacturers, who sincerely attempt to put their knowledge to work for the benefit of the public, and none of whom ever utters a word in criticism of these ridiculous B-complex supplements.

There is not a great deal to say about the potencies. They range from a B-complex 25 which features 25 milligrams of every B vitamin that can be taken in milligrams without danger, and 25 micrograms of the micronutrients like folic acid and vitamin B_{12}, and they range upward, at the present time to a B-complex 125.

Aside from the fact that if you really want your B vitamins to interact to the fullest extent, it takes a great deal more knowledge and study than just including the same weight of everything, the chief objection to all these "balanced" B-complex supplements is that the consumer is paying far, far too much for vitamin potencies that he cannot possibly use. That is true of the B-complex 25 tablets and twice as true of the B-complex 50. There is also a

B-complex 100 and a B-complex 125, which is a tablet so big that if you manage to swallow it, it will feel like a boulder going down.

If you look at the labels of any of these monstrous B-complex supplements, you will see that they contain such ingredients as brewer's or nutritional yeast, desiccated liver, wheat germ, alfalfa, and so on through a long list of names. There are no quantities listed, and there are no quantities worth listing. These are not so much ingredients as added elements that are included in order to give the impression that the tablet is compounded of natural foods. Of course it is not. There is no way you could get that kind of potency from natural foods.

B-complex tablets. There are also available, and not nearly as popular as they ought to be, some B-complex tablets that have been formulated by companies interested in giving their customers the best product possible. Their potencies seem small compared to the "balanced" tablets, but in actuality they are a bit larger than is necessary to satisfy any rational desire or requirement. Their potency numbers do not match because they should not match. They will contain roughly twice as much vitamin B_2 as they do B_1. They will have much more B_3 and B_6 than they do B_1 and B_2, and so on. They are not all the same but each one represents an effort on the part of its manufacturer to put out a genuinely worthwhile food supplement. Moreover, compared to most of the B-vitamin supplements you will see in the same store, they are inexpensive.

If it is a B-complex supplement you are looking for, we recommend such a B-complex tablet or its equivalent in nutritional yeast.

VITAMIN C

Ascorbic acid, with plant material that prevents and cures scurvy, has been known for a long, long while, although not chemically identified until about fifty years ago. Scurvy, a rather horrible disease that caused gums to bleed and teeth to fall out and eventually led to death, plagued seafaring people for as long as there were ships capable of making long voyages. At various times it was found that spruce-needle tea, sauerkraut, and lemons (which the English called limes) would prevent and cure scurvy. And scientists wondered why many animals could live and thrive on a diet of other animals completely devoid of land nutrition, while man would inevitably develop scurvy on such a regimen. The answer was ultimately found to lie in the simple fact that virtually all animals synthesize ascorbic acid in their own bodies, except for man, a few varieties of guinea pigs, and a couple of types of monkeys. Why can't we manufacture our own vitamin C the way our cats and dogs do? It's accomplished by a series of chemical transformations within the body involving both enzymes and coenzymes. Somewhere in prehistory our species lost (or developed without) the ability to manufacture just one of the enzymes involved in the chemical process. Our bodies go just so far and then stop, and we never produce any ascorbic acid. While it would be absurd to put vitamin C in a vitamin tablet for your dog, it makes good sense for his master.

The big question we have to ask ourselves is how much vitamin C we actually require daily, and what we expect it to do for us. The range of possibilities is truly enormous.

Fido produces and uses an amount of vitamin C that is the equivalent of 2 to 3 grams (2,000 to 3,000 milligrams) for an average man weighing about 150 pounds. The vitamin is clearly used in animals to fight against infections of many kinds, and when Fido is actually ill his production of vitamin C may increase to the equivalent of 5 to 6 grams a day. Should we imitate the animals and try to give our own bodies the same proportionate amounts of vitamin C every day?

Not necessarily. Your dog has a faster heartbeat than you do, a higher body temperature, and a general metabolic rate that is considerably faster than yours or mine. The difference gives him proportionately more strength, better resistance to disease, and a considerably shorter life span. These are important differences. Similarly, his use of ascorbic acid metabolically may also proceed at a higher rate than it does in the human body. So it is entirely possible that science may someday establish an upper limit of something like a gram a day that is the maximum of vitamin C the human body is able to utilize. It is possible, but nobody really knows and those who advocate a routine ingestion of three grams a day or more could very well turn out to be right.

What we can be sure of is that while it takes only some 30 milligrams a day of ascorbic acid to provide the certainty of preventing scurvy and remaining in good health, all other things being equal, all other things are often far from equal. There are many qualified investigators who believe that for maximum health benefits, our daily intake of vitamin C should be 2 to 3 grams. In the long run, they may well turn out to be the ones who are right, even though at the present time they have more detractors than adherents. Some of the ways in which vitamin C has been reported beneficial in high potency to people taking it daily or to whom it has been administered, are the following. None has been rigorously proven, none has been disproven.

PREVENTION AND TREATMENT OF THE COMMON COLD. Trials at different places and different times have gotten results ranging from utter failure to very good success. The simplest way to explain the differences is to be aware that the common cold is not one single infection but can be caused by any of dozens of different rhinoviruses. It is entirely conceivable that in a situation in which one type of virus is prevalent, vitamin C will offer no protection at all against the common cold, whereas it may offer very good protection against a different virus prevalent at a different time and place. It is doubtful that the vitamin gives anybody complete protection against colds. However, it is also quite likely that people get protection against a high percentage of potential colds by using high-potency vitamin C, and that when they experience the colds, their duration and severity are shorter.

PROTECTION AGAINST OXIDATION. Vitamin C is one of an important group of preservative materials known as antioxidants. In very brief résumé, what these substances do is prevent other substances from picking up and attaching to their molecules atoms of oxygen. Although we normally think of oxygen as being highly desirable and certainly essential to life, there are many circumstances in which oxygen is highly destructive. Oxygen turns iron to rust. In the special form of ozone, it is the most dangerous portion of photochemical smog. In all lipid foods, oxygen induces spoilage by causing rancidity and it is against this particular destructive activity of oxygen that vitamin C's antioxidant properties offer valuable protection. When fat molecules in the blood are oxidized, they form hydrogen peroxide and other materials that are or may be particularly dangerous. There are some who believe, for instance, that peroxide in the bloodstream is a major stimulator of various types of cancer. The ability of vitamin C to prevent its formation, therefore, is considered a very valuable protection indeed.

CANCER PROTECTION OF VARIOUS KINDS. Sodium nitrite, a special preservative that protects us against botulism in certain types of foods, is widely believed to be a cause of stomach cancer when it encounters and combines with protein materials to form what are labeled nitrosamines. Sodium nitrite is used in virtually all sausage meats from hot dogs to liverwurst, in smoked fish of all kinds, and in corned meats such as corned beef and pastrami.

That threatens a lot of nitrosamine formation, but some vitamin

C present in the stomach will keep it from happening and, presumably, protect us all from this particular form of cancer.

Cadmium, a toxic metal that pollutes the air, is believed to be one important cause of lung cancer. The toxicity of cadmium has been shown to be reduced by vitamin C.

Experiments at a well-known children's hospital have found that vitamin C will in some way prevent the development of leukemia in a population of children in which the number of cases that are to be expected is known.

PROTECTION AGAINST CATARACTS. Not all cataracts. There is one type, however, that is believed to be caused by an aberrant form of oxygen known as superoxide. It is formed, temporarily, by particular types of radiation, notably microwaves. That is why leaking microwave ovens sometimes cause cataracts in users. Because of this and other sources of radiation in the air, the formation of superoxide is increasingly coming to be believed one of the important causes of cataracts. And the ability of vitamin C to scavenge superoxide from the eyes is increasingly coming to be thought an important protection.

PRESERVATION OF YOUTH. Collagen is the body material that occupies the spaces between cells. It has been called a lot of fanciful names and had a lot of magical activity attributed to it. Even without exaggerating its importance, however, we must admit that in appearance at least, the health of collagen and the youthfulness of appearance go hand in hand. This intercellular material is protein in nature and vitamin C is one of its constituents. If it becomes deficient in the vitamin its texture gets thinner and more watery and that induces a kind of collapse of the tissues that makes the skin look older. Not much can be said about it, but it is reasonable to suppose that ample vitamin C helps collagen stay strong and healthy and thus keeps the appearance more youthful.

MINERAL NUTRITION. Calcium and magnesium are both essential elements, vital to health and indispensable in the diet. Yet both are rather difficult for the body to absorb into the blood and to use. Perhaps the best way to improve their absorption is with vitamin C. The mechanism is unknown, but it is now well beyond dispute that more of your dietary calcium and magnesium will be absorbed—up to 30 percent more—and proportionately less will be excreted, if you have a good vitamin C intake as well. In this way, vitamin C indirectly affects the health and strength of bones and teeth and the performance and efficiency of many important enzyme systems in the body.

AS A TREATMENT FOR DISEASE. At various times vitamin C has been reported successful in the treatment of spinal meningitis, mumps, rattlesnake bites, and bee stings, and in prolonging the lives of some cancer patients while inducing some shrinkage of their tumors. It is very hard to believe the wide variety of medical miracles that have been attributed to vitamin C. Yet it should be remembered that in animals this vitamin seems naturally to be called upon as the first response to practically any infection or trauma. Is it possible that the animals know something we don't? In any case, vitamin C is known to do so many things aside from protecting us against scurvy that the desire of the public to use more and more of the vitamin is entirely understandable.

Do you actually need those megadoses, however? Probably not, but we just couldn't say how much you truly do need. At least, unlike the water-soluble B vitamins, a surplus of water-soluble vitamin C will not be stored by the body. It is dissolved in the water that the blood carries and is excreted into the urinary bladder as that water is. Even there, it has been reported a number of times, the surplus vitamin C that the urinary bladder carries is active against any type of urinary infection. So any excess of the vitamin is hardly ever anything to be concerned about.

CAN YOU DAMAGE YOURSELF WITH TOO MUCH VITAMIN C? Of course you can, even though there are enthusiasts who believe and state that you can take the vitamin without limit. You can take a great deal of vitamin C without any serious ill effects, but there is always a limit.

The leading hazard is water loss. Ascorbic acid is really a highly acidic material, which, in sufficient supply, can quickly acidify the entire bloodstream and set the kidneys working overtime to restore the blood's normal, slightly alkaline, condition. Some draining of water in this way is merely an annoyance. Carried too far, it can create other problems. Minerals that are concerned with regulating the amount of fluid within the cells and tissues are lost with the water that is drained from the body and this can lead to a variety of blood pressure problems. One could even become seriously dehydrated without knowing it. The more ascorbic acid you use, the greater the chance that this kind of thing will happen.

Digestive upsets, also, are quite common. Again, it is the acidity of the vitamin that can create problems. In the acid climate of the stomach it is quite at home, but when it passes through into the duodenum and the small intestine, it is a different matter. In those areas the acidity can cause digestive pains and flatulence, and diarrhea is by no means an uncommon result.

If one had such uncomfortable reactions to an excess of vitamin C and went right on taking that much or more, would there be further problems? We are sure there would be, though they are not documented and we cannot say what they would be. But why cast yourself as the guinea pig? If you are already having a bad reaction, enough is enough. Don't ask for trouble.

There is a strong medical opinion, which you may hear from your own doctor, that an excess of vitamin C causes kidney stones. This was investigated thoroughly by the Food and Drug Administration. There is not a single documented case on record, so we must assume that there is no such danger. Many physicians dislike vitamins generally and would accept all too readily a theory that vitamin C is dangerous. If challenged, however, your doctor may be surprised to realize that he has no evidence whatsoever and that, in fact, vitamin C does not cause kidney stones.

TYPES OF VITAMIN C.

Ascorbic acid. All vitamin C is ascorbic acid. For a long while, however, many manufacturers used to claim that there was a "natural" vitamin C that was somehow different, and "ascorbic acid" as an identification was used for the pure product that was made in a pharmaceutical laboratory. Then the secret leaked out that claims about natural vitamin C were all phony and that every vitamin C product was made of the same synthetic ascorbic acid. Today, if the package of tablets is labeled simply ascorbic acid, that indicates it is just pure vitamin C that has not been blended with any associated materials and has not been treated for delayed release or anything like it.

Ascorbic acid has an acidity index (pH) that stands at about 3, which is strongly acidic. When pure ascorbic acid gets into the bloodstream, via digestion, its high acidity causes it to be rapidly filtered out by the kidneys. It can cause increased urination, stomach upsets, and diarrhea. To take it with least reaction, take relatively low potencies—such as 100 milligrams—at a time, and take it around the clock, every hour or two, until it adds up to the daily potency you desire.

Ascorbic acid timed-release (or delayed-release or slow-release) tablets. Such tablets are coated with enteric or some other protein material that partially digests in the stomach, freeing some of the tablet contents of ascorbic acid, while the rest of the tablet passes on into the duodenum for further processing by the body. The theory is that by use of a special coating to retard digestion, a single high-potency tablet can have its absorption spread out over a period of four to eight hours and, in final effect, be transformed as far as the body is concerned into a series of lower-potency tablets taken one at a time. If that were all there is to it, it would be easy to agree on the desirability of the delayed-release technique, even though enteric tablet coatings sometimes cause digestive upsets. But the manufacturers of such tablets—and today that means probably every company in the business—have overlooked or just haven't bothered to investigate the stages of digestion and why it is accomplished in stages.

Digestion begins in the stomach, which is strongly acidic in its climate. The stomach acids dissolve the proteins, including the protein content of grains and vegetables, and the stomach contents, to the extent that they have become acidic in nature, are absorbed into the bloodstream. Thus acids such as aspirin or vitamin C are very quickly taken into the blood and circulated through the body at swallowing. If this is prevented from happening, however, and a large, undigested portion of the vitamin C tablet passes into the duodenum, is it then digested there? That is doubtful, though we have not been able to find any actual biochemical studies.

The climate of the duodenum is quite alkaline, its purpose being to begin the dissolution of fats and other foods that are not affected by the acids of the stomach. It is almost inescapable that the alkaline climate of the duodenum will simply neutralize ascorbic acid being freed from the slow-release tablet, and that what remains will not be vitamin C at all, nor will it possess vitamin C activity.

Thus it seems likely that if you swallow, say, a 500 milligram delayed-release tablet of vitamin C, you will actually get 100 to 200 milligrams of the vitamin through stomach assimilation, and nothing more. The rest of the tablet will be wasted. In other words, the concept of a vitamin C tablet that will slowly feed a high potency of the vitamin into the system is an erroneous concept based on ignorance of how human digestion works. These tablets are considerably more expensive than plain ascorbic acid, and not only are they no better, they are frequently not as effective. Their use is not recommended.

Calcium ascorbate. It has been found possible to buffer, in effect, to reduce the acidity of vitamin C by combining it with calcium, a mineral that is alkaline in nature. Calcium is an essential mineral, important to bones, teeth, nerves, and the heart. Yet the digestive absorption of calcium is not a simple matter. Ordinarily, most of it is lost in the fecal excretions. It has been found that the presence of vitamin C substantially improves and increases the absorption of dietary calcium, which is usually to be desired. It would seem to make sense to combine calcium and ascorbic acid in the same tablet, to accomplish the double purpose of reducing the acidity of the vitamin and bringing more calcium into the body.

Reduction of the acidity of vitamin C can be accomplished by the buffering technique up to a pH of 6, just slightly on the acid side of neutral, without any loss of stability or vitamin C activity. Such buffering seems to accomplish the complete elimination of any stomach upsets or diuretic effect. Far more important, since the kidneys do not frantically remove vitamin C from the bloodstream at its level of reduced acidity, the vitamin remains in the system for a far greater length of time without having to bother with any tricks like the use of slow-release coatings. Actually buffered to a pH of 6, vitamin C should remain substantially in the body for twelve hours or more, and even if you want to keep your level high twenty-four hours a day you should not have to take it more than twice a day. There is one problem, however, which is that the amount of calcium necessary to buffer vitamin C as stated above is disproportionately high. Reckoning that 1 gram of calcium is a desirable intake for an entire day, that amount of calcium will buffer no more than 200 milligrams of vitamin C. So if you want a high potency of vitamin C in your calcium ascorbate, it will provide you with far more calcium than you require and actually enough to create some undesirable health problems.

This is a good product and a desirable one. It is going to take further work and study, however, to bring it to the level of perfection that is desired and that it theoretically should be able to achieve.

Capsules of ascorbic acid. In order to make a practical tablet of vitamin C it is necessary to mix the pure crystalline vitamin with one or more inert materials that make a neater and more durable tablet. Sometimes, however, a physician will recommend that the patient take only the pure vitamin C without any excipients or fillers. The only way to do this is in capsules. There are very few who require this. If you have no special reason for requiring capsules, there is absolutely no reason to pay the extra cost that is involved. They are no better for you and will do you no more good.

Liquid vitamin C. Since vitamin C is fully water soluble, it is easily dissolved in water to provide a liquid preparation. This is a convenience for those few people who find it very difficult to swallow tablets. For anyone else it would be nothing but a nuisance.

Magnesium ascorbate. The rationale for tablets made of magnesium ascorbate is identical with that for calcium ascorbate. Both minerals are essential and dietarily of the greatest importance. The body's absorption and use of both is facilitated by vitamin C, and both are good buffering agents to reduce the acidity of vitamin C to whatever level is desired. The only difference is that calcium ascorbate came first, until someone reflected that if calcium ascorbate was a good product, magnesium ascorbate would be one, too. The one trouble is price. Since there is less demand for magnesium ascorbate, it costs more to manufacture. Since the price is higher, there is less demand. It's a perfectly good product, but considerably more expensive than calcium ascorbate and in no way better. A good product but not a good buy.

Sodium ascorbate. This is by far the oldest and best-tested form of buffered vitamin C. It is the least expensive to produce and is routinely used by many who believe in very high-potency vitamin C. Dr. Linus Pauling who takes upward of 3 grams of vitamin C daily has stated numerous times that what he uses and recommends is sodium ascorbate. When a physician wishes to treat a deep infection or a rattlesnake bite with intravenous injection of several thousand milligrams of vitamin C, it is sodium ascorbate that he uses.

The one problem of sodium ascorbate is that the buffering material is sodium. An accumulation of sodium in the cells of tissues bears a definite relationship to the development of high blood pressure. If your doctor tells you to eat less salt, it is the sodium intake he is trying to reduce. (Salt is sodium chloride.) Many people for many reasons are trying to reduce their sodium intake and certainly want to avoid increasing it. For such people, the sodium in sodium ascorbate makes it something to be avoided. However, there are many, many people who are not in the least bothered by salt in their food or by anything like high blood pressure. Such people can consume sodium without a second thought and apparently eliminate it just as easily. And such people can use sodium ascorbate without the slightest risk.

For those who have no need to avoid it, sodium ascorbate would be by far the form of choice for daily vitamin C. It is well buffered, so that it will remain in the body for a good twelve hours without putting any kind of strain on the kidneys. It will not cause any digestive upsets and it will provide good, usable vitamin C in high or low potency, as you wish.

Acerola. In subtropical climates, notably in Puerto Rico, there grows the acerola berry, which resembles the cherry in appearance and is frequently called the acerola cherry. Ounce for ounce, the berry when picked and eaten ripe has as high a content of vitamin C as any food you might name. Therefore, among those who like to pretend that there is a difference between natural and synthetic vitamin C, the acerola takes on big importance. Supplements of acerola vitamin C are offered with the implication, if not the outright claim, that the tablet's content of dried acerola berries is the source of the natural vitamin C. In actuality, the natural vitamin content of the berries was lost or destroyed during the drying process, and what is actually in the tablet is some dried berries having no nutritional value, to which has been added synthetic vitamin C to make up the desired potency. To this is also added some synthetic cherry flavor and usually some sweetener because cherry flavor doesn't taste like cherry without the sweetener. It doesn't taste like acerola either, but nobody knows that, and the suggestion of cherry makes people feel they are eating the real thing. This type of product is a fake that is best avoided.

Rose hips. This, of course, is the best known of the phony sort of vitamin C tablets. Rose hips have been famed as a vitamin C source since World War II, when a sugar shortage in Sweden made it impossible to manufacture vitamin C, and fresh fruits and vegetables were in even shorter supply than is normal for the sunless northern countries. It was found that rose hips, which are seeds and which are formed abundantly on all rose bushes and vines if they are not removed to promote flowering, were excellent sources of vitamin C. Picked in the fall, they could be kept for several months and used to brew a tea or even as an ingredient in preserves, though their flavor is bitter and unpleasant.

From this historic necessity, there grew a host of rose hips products. Alas, it was quickly learned that the vitamin C content of rose hips does not last forever. It is rather short-lived. Thereafter, what is left is a woody seed that contains either no vitamin C at all or very damn little. This was the material that was packaged for many years as the truly natural and the superior vitamin C product even though the packagers knew full well that if they wanted to claim any vitamin C potency at all, they could only do it by adding synthetic ascorbic acid. Today the ability to make potency claims is better controlled, and the labels of the same products will now read something like "Vitamin C with Rose Hips," with the type composed in such a way as to give the impression that the rose hips are the source of the vitamin C.

It is a grand public delusion. The belief in rose hips has become so widespread that there are many health food stores in which you could not find a vitamin C product that does not contain rose hips. It doesn't matter very much. It no longer costs anything to add rose hips to a vitamin C tablet and if people believe it gives them something extra, why not let them have it? Okay. It's as useless and space filling as any other tablet filler, and it costs no more. Just so you know.

Vitamin C in its various forms is available in potencies from as low as 50 milligrams per tablet to a full gram (1,000 milligrams) or perhaps more. How do you choose the proper potency for you?

50 to 100 milligrams. Taken at one time this is the maximum useful dose you can take of plain ascorbic acid. To build it into a high potency intake, repeat the dose every two hours.

200 milligrams. This is the top dose from which you can expect any effect from a delayed-release tablet. That is about as much as will be released within the two hours or so that it takes food to clear the stomach. Whatever passes lower down in the digestive tract is waste. Delayed-release tablets are usually at least 250 milligrams, more often 500 milligrams or so; 200 to 250 milligrams represents a sensible choice.

Two hundred milligrams is the top dosage of calcium ascorbate that you should use to avoid absorbing a surplus of calcium.

500 milligrams to one gram. Even higher potencies are readily available, but you will not actually absorb and use all that vitamin C even though it is in the tablet. The only exception is sodium ascorbate, if you are able to take that much sodium without any ill effects.

To obtain a high potency of dietary vitamin C, of let us say 1,500 to 2,000 milligrams daily, the best and perhaps the only technique remains to use ascorbic acid 100 to 200 milligrams at a time and keep repeating the doses frequently around the clock. To avoid any digestive problems, it helps to drink a buffering material such as milk right along with the tablets.

VITAMIN D

There is not a great deal to say about vitamin D, inasmuch as it is not generally available in most places as a single food supplement, and where it is available it is only with the strictest limitations. The reason for this is that the vitamin, though certainly essential, indispensable to us in important ways and one that we need in full measure, is also dangerous if taken in excess. So dangerous is it considered, in fact, because of the serious damage it can do to infants and children, that there is just about no variety possible in the sale of vitamin D, potency wars are out of the question, and all that is left is a vitamin that, whether you buy it singly or in combination, is limited to 400 International Units (IU) per dose. No glamor. No way to use it to lure a customer from a competitor. Just plain old absolutely essential, health-building vitamin D.

Actually, there is a surprisingly wide range of materials that are considered vitamin D. They are all the vitamin, because when they are incorporated into the human body, they all have the same hormone-like activity that is needed for the use and regulation of calcium. Whenever a vitamin's potency is measured in IU, what is actually being measured is a certain biological activity. Any substance that brings about that particular biological activity can therefore be considered to be the vitamin and is so considered. In the case of vitamin D, the activity is the deposit of the mineral calcium into bones and teeth, in the course of which a certain amount of free mineral in the bloodstream may also result from the vitamin D. Cholesterol under the skin, acted upon by sunlight, is transformed into cholecalciferol, a form of vitamin D. Ergosterol, blended into milk and then exposed to ultraviolet light, is transformed into ergocalciferol, another form of vitamin D. And there are many, many more. All go through further transformations in our livers to finally become the hormonal substances that make it possible for hardening, solidifying calcium to be deposited in bones and teeth, from which other hormones may have withdrawn them in response to temporary body needs. And any material that the liver can employ for this purpose is rightfully called vitamin D.

In northern regions of limited sunlight many children used to grow up with bones that were bent instead of straight and that broke far too easily, because lacking sunlight, they lacked vitamin D. It was ultimately discovered that cod-liver oil would prevent or cure rickets and keep the children in much better health. In the United States, where practically all families can afford milk for their children, it was cleverly decided that the addition of vitamin D to milk would give children the vitamin D they need and simultaneously provide them with the calcium on which the vitamin D acts within our bodies. That approach has its problems, however. Most of the dark-skinned peoples of the world, after early infancy, lose the ability to produce the enzyme lactase, which is responsible for the digestion of milk sugar. Such people, as a consequence, tend to develop diarrhea and flatulence when they drink milk. Milk cannot be used as a source of vitamin D for them. So there is a need for vitamin D supplements, and it is probably unfortunate that so much hullabaloo has been raised about their possible toxicity that they have become harder and harder for people to find.

That may be one of the reasons that, while the incidence of rickets decreases year by year in the children of the world, its adult counterpart, osteomalacia, is definitely on the increase. Osteomalacia, which is most common in older adults, is very little different from rickets. The only significant variation is that growing bones, insufficiently mineralized in rickets, tend to bend under pressure and the growth of rachitic children is stunted. When full-grown adults develop the same disease, their growth is not affected. Otherwise there is no difference and both are due to deficiency in vitamin D.

It seems absurd. Vitamin D is the easiest of all vitamins to obtain, since all you have to do is expose your skin to sunlight. Yet the sun does not shine often in many northern countries and when that problem is complicated by pollution of the air, which darkens the skies with smoke and shuts out the rays of the sun, then it becomes one of the unpleasant facts of life that in such regions you cannot get enough vitamin D from the sunlight and must therefore obtain it from your diet.

It has already been pointed out that vitamin D supplements in potencies of more than 400 IU are prohibited by FDA regulations. If you can find a vitamin D supplement, the potency will almost invariably be 400 IU. The easiest way to get it is in combination with vitamin A. You can choose from a variety of supplements, any one of which will give you 10,000 IU of vitamin A plus 400 IU of vitamin D.

In most cases, your biggest concern about vitamin D will be to make certain that you don't get too much. An excess results in a surplus of free calcium in the bloodstream. One of the common results is the formation of kidney stones, a medical problem that is one of the ultimately painful ones. It is free calcium in the bloodstream that combines with cholesterol and certain proteins to form the plaque of atherosclerosis, blocking off one or more arteries and seriously impeding the flow of blood carried by the arteries. The toxic effects of the vitamin are most dangerous when it is given in excess to infants and small children. How much is too much? A healthy adult can actually take as much as 1,000 IU a day with no fear of any ill effects. Children are closer to the borderline and really should not take any vitamin D-containing supplements if they play in the sunlight and drink irradiated milk.

VITAMIN E

A lot of what you think about vitamin E depends on whether you consider it a vitamin or a drug. It is a vitamin—a dietary essential without which people would sicken and die. However, there is a small quantity of vitamin E in many foods, and the small amount that you obtain from your diet if you just eat without any thought of your vitamin E intake is apparently enough to prevent anything like a gross deficiency of the vitamin. At least, it has never been possible for anyone to prove that a particular symptom or group of symptoms is a vitamin E deficiency disease. The one exception is in newborn and very young infants, in whom an inadequate amount of vitamin E can result in one type of anemia. Otherwise all that we know about vitamin E deficiency disease relates to animals, in whom it is possible to induce a vitamin E deficiency under laboratory conditions, and in whom that deficiency will lead to abortions and stillbirths in pregnant females and generally to cystic fibrosis in many cases.

So in terms of preventing deficiency disease, one really does not need a vitamin E supplement at all. However, there has been enormous experimentation, both clinically and in the laboratory, to determine what properties vitamin E possesses and what kind of therapeutic use can be made of those properties. Over the years, a stunningly impressive, wide range of attributes have been claimed for this vitamin. The quantities of this vitamin that are bought and sold annually amount to big business. Yet virtually all its use is as a drug, and those who use it do so to obtain the benefits of druglike properties that are claimed for the vitamin.

Here is a list of the ways that some physicians, some research scientists, and millions of people believe that health benefits are obtained from vitamin E:

TO PREVENT HEART ATTACKS. Vitamin E is claimed to be fibrinolytic. That is, it is believed to dissolve fibrin, one of the materials that go together to form blood clots. By dissolving fibrin, the theory goes, the vitamin either reduces or eliminates clots in the arteries. This helps to maintain the steady supply of blood to the heart, and thus prevents the most common form of heart attack. This idea is accepted and promoted by some members of the medical profession, but rejected by most. It is widely accepted within the lay public.

TO TREAT HEART ATTACKS (MYOCARDIAL INFARCTION) AND FACILITATE RECOVERY OF THE PATIENT. As used by a number of practicing physicians, vitamin E is believed to strengthen and improve the heart action by increasing both the blood supply and the oxygen supply to the heart. By strengthening the action of the heart, it is believed also to increase the blood pressure in some cases and special precautions are taken with patients who have high blood pressure problems.

TO REDUCE OR ELIMINATE ANGINA PECTORIS. The severe chest pains which stem from cardiac problems are actually caused by oxygen insufficiency. Working as an antioxidant, vitamin E does conserve the oxygen that is in the bloodstream and in that sense, to some extent increases the amount of oxygen available to the tissues. The increase may be significant in some cases, in others so slight as to be meaningless. As a treatment for angina, vitamin E is not reliable, though occasionally successful.

TO PREVENT PULMONARY EMBOLISM. There are a few surgeons who routinely use vitamin E before and after major surgery to protect the patient against one frequent complication of surgery, the formation of blood clots in the veins of the legs, which are subsequently carried to the lungs where they become deadly. The surgeons who use the fibrinolytic properties of vitamin E in this way do have comparative figures showing the technique to be highly successful.

TO TREAT VARIOUS CIRCULATORY PROBLEMS OF THE LEGS. Some people take vitamin E in the belief that, by dissolving blood clots, it will improve the passage of blood through the veins and thus reduce or even eliminate varicose veins. Inasmuch as pregnancy almost invariably induces some varicosity, practically every woman might potentially take advantage of this property of vitamin E, if it actually works. It has certainly been successful for many thousands of women, but there is no information whatsoever as to what percentage of women can be helped in this way or how reliable the treatment is. The same properties of vitamin E already discussed, sparing the oxygen supply in the blood and reducing blood clots, are believed by some to make it an important adjunct in the treatment of diabetes. Regular use of the vitamin is believed to improve the circulation of blood to the feet, which in diabetics frequently are deprived of enough blood and become gangrenous.

That vitamin E is helpful in diabetes has been misinterpreted by some to mean that it will reduce and regularize the levels of blood sugar. It will not. Vitamin E is not a treatment for diabetes and no diabetic should attempt to use it in that way.

Another problem of blood circulation to the legs is intermittent claudication, the development of severe pains in the legs when they are used for walking, which makes it impossible for the victim to walk any distance. Vitamin E has been reported very helpful in some of these cases. It will not help in every case.

TO TREAT PURPURA. Purpura is the unexplained and apparently reasonless bursting of capillaries followed by the formation of bruises. Vitamin E has eliminated this problem from the lives of numerous people. Again, it is far from being a universal cure and may do no good at all for as many people as it will help.

TO OVERCOME MALE IMPOTENCE. Vitamin E is useless for this purpose. The early investigation and development of the vitamin arose from its discovery as a factor that would prevent stillbirths in laboratory rats showing this problem. Such stillbirths were later shown to be caused by a deficiency of the vitamin. Because of this early experience, it came to be believed that vitamin E was somehow an answer to sexual problems and an improver of sexuality. There is always a big demand for products that promise sexual miracles and so a number of fast buck operators promoted vitamin E on this basis. The myth still persists, though it has been repudiated dozens or hundreds of times by all scientists who have ever looked into it. Vitamin E has no effect on male potency.

TO IMPROVE FEMALE SEXUAL RESPONSE, FERTILITY, ETC. If you buy vitamin E for this purpose, you are fairly surely wasting your money. The vitamin to some small extent is antagonistic to the female hormone, estrogen. In those very few cases in which infertility is caused by an excess of estrogen in the woman's system, vitamin E might be of some help though it is not nearly as reliable or efficacious as drugs that your physician can prescribe. It will not increase your sexuality nor will it improve your ability to reach sexual climax. As a sex vitamin, E has no value and will do you no good if that is what you are seeking.

TO PROLONG LIFE. To live longer without becoming too feeble to enjoy it is one of the perpetual dreams of mankind. Vitamin E may well be one element that will contribute to realization of that dream. The belief that it is valuable in this respect relates to the antioxidant properties of the vitamin. It is believed by a good many research scientists, most of them biochemists, that a major cause of some diseases is the oxidation in the bloodstream of susceptible materials such as fats. It is well known that when a fat oxidizes, a fancy way of saying that it becomes rancid, the unpleasant taste and odor are caused by the formation of hydrogen peroxide. In the bloodstream this leads to deformation of molecular fractions or aberrant molecules that are known as free radicals. And when free radicals are incorporated into normal tissue they are believed to form or cause the formation of cells that are aberrations. The result is believed sometimes to be a cell that flourishes in the human body, though it does not belong there. One obvious example is the development and growth of a tumor.

What an antioxidant does is prevent the joining of oxygen to fat molecules or other molecules, thus preventing rancidity and spoilage in food and doing very much the same thing in the bloodstream. Vitamin E is a strong and effective antioxidant. By preventing much free radical formation in the bloodstream, it is believed to prevent much development of disease and in that way to prolong healthy, active life. Many experiments conducted with short-lived animals under laboratory conditions have shown that it does just this. Corroboration in terms of the human life span has never been forthcoming and may never be.

It has also been found that when living cells are cultured in the laboratory, usually to determine how many times they will reproduce themselves before cellular death occurs, the addition of vitamin E to the culture medium will prolong the life of the cell to about double what it would otherwise be. No one has even speculated yet as to why or how this should be so. But it does work. If you think the vitamin will do as much for you, you certainly ought to be taking it.

TO PREVENT SCARS. Vitamin E is also used as a dressing on healing wounds of all kinds, including burns. Even physicians who use it do not claim to know why it works, but the vitamin has shown itself quite successful at reducing the amount of scarring one would normally expect from any particular injury. In many cases there are no scars at all where one knows that scars should have formed. In many more, what would have been expected to be a prominent and ugly scar is reduced to something so inconspicuous it can hardly be seen and is easily covered with makeup. It really works and should probably be used more widely than it is.

TYPES OF VITAMIN E. Vitamin E is measured in international units, thereby largely eliminating any distinction that might exist in anyone's mind between the natural and the synthetic. An IU of vitamin E is a certain amount of biological activity—in this case, the activity of one milligram of dl-alphatocopherol acetate. Since, when you take a vitamin, your objective is to take its biological activity into your own body and utilize it, it can hardly matter to you whether the basic material is more or less active biologically as long as you get the same number of international units. In other words, if vitamin E extracted from corn is 20 percent more active than vitamin E from the pharmaceutical company, a hundred units of the synthetic vitamin E will contain 100 milligrams of dl-alphatocopherol acetate, whereas 100 units of the d-alphatocopherol acetate, extracted from corn will weigh only about 80 milligrams. But in either case, you will be getting exactly the same amount of biological activity and it can hardly matter much to you which type you are getting it from. Having cleared up that question, we hope, let us go on to the types of vitamin E that are available.

Alphatocopherol. This is pure vitamin E. If it is preceded by the small letter d in labeling, that indicates that it is the natural vitamin derived wholly from a natural source such as corn oil. If it is preceded by the letters dl, that indicates that it is synthetic. As we explained above, the biological activity per international unit is identical and there is really no reason to prefer one above the other.

Mixed tocopherols. Alphatocopherol is the accepted standard and is vitamin E. In nature it is frequently accompanied by what are known chemically as isomers—materials that are nearly identical chemically with only slight variations. There are a number of these and they are identified by the letters of the Greek alphabet. It is only the first four, alpha, beta, gamma, and delta, that have any nutritional significance. Each of these four possesses some antioxidant activity and presumably is of nutritional value.

When you buy a product that is labeled "Vitamin E—Mixed Tocopherols—100 IU" that product contains per capsule 100 units of alphatocopherol plus some beta, gamma, and delta of no specified potency. To the extent that it contains mixed tocopherols, you are actually getting something in addition to the 100 IU of vitamin E specified on the label, and it is probably worth a little more money. However, there is never a specified potency of the beta, gamma, and delta fractions, and the amount of them that is included could easily be so little that it is really not worth mentioning. There is no way of telling. The store manager can't tell, either. This being the case, if you want extra antioxidant activity, probably the best way to get it is to buy a higher potency of alphatocopherol and know what it is that you are getting. No one has yet found any value or virtue in the other tocopherol fractions that is not possessed by alphatocopherol.

Vitamin E in oil packed in capsules. Most vitamin E is marketed in this particular form. The vitamin occurs naturally in fats and oils in which it will remain dissolved and will consequently be easily absorbed digestively. The actual oil that is used is seldom identified and might well be any oil that has been accepted as fit for human consumption. The one thing of which you can be sure is that it is not the original oil from which the vitamin was extracted. The original oil cannot be packed as a vitamin supplement because there is no way to measure or to regulate the precise potency of vitamin E per a given number of minims. Therefore, the vitamin must be extracted from its original source to be added in measured amounts to the oil that is going to be encapsulated. The capsules are most likely to contain cottonseed or corn oil, both of which are usually available in good supply and inexpensive. At special times, the manufacturer may be unable to obtain the cheaper oils and have to use sesame, peanut, sunflower, or what have you. There is no reason to suppose that one oil is preferable to another for this purpose. If you happen to be allergic to corn, say, or to sesame, you had better take no chances and get the dry vitamin E that is packed in tablets.

Vitamin E emulsified in lecithin. This product is relatively scarce. It may well take some hunting to find it. Yet it does offer possible advantages that may make it quite desirable to some. Lecithin is itself both a lipid and an emulsifier. It is believed by many to act as an emulsifier in the bloodstream, particularly in relation to cholesterol. It is thought that by shattering the globules of cholesterol and dispersing them well through the blood, lecithin prevents cholesterol from clumping and therefore is an active agent to prevent arterial plaque and atherosclerosis. Usually the same physicians and lay authorities who endorse vitamin E as a valuable aid to the heart are also in favor of a regular daily intake of lecithin. The two nutrients combine well, the vitamin E being well dispersed through the lecithin and absorbed into the bloodstream as readily as from any other lipid medium.

Vitamin E skin cream. Vitamin E is one of the few vitamins that does actually penetrate the skin and that, when rubbed in either in a cold cream or a moisturizing cream, will get past the surface layer of dead skin and down to the living tissue beneath. Does that, however, mean that the vitamin improves the skin? There is practically no positive or negative evidence. There are a good number of people who believe that the antioxidant properties of vitamin E protect the lipids beneath the skin and prevent the formation of blackheads and similar types of blemishes, while preserving the lipids that keep the skin moist and smooth. For a while the marketing of skin creams containing vitamin E was a major fad, taken up and vigorously promoted by all the leading cosmetic companies. As is their way, they have now passed on to newer fads, but there are still commercial cosmetic lines of vitamin E creams obtainable at just about any cosmetics department or drugstore. They are little different from the vitamin E creams you will find in a health food store, except that the ones in the health food store may well have no perfume. Such creams are quite expensive wherever you may get them.

We suggest that these cosmetic items are not worth their premium prices unless they produce unusually fine results for you. The only way to find out is to buy the smallest package you can get and try it. If it really gives you a definite improvement in your skin's health and appearance, it may well be worth whatever it costs to you. If it doesn't, if it's no better than any other cold cream or moisturizing cream, stick to the one that costs the least.

Vitamin E ointment. This is simply vitamin E dispersed through a heavy lipid base, usually petroleum jelly, suitable for dressing a skin injury such as a burn or a wound. It is inexpensive and despite the fact that your doctor might not approve, it has been quite successful at minimizing scarring while the wound heals. The ointment usually comes in a tube and is something good to keep in your medicine cabinet or first-aid kit.

Water-dispersible vitamin E. There are always some people whose digestive system cannot tolerate oils or who, because they are vegetarians, do not want to put capsules made of gelatin into their stomachs. For such people, needless to say, chemistry has found a way to produce vitamin E in a dry form that will dissolve in water and thus is not dependent on oil. The dry vitamin is packed in tablets in all the same potencies as the encapsulated liquid. It has the same biological activity and you can certainly use it if you have any reason to avoid the capsules. It is a little more expensive, however, and does not give you anything more.

Wheat-germ oil with vitamin E. For many years wheat-germ oil was highly touted as a high-potency source of vitamin E. Hundreds of thousands of people bought and took wheat-germ oil in the belief that they were thus supplying themselves with a high daily ration of vitamin E in its most natural form. In actuality, they were getting little or no vitamin E in the oil. It is a fairly rich source of the vitamin when it is immaculately fresh, but the vitamin functions as an antioxidant preservative and is quickly used up or lost as the oil stands on the shelf. Today too many people have gotten impatient with the misrepresentation for it to continue. Today the label on the bottle will say Wheat-Germ Oil with 25 IU or 50 IU per teaspoon added. As was always the case, if the oil is to contain an assayable potency of vitamin E, the vitamin must be added to it.

Other than its supposed richness in vitamin E, we know of no particular reason why you would prefer wheat-germ oil, which is a good polyunsaturate but quite expensive, over the less expensive and equally good corn, soy, peanut, and other vegetable oils.

Vitamin E comes in the following potencies:

30 IU. This low potency of vitamin E is not widely available and is not easy to find. It is recommended by some nutritional authorities for those who wish to improve their nutrition with vitamin E but have kidney problems. To avoid aggravation of kidney difficulties or an increase in blood pressure, it is recommended that these people start with a 30 IU dose, take it once a day for a month, and then double it to 60 IU. In this way, it is believed, they will be able gradually to take high potencies daily.

90 IU. The rationale for this quantity is exactly the same as that for 30 IU. Different authorities hold different opinions and some of them recommend starting a vitamin E program at the 90 IU level, believing that is safe and cannot possibly cause any rise in the blood pressure. Since it is recommended, and some people ask for it, it is packaged and can be found with a little effort.

100 IU. This is the lowest standard dosage that is recommended for or used by people with no particular health problems that might be affected by the vitamin. There are many who believe that 100 IU a day is about as much vitamin E as a person is able to utilize. For example, the scientists whose experiments showed that vitamin E can greatly prolong the life of the individual cell in a laboratory culture consider that as much of such an effect as can be gained by a living person will be provided by a dosage of 100 IU a day.

200 IU. It is common advice from those who seem to know the most about vitamin E that everyone starting on a program of using the vitamin should start with a low dosage and increase it gradually. In most cases this means starting at a dosage of 100 IU and then doubling it to 200 after a month or two. It is about the only rationale for packaging the vitamin in this particular potency.

400 IU. As noted above this should not be considered a potency for beginners. Many of the physicians who use vitamin E in their practice believe that 400 IU is the desirable maintenance dosage, which, after being attained slowly, should be continued for the rest of a person's life. Since vitamin E is a fat-soluble vitamin that is not excreted and whose surplus is stored in the liver, there is no necessity to separate the dosages through the day and it makes sense to package it as a single daily dose. Even the greatest enthusiasts for vitamin E consider 400 IU an adequate quantity to prevent the formation of blood clots in the leg veins and in the arteries and to perform all the antioxidant activities that a hostile environment and badly processed foods might make necessary.

600 IU. This is a therapeutic dosage and, generally speaking, it should not be used except upon professional advice. It is a potency level of vitamin E that is used by some cardiologists in the treatment of heart attacks in much the same way that most cardiologists use anticoagulant drugs that are acknowledged to be dangerous, but whose advantages outweigh the dangers.

There is only one circumstance in which a dosage as high as 600 IU of vitamin E can be used without professional guidance. Those who have been taking the vitamin for years sometimes become so adjusted to the intake that it no longer has the desired effect, even though that effect has been secured over a period of time. To make this clear, a person might have ended his intermittent claudication or purpura with a daily dosage of 400 IU, only to find after a couple of years that the problem is returning. In such a case, one can safely increase the dosage to 600 IU or even 800. It will usually be found that this increase in dosage will fully restore the effect that is sought.

800 IU. Aside from increasing a smaller dosage that has become ineffective over a period of time, there is really no reason why anybody not advised to do so by his doctor would want to buy and take vitamin E at a potency as high as 800 IU. Nevertheless many people do, because they have been swept up in what has been called the "Megavitamin Revolution" and have come to believe in astronomical doses of all vitamins. Fortunately, E seems to be the least toxic of all vitamins and though it is only reasonable to suppose that overdosage should have ill effects, none have yet been demonstrated.

1,000 IU. As this volume is being produced, this is the ultimate in purposeless and nonsensical high potencies of vitamin E available in the retail stores. In a couple of months even higher potencies may become available because people do have this profound if erroneous conviction that if a little of something is good for you, more must be better. There is no rational purpose to a vitamin E supplement this potent. It is not recommended. Nevertheless, it is widely available and many people will go right on buying it. We hope it does no harm.

VITAMIN K

This vitamin really requires hardly anything in the way of discussion. It is a regulator of the ability of blood to clot. It has a truly powerful effect in promoting clotting. But as we live and as we eat today, it is practically never that anyone is bothered by an inability of his blood to clot. The exception is hemophilia, which is not a vitamin K deficiency and is not treated with vitamin K.

For practically all ordinary circumstances, if we have a clotting problem, it is that our blood clots too easily and too fast.

In other words, there is just about no one who needs more vitamin K than he is already getting from his food. We get small quantities in green, leafy vegetables and those small quantities are as much vitamin K as anybody needs. There is no reason why you should ever need a supplement of vitamin K and you should really never take one except on the advice of your physician.

Nevertheless, there are people who will buy anything that is a vitamin and just as surely there are others who will sell to them. Vitamin K is available as a supplement in potencies up to 100 micrograms. This is a very small and harmless dosage. If you needed it for any medical purpose, your doctor would prescribe something like 10 milligrams. One hundred micrograms is only one hundredth of that amount and will neither harm you nor do you the slightest good. There is no reason whatsoever to buy it or take it.

VITAMIN P

Vitamin P is not recognized as a vitamin in the United States. It was discovered in Hungary in the 1930s and comprises a group of factors found in fruits and vegetables that have a heavy white pulp. Oranges and bell peppers are among the prominent suppliers of vitamin P, which is known in the United States as bioflavonoids. The discoverer, Nobel laureate Szent-Györgyi, suggests that bioflavonoids may be so widespread in the American diet that no deficiency serious enough to lead to disease is ever found in this country, whereas in Europe where he was working in that time of economic depression there was a definite medical entity recognizable as a deficiency of bioflavonoids, and it was perfectly reasonable to name the material vitamin P (for permeability). The chief role of bioflavonoids appears to be to strengthen the walls of the capillaries, giving them stronger resistance to breakage and rendering them less vulnerable to seepage. Women at the menopause and others sometimes bruise very easily, bruising technically being the rupture of one or more capillaries with subsequent formation of a small area of discoloration and tenderness. It has sometimes been possible to treat such bruising very successfully with bioflavonoids.

Although information is not clear-cut, it appears that the two most important bioflavonoids are hesperidin and rutin. Hesperidin is one of the bioflavonoids obtained in the pulp beneath lemon and orange peel, while rutin is derived from the bran of buckwheat. Both these bioflavonoids have been used successfully, though not invariably so, to treat bruising and capillary fragility. In addition, more recent studies have found that they possess antioxidant activity, that they help to prolong the activity of adrenaline, the chief hormone secreted by the adrenal glands, and that they will help to remove a surplus of copper from the blood.

Although rutin is an exception, generally the fruits and vegetables that are richest in vitamin C are also the richest sources of bioflavonoids. That is true of citrus fruits, fresh rose hips, bell peppers, paprika, and black currants. Because of this association in nature, many have assumed that vitamin C and bioflavonoids interact and support one another's biological activity. There is no convincing evidence that this is so, but neither has it been disproven. Vitamin manufacturers cater to the idea by combining the two into single tablets. In fact, if you want to add bioflavonoids to your diet, it will be easier to find them in combination with vitamin C than to find them as separate bioflavonoids. There is no objection to the combination except that usually there is no stated potency of bioflavonoids and you may actually be getting very, very little vitamin P in your tablet.

To be sure of what you are getting, look for a package offering rutin, citrus bioflavonoids, hesperidin complex, or mixed bioflavonoids. The potencies will range from 50 milligrams to 150 milligrams. The price should be quite low. All bioflavonoid products are natural because it has never paid anyone to reproduce them in the laboratory.

MINERALS

In addition to the vitamins, there is a goodly number of minerals that are equally essential to human health. They tend to be materials that the body uses directly to manufacture physiological structures, as for example it uses calcium to make up the basic material of bones and teeth and similarly uses iron to manufacture hemoglobin, which is material in the red blood cells that transports oxygen to all the organs and tissues. Minerals, like vitamins, sometimes act as coenzymes that must be present in the body before a particular enzyme system is able to synthesize and to function fully, and, again like vitamins, are sometimes incorporated into the very structure of the enzymes.

What, then, is the difference between vitamins and minerals? The differences are chemical. The minerals come from the earth, whereas the vitamins come from plants that feed upon the earth. Minerals are all chemical elements, whereas the vitamins are chemical compounds that are synthesized by living matter. Life originated in the sea and all the essential minerals can be found in seawater. None of the vitamins is. Thus, though vitamins and a group of minerals labeled essential are indispensable to human life and to human health as well, there are differences between them that would reasonably divide them into separate categories.

Another distinction of minerals, at least in terms of health food products, is that not all of them are considered desirable and some are out-and-out toxic and should only be avoided. Aside from that problem, however, there is a small group of minerals that are dietarily essential and certainly important, yet which you will never find in a health food store for the simple reason that somebody many years ago developed a prejudice against them and condemned them as to be avoided.

A good example of this is sulfur, which is certainly essential and extremely important to the formation of all protein tissues because sulfur is incorporated into the very structure of some of the amino acids. Nevertheless, sulfur was one of the important elements in the so-called killer fogs that used to plague London and a few other industrial cities elsewhere; peculiar climatic conditions would cause concentrations of factory smoke for days at a time, killing some of the people who breathed the resulting horrible mixture of smoke and fog. Sulfur was also for some time erroneously considered the element responsible for the genital cancer that used to afflict chimney sweeps. Some of the original enthusiasts for natural living decreed that sulfur was bad for you, and consequently not natural. Since that time, this valuable and essential mineral, extremely important to health, has been adjudged an enemy. Such harmless products as raisins cured with sulfur have been decreed undesirable, and you will never find a sulfur supplement or a product containing sulfur in a health food store.

Fortunately, chicken ranchers see to it that their hens get enough sulfur in their feed, and if you eat eggs, you are getting a good enough supply of sulfur for your needs. It is true of sulfur, as it is of most of the dietary minerals, that if you eat a sensible diet containing substantial quantities of raw fruits and vegetables, you are quite possibly getting all the minerals you need right in your food and may require nothing more. There are a few exceptions to this which we will describe below.

The essential minerals that you will find available as dietary supplements are as follows:

CALCIUM

This is one of the minerals for which supplementation may be important, simply because we need so much of it. The most conservative estimate of how much calcium a normal adult requires is 800 milligrams daily, absorbed and put to use. Other expert estimates of the requirements range to as high as 1,400 milligrams a day. If you drink at least a pint of milk a day, like to eat cheese and other dairy products, and also have a liking for green, leafy vegetables, you are getting as much calcium as you require straight from your diet. In most cases, however, some calcium supplementation is helpful.

What does it help? In the first place, calcium with the proper assistance of other nutrients such as phosphorus and vitamins A and D enters into the structure of our bones and teeth, making them hard, dense, and resistant to decay and breakage. This is particularly important as we grow older, because a chronic calcium insufficiency will inevitably lead to bone demineralization. Loss of mineral in the jawbone leads to loss of teeth. Loss of mineral in the bones everywhere else induces a brittle, spongy structure that makes the bones fragile and easily broken. The broken hips that are so common, tragic, and frequently fatal among the elderly result from calcium deficiency.

Calcium is one of the nutrients that are important to the nervous system. It is a regulator of the heartbeat and is just what the doctor ordered for certain types of very painful cramps, including the type that occurs in the calves of the legs while a person sleeps and a type that hits women during pregnancy.

A sufficient supply of calcium is obviously a basic objective of anybody's diet. Nevertheless, calcium intake can be overdone and in some circumstances that can be quite dangerous. Ordinarily, a surplus of calcium will be harmlessly excreted and do no harm at all. If, however, we happen to be overly efficient absorbers and users of calcium, if, for instance, we take in a lot of vitamin C, spend a lot of time in the sunlight, or just have the kind of metabolism that latches on to calcium and doesn't like to let go, we can quickly build up a serious surplus of calcium in the bloodstream. Such excess calcium tends to accumulate in special locations where it can not only cause pain and discomfort, but shows up prominently in X-ray examinations and be easily misdiagnosed. A calcium spot in the lungs has the appearance of tuberculosis. Surrounding an ovary, it looks like cancer. It can lead to medical treatment that would be quite injurious to a person not requiring it. Surplus calcium in the arteries is deposited in forming arterial plaque, increasing the problem of narrowing arteries that we know as atherosclerosis.

So you must be careful that your calcium intake is neither too much nor too little. A measured intake of no more than 1 gram a day of supplemental calcium is suggested. It may be obtained in the following types of supplements:

BONE MEAL OR BONE FLOUR. Widely advocated and used as a calcium supplement, this is actually as inefficient a supplement as you are likely to find. It is a simple product—the long bones (legs and ribs) of cattle, pulverized and sterilized. It is sold in bottles of powder and in tablets, and if you have any reason for preferring it that way, you can also get it in capsules. The mineral content of this powdered bone product is the same as that of the bones from which it is made—approximately two parts calcium to one part phosphorus with small amounts of such bone-hardening minerals as strontium, fluorine, and magnesium. Because we usually eat a surplus of phosphorus in our normal diets, the phosphorus in bone flour promotes excretion rather than absorption of the calcium it contains. So even though you take bone meal tablets equivalent to a gram of calcium daily, you have no way of knowing whether you are actually absorbing that calcium or just passing it through your body to be excreted with your surplus phosphorus.

Bone meal also contains very small quantities of lead, arsenic, fluorine, and other materials that a living body deposits in bone and of which one would not want to accumulate too much.

Bone meal is prepared with or without the marrow that was contained in the bones. It sometimes has marrow added. It may come with or without vitamin D, which facilitates absorption of the calcium. It is a relatively inexpensive supplement and far more popular than it deserves to be.

CALCIUM ASCORBATE. This product can be an excellent calcium supplement. Though it is primarily designed as a better form of vitamin C (see listing under VITAMIN C), it is a combination form that greatly facilitates the absorption of the calcium in the product also. Its problem is that the label on the bottle will state the potency of vitamin C contained in each tablet and often ignore the calcium potency. In actuality, it takes a lot of calcium to buffer ascorbic acid as is done for calcium ascorbate. Thus, if you are taking this buffered product in order to be able to increase your vitamin C intake, you will probably be ingesting and absorbing too much calcium. It is recommended that you take no more than 500 milligrams a day of vitamin C as calcium ascorbate. This should give you about the right amount of calcium, and it should be well absorbed. Take any additional vitamin C in another form.

Calcium ascorbate is sold only in tablets. The potencies are stated as potencies of vitamin C and range from 200 to 1,000 milligrams.

CALCIUM LACTATE. This is a milk product containing calcium that is free of phosphorus, which therefore ought to be far better absorbed and utilized than any calcium-phosphorus combination. Lactic acid from milk, which is said to facilitate the absorption of calcium, is combined with it into the one product. It comes in tablets and powder. It is normally offered in smaller tablets providing 200 or 250 milligrams of calcium per tablet, permitting you to take a fairly precise dosage of calcium each day.

DICALCIUM PHOSPHATE. In this product, for whatever reason, calcium is bonded with phosphoric acid in a precise ratio of two parts of calcium to one part of phosphorus. This is essentially a pharmaceutical preparation available for use when both minerals are desired in just about the same proportion as in normal bones and teeth. It may well be a better choice than bone meal, because you can be sure it is free of lead and any other toxic materials.

DOLOMITE. This product is sold as a magnesium supplement, but since it contains more calcium than it does magnesium, it obviously can be used as a calcium supplement as well. In actuality, it is a type of limestone rich in magnesium, abundant around the world. The problem with this particular product is that it contains nothing to facilitate its absorption. Therefore, unless you take the trouble to ask yourself what else you can put in your diet to facilitate absorption of the minerals in dolomite tablets, it is quite likely that most of the calcium and magnesium will be excreted without ever being put to use in your body. The proportions of calcium and magnesium cannot be stated because they vary from one batch to another. Dolomite, like bone meal, is quite likely to be contaminated with various nondietary and toxic minerals that happen to have an affinity for calcium or magnesium or both. Strontium 90, the radioactive isotope, is among the possibilities.

EGGSHELL CALCIUM. Eggshells are nearly pure calcium and to some people who want pure calcium free of any phosphorus, the eggshell seems a desirable natural source. We know of nothing wrong with this product except that purifying and then pulverizing eggshells seems an unnecessarily laborious way of obtaining calcium, which is the identical mineral no matter what its source. Eggshell calcium is sold in tablets.

OYSTER-SHELL CALCIUM. The oyster shell, like the eggshell, comes close to being pure calcium. The same is true of the clam shell and the snail shell, neither of which has yet been used for a calcium supplement, though they could be as logically as the oyster shell. The theory behind the use of oyster shells is that, in addition to calcium, they contain the wide variety of trace minerals from seawater. Because they come from the sea, oyster shells are very high in sodium and are probably best avoided. This product is not a popular one and if you wanted it, you would find it hard to get. Nevertheless, it exists. It comes in tablets and its potency is stated as a weight of calcium per tablet. It's truly hard to see why anyone would bother.

Calcium will also be found in all multimineral preparations.

CHROMIUM

Until fairly recent times, the idea of looking for a reliable daily source of chromium in the diet would have seemed laughable. Chromium is a mineral that even in small quantities can be highly toxic. Yet in microscopic traces, measured in thousandths of a single milligram, chromium has turned out to be not only a valuable mineral but an essential one. In remarkably small traces, chromium enters into the functioning of the human pancreas in its most important activity—the manufacture of the hormone insulin.

In the deficiency or outright absence of chromium, the pancreas will go on producing insulin but the hormone will lack effectiveness. It will not be able to function as it should. The function of insulin is to regulate the levels of glucose in the bloodstream by combining with a surplus of glucose and carrying it out of the blood and into the cells and tissues where it is either burned (oxidized) for the production of energy or converted into fat to be stored for future energy needs.

Ideally, the production of insulin would be so fine-tuned that the level of glucose in the blood would always be the same within very narrow limits, the level being determined by the demand of the brain for glucose. This form of sugar is the basic food of the brain and must not be too much or too little. Too much glucose in the blood, which the body is unable to remove, is the condition known as diabetes. The oversupply of food to the brain gradually leads to coma and to death. An undersupply, the condition known as hypoglycemia, or low blood sugar, causes a reduction in energy and leads to many nervous symptoms, including emotional depression and suicidal tendencies.

To guard a person against both diabetes and hypoglycemia, the pancreas must receive its daily quota of chromium in a particular form that is biologically active. It is no use licking the chrome plating on your car's door handles. Though it is the same mineral, if you can get it off the handle it will either poison you or be neutral and worthless. The chromium that your pancreas requires to the extent of a few micrograms a day is now known scientifically as glucose tolerance factor, commonly abbreviated as GTF.

GTF was first found in wheat bran, and after a good bit of study was identified as a factor manufactured by the bacteria that live on the whole wheat berry. Further study found that GTF was most abundant in brewer's yeast. It turned out to be trivalent chromium bound to some unidentified protein factor in the yeast that somehow mediated the assimilation of the chromium and its absorption by the pancreas, where it was used in the manufacture of high-quality insulin.

By now it has come to be recognized that GTF, which is chromium in the special form acceptable to the pancreas, is a dietary essential. It is included in most multimineral preparations, though it is still advisable to read the label carefully and make certain that the chromium the tablet contains is actually identified as GTF. Otherwise, it may be there as chromium but still be nutritionally useless.

Aside from the multimineral route, there are two ways to supplement your diet with GTF chromium. One is to take brewer's yeast every day, and for this you can even get a high-chromium brewer's yeast, which is produced simply by feeding more chromium to the yeast culture, and leaving it to the yeast to transform it into GTF. There are also GTF chromium supplements giving a measured potency of from 20 to 100 micrograms of chromium, chelated to one or another amino acid that has been found to make the conversion that gives chromium GTF activity.

If you opt for brewer's yeast, it can be bought as a powder, as a powder packed in capsules, or as bottled tablets. It can be added to food by sprinkling it on salads or adding it to a blended drink, etc., but the taste is usually quite bitter. You can also get debittered brewer's yeast, but the process by which the bitterness is removed is not entirely successful and you may like the resulting flavor even less. You'll probably do best to take it in a way that permits you to swallow it without tasting it at all.

Perhaps the most pleasant way of all to get your daily GTF is to drink a glass of beer every day. It is a good source.

COPPER

Copper is one of the essential minerals, being necessary (along with iron) for the formation of hemoglobin, the pigmented material of red blood cells that transports oxygen from the lungs to the heart and thence to all the organs and tissues of the body. However, a healthy adult weighing 160 pounds requires about 2 milligrams a day of copper. The average intake from food alone is more than 3 milligrams, and if the plumbing system of your home happens to use copper pipes, your daily intake may well be 5 or 6 milligrams. You have no need of copper supplementation. If you use a multi-mineral and copper is one of the minerals it contains, watch out. It is a good assumption that the maker of that multimineral is more interested in impressing you with a long list of contents than he is in trying to produce a product that will be best for your health.

Toxicologically, copper is classified as one of the heavy metals. That means it can be poisonous, even fatally poisonous to the human body. A surplus of copper stored in the body can lead to atherosclerosis and high blood pressure and can induce hyperactivity and serious malfunctions of the brain. So it makes better sense to try to reduce your copper intake rather than augment it. If you think you may have too much copper, check your water pipes and if they are made of copper, try using bottled water from another source. If your doctor should find an excess of copper in your system, he has effective ways of removing it.

We advise against using any mineral supplement that contains copper.

FLUORINE

Fluorine is one of those essential elements that the health food and natural living movement has decided, in its own eccentric way, is an enemy of health that is to be avoided and fought against rather than included in the diet. Pure fluorine is a gas that could not be used for dietary purposes. To add it to a city's water supply or otherwise make it available for ingestion, it must be formed into a salt by combination with some other element. The most common form in which fluorine occurs in nature is calcium fluoride, and the form in which it is added to drinking water and vitamin supplements is sodium fluoride or some slight variation.

This book has no way of solving the ongoing debate about fluoridation of municipal water. It is true that at a very low level, encouraging the ingestion of about 1 milligram a day of sodium fluoride, fluorine will increase the hardness of children's teeth and reduce cavity formation, exerting this prophylactic effect up to about seventeen years of age. It is also true that about 10 percent of the children drinking fluoridated water will show signs of toxic reaction to it, such as chalky patches or black spots on their teeth. Proponents of 1 milligram a day of fluoride in the diet say that it is not dangerous. Opponents point out that sodium fluoride is routinely used as an enzyme poison in experimental laboratories, that for that reason it is a highly effective rat poison, and that it must over a period of time do damage to human health, even at the low intake of 1 milligram a day. All natural health publications and health food stores and organizations are dedicated in their opposition to any kind of dietary intake of fluorine, even though it has been named one of the essential minerals for its effect in hardening the teeth and bones.

You will not find fluoride offered for sale in any health food store, yet it is there and you can buy it if you wish. All bone meal has a content of calcium fluoride, in all probability enough to give you a dietary intake of 1 milligram a day of elemental fluorine. Dolomite may also contain calcium fluoride or magnesium fluoride, or both and, you may be sure, so will oyster-shell calcium. There is no good reason to suppose that the fluoride content of these calcium supplements does any kind of harm. This is the only way that fluoride is obtainable in a health food store. If you want a measured daily supplement, you will have to get it from a drugstore vitamin and mineral supplement.

IODINE

This essential element regulates the size and activity of the thyroid gland. The thyroid, in its turn, regulates the rate at which the body oxidizes glucose to produce energy. This is such a basic activity that iodine, even though it is very much a Johnny-one-note of a nutrient, remains extremely important. What's more, its dietary intake does present some problems, even though our requirement is only on the level of some 10 micrograms a day—a small fraction of a single milligram. Iodine deficiency leads to goiter, a spectacular enlargement of the thyroid gland that is accompanied by sharp irregularities in its activity and production of the thyroid hormone, thyroxine. Goiter can induce severe and unwanted weight loss, an uncomfortably nervous state, heart palpitations, and blood vessel complications—all for lack of 10 micrograms a day of iodine. Or it can slow down the entire metabolism, inducing obesity with cardiac and nervous complications. The existence of the famed goiter belt in the American Middle West is sufficient evidence that we cannot rely on our food supply to furnish us with enough iodine, even though we require so little. Where the soil is deficient in iodine, the food will be, too, and even a carefully balanced, excellent diet will not protect against iodine deficiency.

The incidence of goiter has been greatly reduced by the simple means of adding traces of iodine to table salt, considered the most universal of all foods and therefore the one most likely to supply adequate amounts of iodine to everybody. It has been a good public health measure but far from a perfect one. The biggest problem is that many people avoid salt, chemically sodium chloride, because their blood pressure is high and reduced sodium intake is frequently a help in this situation. It is estimated that some forty million Americans have high blood pressure whether they know it or not, and there are many more who have become persuaded quite correctly that they have no need for table salt and are better off without it. So there are truly great numbers of people who do not eat iodized salt, and can easily become iodine deficient.

There are no iodine supplements, as such, available anywhere. Kelp is offered in practically every health food store as a source of iodine. It is a type of seaweed, dried and chopped down to fragments small enough to be sprinkled onto food. Coming from the sea, kelp contains a great deal of sodium, just as iodized salt does, and should be avoided by millions of people who require a low sodium diet. The iodine content of kelp is often too high for safety, since a surplus of iodine can be highly toxic.

Kelp is not recommended as an iodine source. If you are able to eat any type of ocean fish or shellfish twice a week, that is probably the best way to get a good yet reasonable iodine intake. If you are not, then your best bet is a multimineral tablet that contains a measured and declared potency of iodine. The iodine content should be from 10 to 20 micrograms daily—no more.

IRON

Everybody knows about iron. For at least sixty or seventy years it has been well advertised that there is a blood disease called anemia that makes victims feel tired and dragged out and is caused by a lack of iron. Misleading information in ads has, over the years, persuaded hundreds of millions of people to self-diagnose all kinds of symptoms of illness or just plain getting older as iron deficiency anemia and to treat it by taking iron preparations. As a result, there is an entire generation with a high incidence of severe pain and loss of liver function caused by the storage of too much iron in the liver.

Since then the government has gotten a handle on the problem and has managed, at least, to restrict the kind of claims that can be made for iron products, which has reduced the demand and thus reduced the incidence of iron storage disease. It is still an important problem, however, and one of which you should be fully aware in considering whether you need an iron supplement and how big it should be.

Iron is integral to the body's ability to manufacture hemoglobin, the red pigmented material in the red blood cell that carries oxygen through the body. It is true that if your body lacks iron, the hemoglobin content of the blood will be reduced, the blood will have less capacity for transporting oxygen, and cells needing oxygen to produce energy for whatever reason will become fatigued sooner. There are also dozens of other reasons why people become fatigued and don't have as much pep as they used to. The most common is that they are getting older. There are also many diseases that have nothing to do with iron that make people feel more tired.

It has been determined that an adult in good health weighing 140 to 160 pounds actually uses 10 to 12 milligrams of iron a day in the manufacture of new red blood cells. Iron is rather plentiful in food and anyone who eats a normal diet that includes some red meat gets that much iron from his food and requires no supplementation. There are, however, some conditions that raise the iron requirements and make some kind of supplementation desirable for millions of people. Women between eleven or twelve and fifty have a monthly menstrual cycle in which blood is lost. In order to replace that lost blood each month, a woman has been calculated to need from 1 to 2 milligrams a day more iron than she is likely to get from her food alone. Does that mean that 2 milligrams a day of additional iron will take care of her needs? Not really. If it is elemental iron that she gets, her actual absorption and utilization of it will probably be no higher than 10 percent. On the other hand, there are many iron preparations that offer more efficient absorption than elemental iron. In taking them, it is wise to compensate for the greater efficiency by taking lower potencies.

There are other reasons for requiring supplemental iron. One of them is pregnancy. There are various kinds of internal bleeding that increase the demand for new blood. And sometimes one un-wittingly does something that just uses up the iron faster. For example, vitamin E is recognized as an antagonist of iron and will tend, if you take a lot of the vitamin, to increase the amount of iron that your system requires. A heavy smoker will have much of his hemoglobin bound up with carbon monoxide and thus unable to transport oxygen, creating a need in his blood for more red cells and more hemoglobin. And so on. There are many reasons why some iron supplementation may be desirable or downright neces-sary. If it is, you should certainly try to get as much iron as you need, while being very careful not to get too much.

TYPES OF IRON SUPPLEMENTATION. Chemically, there are an amazing number of kinds of iron salts available for use as sup-plements. This appears to have come about simply because none of them is entirely satisfactory and the pharmaceutical companies have kept producing new kinds, looking for more predictable and reli-able results to be gained with less discomfort. In terms of what you can buy without a prescription, however, there are really only three:

Ferrous sulfate. This is the most efficient and most effective iron salt. It is absorbed well and its efficiency is close to 100 percent. It will sometimes produce discomfort in the stomach and it might induce many kinds of digestive distress. However, such side effects are directly proportionate to the amount that is actually swallowed. Ferrous sulfate will fill your needs with a very low dose. Five mil-ligrams of iron as ferrous sulfate is the most you should ever need in twenty-four hours, unless you are under medical supervision and are actually treating a recognizable anemia. By keeping the dose down, you'll also keep the side effects down.

Ferrous gluconate. Because there is a strong prejudice against sulfur among health food devotees and their gurus, it is a common practice to substitute the glucose salt (gluconate) wherever medical practice has found the sulfur salt (sulfate) to be effective. In a wide range of medications it has been found that the sulfur salts of elements are the ones that work most effectively and they have become the standard medications. The gluconates seem never to be as efficient and are used chiefly because glucose is not sulfur. In the case of iron, the consumer is lucky. Ferrous gluconate is fairly efficient, though it does not compare to ferrous sulfate for efficiency. You would need perhaps 10 milligrams a day of iron as ferrous gluconate in order to enrich your dietary intake by 2 milligrams.

Ferrous ammonium citrate. About the only reason this is sometimes used is that it is fully soluble in water and thus goes well in a liquid tonic. The iron absorption efficiency is low and uncertain and is probably little better than the 10 percent efficiency that elemental iron possesses. If you *must* take your iron supplement as a liquid, this is what you are going to get. It does not have much to recommend it except ease of swallowing.

Protein-chelated iron. This involves a somewhat newer and still novel chemical trick to get elemental iron into the system. When it is done properly, molecule by molecule, the iron is attached in a chemical bonding to an amino acid, one of the constituents of protein. The reason for doing this is that the amino acid is more readily accepted to enter the bloodstream through the stomach or intestinal wall, whereas the elemental iron by itself would not be so accepted except to a very limited extent. It is precisely the same reason that iron is formed into a sulfur salt as ferrous sulfate, because the sulfur is more readily accepted by the body than is the iron. It gains admission for itself and carries the iron along with it. In the case of the protein chelates, it is an amino acid that runs interference and brings the product to the goal. However, not all amino acids are equally efficient at this work. Since the one that is used is rarely specified, it is impossible to predict whether any given brand of protein chelate will offer high efficiency absorption or low efficiency. Thus, though the principle is a good one, the effects are too uncertain and it really makes better sense, for daily iron supplementation, to choose low-potency ferrous sulfate and know exactly what you are getting and what it is going to do for you.

Blackstrap molasses. This is a rich natural source of iron—perhaps too rich. If you were to use it as molasses was once used, as a sweetener for coffee or tea, instead of sugar in baked goods, and as a substitute for butter to use with bread and cereals, your daily intake of blackstrap molasses might easily furnish you with enough iron each day to cause the very serious iron storage disease. Fortunately, we doubt if anyone uses blackstrap molasses that way today. Today you can get either capsules or tablets that offer small quantities of blackstrap molasses with iron added to achieve a stable potency. The potencies range from 10 milligrams of iron to 25 and if you like this product, your choice should be the lowest potency you can get. More is not better, and 25 milligrams of iron is just too much for daily intake.

Desiccated liver. Since liver stores iron, it is always a good, reliable source of iron. Eating whole liver is probably the most effective way of all to supplement your iron intake. To obtain a significant amount of iron from desiccated liver tablets, however, you would have to take a great many of them. Multiply the weight of the desiccated liver by four and you get a good approximation of how much of the nutrient values of whole liver you are getting. Thus you would have to eat a whole ounce of desiccated liver to get the equivalent of a quarter pound of whole liver. That's a lot of tablets and practically no one is ever going to do it. Since it is variable, desiccated liver tablets do not claim or specify any potency of iron and there is no way to tell just how much iron you are getting from them. They do contain iron, however, and in the most absorbable form known—heme iron. If you don't really require any supplementation at all but just want to make sure, a few desiccated liver tablets every day is a good choice.

Tablets and capsules of iron supplements are offered in potencies up to 125 milligrams of iron, and perhaps even more. Such potencies are dangerously high. They should be avoided. Even at the low 10 percent absorption rate of elemental iron, a 125 milligram supplement would give you an effective 12.5 milligrams in your body, which could only be justified if your diet contained no iron whatsoever. That is impossible even if you are the strictest of vegetarians. To take a supplement that big is to look for trouble and very likely to find it.

It is strongly recommended that before you buy any iron supplement, you consult the information above and choose one that will provide no more than a few milligrams of assimilated iron.

MAGNESIUM

Magnesium is everywhere. It is abundant in seawater. It is a constituent of chlorophyll and therefore it is to be found in all green plants. The hard water that most of us use for drinking is usually abundant in magnesium. We get dietary magnesium from nuts and seeds, from whole grains, and from many additional vegetables such as tomatoes, as well as all those that are green in color and contain chlorophyll. Yet in spite of the wide abundance of this essential mineral, most of us would run a small deficit in our daily consumption of magnesium if we depended on food and water alone for our supply. The most authentic estimate seems to be that we require 600 to 700 milligrams a day of magnesium for optimal health, and that normal consumption from all dietary sources falls about 200 milligrams a day short of the ideal.

Why do our bodies want so much magnesium? Well, it plays several important roles in human physiology, in the course of which it gets used up at a fast rate. As a matter of fact, there is probably not a single function of the human body into which magnesium does not enter in some way and play some role, so as with some other universal requirements such as oxygen and glucose, if the body does not have enough magnesium it actually becomes inefficient all over and in every way.

Here are just a few of the important roles played by this particular essential mineral:

Magnesium is a heart nutrient and is successfully used by some physicians both to treat and to prevent heart attacks, with statistical evidence giving strong indication that magnesium is highly successful in both regards. It has been found in many studies that hard drinking water that is high in magnesium greatly reduces the incidence of heart attack among the people who drink it. Magnesium enters into the structure of bone, and when there is more magnesium in the bone, the bone is harder and far more resistant to breaking. Although magnesium is neither a treatment nor a cure for cancer, and cancer is in no way directly related to magnesium deficiency, it has still been found that people with high magnesium diets or living in regions where the soil is rich in magnesium have statistically less tendency to develop cancer over the years than their counterparts whose diets are low in magnesium. This, in all probability, is simply because the low-magnesium people have less enzyme efficiency, which reduces the efficiency of all their bodily functions.

Magnesium presents one problem to us, however. Elemental magnesium or the mineral in any form that the body does not absorb well acts as a laxative. For about a hundred years, many of the standard laxative preparations have been based on magnesium. And so, when you decide to supplement your diet with plenty of magnesium because this mineral is so universally important, you had better make sure that you get the magnesium in a form that your body is going to absorb from your digestive system. Otherwise, all the magnesium will do is set up a slight irritation in your intestines that will induce the accumulation of additional liquids and have a laxative effect. Even if you happen to need a laxative, the magnesium that you do not absorb will certainly confer no nutritional benefits upon you.

TYPES AND POTENCIES OF MAGNESIUM SUPPLEMENTS.

It seems strange that with regard to magnesium, accepted as a highly desirable food supplement, there are no potency wars and none of the supplements offered would overdose a normal adult taking it. When you realize that the makers are afraid of inducing a cathartic effect, it all becomes clear. Whatever the reason, the supplements providing magnesium seldom go over 150 milligrams or so of the mineral and usually offer even less, so that you have to take several tablets in order to get 200 milligrams of magnesium. This is all to the good and eliminates any need for close scrutiny of magnesium potencies. You would have to try really hard to overdose yourself.

The types of magnesium supplements you will find available are:

Dolomite. This is just plain limestone from a lime deposit that lay underneath the ocean at some time in the distant past and thus absorbed large quantities of magnesium from the ocean water. The magnesium in dolomite is elemental and is more likely to have a laxative effect than it is to be absorbed. In fact, many people have found that they have no digestive effect on dolomite whatsoever and that the whole tablets pass through them unchanged. Digestion might conceivably be improved by supplementing the stomach acid and increasing the volume but it hardly seems worth the trouble. Dolomite is also very likely to contain toxic adulterants such as arsenic and lead and excessive amounts of fluorine. There are better and safer magnesium supplements.

Magnesium aspartate. Aspartic acid is a nonessential amino acid, which is to say that our bodies normally synthesize as much as we need and we do not require any from outside sources. However, the salt of magnesium combined with aspartic acid has long been considered a valuable mild tranquilizer and improver of the nerves. Combining magnesium with aspartic acid does seem to improve the efficiency of absorption and provide one good way of not only taking a magnesium supplement but actually getting the mineral into the system where it can go to work for your health.

Magnesium ascorbate. The only thing that seems to be wrong with this supplement as a source of magnesium or of vitamin C is that it is very expensive to manufacture and consequently very costly at the retail level. Magnesium ascorbate provides a buffered form of vitamin C that permits it to stay in the bloodstream considerably longer to the greater benefit of the user. Vitamin C, in its turn, improves the absorption and use of the magnesium with it—it is indeed a happy wedding. It is doubtful, however, that it is worth the very high cost.

Magnesium orotate. This particular form of magnesium is used in central and northern Europe in the treatment of heart disease. It is believed to carry magnesium directly to the heart muscle better than any other form of the mineral. In treating patients who have already had a heart attack, some European physicians believe that the use of magnesium orotate prevents recurrence and builds cardiac health and is therefore an important tool for them. That would make magnesium orotate less desirable as a general magnesium supplement, inasmuch as the mineral would be concentrated in the heart rather than distributed throughout the body as it normally should be.

Protein-chelated magnesium. Magnesium has been well tested for the efficiency of absorption after it has been bonded to any of several amino acids. Methionine seems to be the amino that provides the most effective bonding and the best absorption and use of the magnesium. If the label of the product indicates that the magnesium is indeed chelated with methionine, you can buy these tablets in confidence that they will give you the benefits they are supposed to. If the product is just called a protein chelate, you really have no way of knowing and it may be quite effective or less effective or not effective at all. We consider it well worthwhile to look for the methionine-chelated product. In the case of magnesium, there is no competition with the normally superior absorption offered by combining with sulfur. Magnesium sulfate has a definite cathartic effect, stimulating the production and release of large quantities of liver bile. Do not buy magnesium sulfate for any purpose except cathartic. And that leaves methionine-chelated magnesium the undisputed best and most desirable product for anyone who wants a regular daily supplement of his magnesium intake. Take these tablets to provide up to 200 milligrams a day of supplemental magnesium.

MANGANESE

Our requirement for this essential trace element is about 5 milligrams a day from all sources. Those of us who have a liking for whole-grain breads and nuts and seeds for snack foods will easily exceed our manganese requirement. Others with different dietary preferences will still get some manganese in their food but may well run a deficit of 1 to 2 milligrams a day. This is a tiny amount and no one is offering it as a distinct dietary supplement. Any multimineral tablet that you get, however, should contain 1 to 2 milligrams of manganese just to be on the safe side. If you should have a little excess, it will be harmlessly excreted.

Small as the quantity is of manganese that we require, it is truly essential and we cannot do without it. The mineral is a catalyst that serves to activate some of our most important enzyme systems. It has long been noted that there is a connection between diabetes and atherosclerosis, and that diabetics have a strong tendency to wind up with atherosclerosis and ultimately to die of heart disease. The key to the connection may well be manganese, a deficiency of which will leave imperfections in the insulin that is produced by the pancreas and render the insulin less effective in removing sugar from the bloodstream. People with a chronic deficiency of manganese will frequently become diabetic, and people who are manganese deficient have a much stronger tendency to develop atherosclerosis. Conceivably improvements in the dietary intake of this trace mineral by as little as 1 or 2 milligrams a day could serve to prevent much diabetes and many heart attacks.

Not available as a single supplement, manganese is most easily obtained as one of the minerals in a multimineral supplement. There seems to be no problem with absorption. You can also increase your intake by eating wheat germ and whole-grain breads and cereals.

MOLYBDENUM

A dental officer studied some 30,000 Navy recruits who passed through the Great Lakes Naval Training Station. He found there were only a couple of hundred who had never had a cavity in their teeth, and these came from two small geographical regions—one in Ohio and one in Kentucky. The only similarity between the two regions was that both had soil and a water supply rich in molybdenum. Obviously this mineral, which we need only in the smallest traces, has a lot to do with dental health. The information emerged, however, at a time when the fluoridation of municipal water supplies was receiving a great push and the fluoridation opponents did not want any distractions. The information about molybdenum was simply ignored and to this day it is not known how and why the element has such a beneficial effect on teeth and perhaps on bones.

It is an activator of a few enzymes and most interestingly, an antagonist of copper, so that particularly those people who have too much copper in their systems will benefit by a little dietary molybdenum, which will carry the copper out of their bodies.

The body excretes any excess of molybdenum that cannot be used, so the trace element is in effect nontoxic. It cannot hurt you and can only do you good, so there is every reason to insist that there be a little molybdenum in your multimineral supplement. Eating whole grains and seeds will also supply a trace of the element. You can't expect perfect teeth, because there is reason to believe that molybdenum nutrition must begin before birth, during the mother's pregnancy, to produce that kind of dental perfection. On the other hand, you could hardly include regular daily traces of molybdenum in your diet without deriving some benefit.

PHOSPHORUS

Phosphorus is the one element that is so abundant in our food supply that there is really no need to think about it at all. There is phosphorus in just about everything from the milk you drink to the bread and meat you eat. Even a can or bottle of soda water has a high phosphorus content. In fact, we are very fortunate that an excess of phosphorus tends to be harmlessly excreted, since an excess of phosphorus is what most of us have most of the time. It does no harm. As it is excreted it will take the calcium out of the body with it, but only such free calcium it happens to encounter in the bloodstream. The calcium in bones, teeth, and nerves— calcium that is bound in any way—will not be removed from the body by surplus phosphorus. It is only the new calcium—the gram or so that each of us should be getting every day—that is endangered by too much phosphorus. Thus, if we use bone meal as our calcium source, after a while we may well learn to our dismay that we just haven't been getting the calcium we thought we were. Its accompanying phosphorus has taken it right out of our bodies.

That is really what you have to know about phosphorus. It is important to you in many ways. It builds stronger teeth and bones and plays many biological roles. It is true, for example, as your grandmother used to tell you, that eating more fish makes for more positive and more acute brain activity, and that is because there is a lot of phosphorus in fish.

You don't have to worry about phosphorus supplements, however. And you won't even find them in most health food stores. Multimineral tablets frequently include no phosphorus and if they do, it is simply a few token milligrams with no nutritional significance but simply as a nod to completeness. You're getting plenty of phosphorus now and don't need any more.

POTASSIUM

You hear a great deal about potassium, because there are truly a lot of potassium deficiencies around. That is because there are so many valid medical reasons why people should reduce the amount of fluid in their bodies. Diuretics are intended to remove sodium that binds water within the cells and tissues. But as the water and sodium go out, so does potassium, which is frequently not replaced. The result is weakness, irregularities of the heartbeat, and sometimes a greater tendency of the body to accumulate unnecessary and undesirable water; now and then a potassium deficiency can even lead to death. It is indeed a complicated relationship between potassium and sodium, a kind of love-hate relationship that can cause unpredictable developments. The best evaluation of whether your body contains enough potassium and whether you need more is how you yourself feel. Less than with any other mineral, there is no numerical guide to how much potassium you ought to have or how much you ought to take in every day.

From the individual cell up to large and complex body structures, sodium acts to keep fluid in the body and potassium acts to remove it. Between them, the two elements should and usually do maintain a delicate balance that regulates how much fluid there is in the cell or in the body. Unfortunately, sodium chloride, which we call salt, has the quality of improving the flavor of just about any food—even sweets. We use a lot of salt and we get too much sodium in our bodies. If we habitually exercise hard, or if we live in hot climates where we lose a lot of fluid by sweating, or if we just have the right kind of metabolism, we are able to get rid of all that surplus sodium. Otherwise, we swell up periodically under the influence of estrogen or we gradually gain weight as our tissues accumulate fluid, and as our weight increases, demanding an additional volume of blood to feed our tissues, our blood pressure rises with more blood traveling through the same blood vessels, threatening a sudden breakage of one of those blood vessels. To guard against stroke, the doctor gives us drugs to increase our urination and thus remove fluid and sodium from our bodies. But whether it be by diuretic drugs or by sweating, the fluid loss removes not only sodium but other minerals as well, chief among them being potassium.

The sodium goes down to a more acceptable level at which total body fluid and blood pressure drop, but the potassium level drops, too, slowing down the process of converting sugar into energy, making the transmission of nerve impulses more erratic, and leaving the heart muscle without its proper nutrition, which weakens the heartbeat. Athletes have learned that heavy sweating will bring on this kind of sudden collapse unless they guard against it, so they take extra potassium before and during competitions.

What about the rest of us?

The way we get extra potassium, if we're not going to lose it again in the next hour or two of playing football, is a critical one. Doctors are very reluctant to recommend potassium supplements because they often cause indigestion right in the stomach, and sometimes stomach ulcers. To prevent these unpleasant symptoms, some potassium supplements have enteric coatings that prevent digestion in the stomach and carry the tablet unchanged into the small intestine where it is digested. In that location tablets have been found to cause ulcers as well, and have been blamed for the initiation of cancer. So your doctor would much rather that you get any supplemental potassium you need from food, which is not too difficult if you really try.

Raisins and prunes and the grapes and plums from which they are made are all quite abundant sources of potassium. So are bananas and whole oranges. Nuts, seeds, and whole grains are fair sources and just putting some concentration on these foods could take care of your potassium needs very nicely, even if you are using diuretics. If you can't get oranges right now and you hate raisins, then you have a problem and you might well have to take a potassium supplement. If so, please be aware that this is a very tricky mineral and you don't want an excess of it, any more than you want a deficiency. If you know you need supplemental potassium, take it as long as your symptoms of deficiency persist, and as soon as you are rid of the symptoms, stop the potassium supplementation as well. That way you will gain all the benefits of a good potassium supply without risking the ill effects of too much.

TYPES AND POTENCIES OF POTASSIUM SUPPLEMENTS. Whether as a single, individual potassium supplement or as one factor in a multimineral, potassium is offered in relatively small potencies because the makers are afraid of ill effects from large ones. Manufacturers have decided that the potencies should be under 100 milligrams in all cases. That means that some of them are offering 99 and a fraction milligrams to stay just within the limit, while others keep their products down far lower. Thirty or 50 milligrams a day would seem a sensible level to provide needed extra potassium yet avert any ill effects.

Potassium aspartate. When people complain of easy fatigue and nervous jitters, and perhaps of loss of interest in sex, potassium aspartate and magnesium aspartate are frequently recommended to be taken together. Why these two elemental salts should be of particular value in this kind of complaint, typical of middle-aged people, is by no means well understood. The two mineral salts are used rather like aspirin, which has been alleviating pain for a hundred years even though how it does so is still not understood. In the same way, for reasons unknown, potassium aspartate and magnesium aspartate taken together are far more effective than either one taken separately. In treating what has often been called "housewife's syndrome," they provide perfectly good daily supplements of both minerals.

Potassium chloride. This product is widely used as a salt substitute and for the purpose is a pretty good product. It does not really taste like salt nor does it have the same wonderful flavor-enhancing quality that salt has. But it does have a certain bitterness that people who must give up salt find better than nothing at all. And while helping somewhat with the flavor of your foods, it does also supply replacement potassium for what is being lost through diuretic therapy. Potassium chloride comes in small shaker bottles and is an easy safeguard for the millions who are or should be reducing the sodium content of their bodies.

For those who are not using diuretics but merely would like to reduce their sodium intake, there is a product called Lite Salt that is half table salt (sodium chloride) and half potassium chloride. This makes a very acceptable substitute for table salt in flavor, while it cuts in half the amount of sodium that you add to your foods and simultaneously increases your potassium intake. It's a very good product as long as you don't make the mistake of thinking it's of value for high blood pressure.

Potassium gluconate. Supplement manufacturers are very fond of the gluconates for a few simple reasons: They are quite cheap to manufacture and they can be called "chelated" without offending the Federal Trade Commission. Thus they can capitalize on a fast-growing demand for protein-chelated minerals and mislead a good number of customers into thinking they are getting protein chelates when all they are getting is the cheaper and less effective gluconates. These two reasons are enough to explain why potassium and other gluconates are so commonly found in health food stores. Not that there is anything especially wrong with potassium gluconate. It simply provides less efficient absorption and more waste, so that you have to use more of it to get the same effect. With potassium, where overdosage may be a real problem, that may even be a real protection for some.

Protein-chelated potassium. Only recently developed to improve the efficiency of animal feeds, in an area where business requirements demand the very best, protein-chelated minerals in general and protein-chelated potassium specifically have proven themselves superior to other types of supplements. The problem here is that while many minerals are essential to human nutrition, the body is adapted to taking them in only as constituents of food. Whatever the mineral may be, if you swallow it not as part of the wheat berry or a tomato but as the elemental mineral, the body will be reluctant or downright opposed to receiving the mineral. It will travel from one end of the digestive tract to the other and never get into the bloodstream. So in trying to get a greater supply of any mineral into the body, the problem is always to bond it to some other material that the body will accept and absorb far more readily. The individual amino acids that are combined into the various forms of protein have, to date, been found to be the most efficient bonding materials for most trace minerals. One amino acid will also be more efficient than another, but the relative efficiencies are a matter of debate at this time, rather than of hard and fast knowledge. Methionine has been given enough testing so that we can recommend it as the best chelating protein. That is not to say that others are not as good, but merely that we have no proof that they are. In any case, if you require supplemental potassium, you will find the protein-chelated tablets faster working and more effective.

Let us stress once more that it is easy to get a surplus of potassium in the body and it is no joking matter. It is one area in which you really should have professional advice before you go ahead to take supplements. You will also find potassium in any multimineral supplement you decide to take. Careful checking of the amount so provided against what your daily need would reasonably be is advised. For a person in normal health, the supplement providing 12 to 20 milligrams of potassium a day is preferable to the one that provides nearly 100 milligrams.

SELENIUM

Selenium has been with us for billions of years, yet in a way it is a new nutritional discovery. There is a cattle disease known as the blind staggers that is caused by too much selenium in the diet; and for a long, long while that was just about all that anybody really knew about selenium. It was listed as one of the toxic minerals and people were warned to stay away from it. Then, in the course of study of how vitamin E works, it was found that just a trace of selenium in the diet makes vitamin E far more active, and that selenium might have some nutritional purpose after all. When the significant fact came to light that breast cancer, one of the fastest increasing types in the United States, occurs at a far lower rate in Japan, it led to new studies that concluded that more selenium in the diet was what protected the women of Japan. Studies have found that selenium is an antioxidant in its own right, as active and as potent as either vitamin C or vitamin E. It has been found to have strong potential against infection and, by reducing inflammation, to reduce the pains of chronic arthritis. In fact, just about everywhere you look these days, selenium has been found to possess unexpected therapeutic value. The element has been transformed from one to be avoided to one that is recognized to be essential to human health and highly desirable in a larger quantity than we are liable to get from food alone.

Today the desirability of supplemental selenium is not only admitted but is something of a fad. The makers of combination products have found that by adding just a little selenium to their tablet they can sell a lot more of it, and they are doing so. This raises the possibility that you can unwittingly give yourself a toxic overdose because you are getting selenium from too many sources. In nature, where the major sources are shellfish, followed by fish, seaweed (which few of us eat), and the organ meats such as liver and kidneys (which we do not eat very often), the danger of a toxic dose of selenium is minimal. Even though the safe limit is only about 1 milligram a day of selenium from all sources, it was nothing to be concerned about until the element started appearing in so many health food products. Now you have to watch yourself. It is all too easy to take a multimineral, a stress supplement, and an antioxidant combination, each containing a safe amount of selenium, to eat clam chowder and a lobster tail for dinner and to start experiencing some of the unpleasant symptoms of selenium overdose. Protect yourself by watching your total intake.

TYPES AND POTENCIES OF SELENIUM SUPPLEMENTS. In the past couple of years a technique has been developed to produce a high-selenium nutritional yeast, whether brewer's or otherwise. The relationship is a natural one. Brewer's yeast has long been recognized as the most reliable source of nutritional selenium. However, it is always difficult to say that a food will contain exactly so much of a particular constituent. You cannot, for instance, sell an orange as a supplement containing 80 milligrams of vitamin C, even though that may be the value that food tables list. A food table value is an average, but a food supplement must contain a precise weight, verifiable by assay. And that is just what a new technique of culturing high-selenium yeast has made possible. So popular has yeast of uniform selenium potency proven, that it has virtually driven all other types of selenium supplements from the market. If you should happen to see a bottle of tablets containing elemental selenium or even a protein chelate, it has probably been standing on the shelf for a long time. What is available in today's fresh products is either tablets or capsules of high-selenium nutritional yeast, in potencies ranging from 50 to 200 micrograms. You can also get the same potencies in the same high-selenium yeast in a multimineral tablet.

SODIUM

It is perhaps strange to list sodium here. Although sodium is an essential mineral, you will never find a sodium supplement on sale in any health food store in this country. It is doubtful whether you will find one even in a drugstore. The reason, of course, is that sodium chloride, which is common table salt, is such an effective flavor enhancer that it is added to just about everything. Sodium is an essential mineral, but so plentiful that if we never added a single grain of salt to anything we eat, we would still be getting plenty of sodium. Although some people seem to be able to handle enormous sodium intakes and never suffer an ill effect, as a general rule we would all be better off to reduce our intake of sodium. And that is why sodium is listed here.

Whether you realize it or not, even among the products of the health food store there are a few that are high in sodium and that you ought to watch out for unless you are sure that you can handle an increase in your sodium intake. One of them is sea salt, which is offered as a more natural substitute for the salt extracted from salt mines. Sea salt is promoted as offering a wide range of trace minerals from the sea, which is presumed to make it easier on the human system. There is no evidence of this. It contains just as much sodium, and if you are under medical orders to avoid or limit your sodium intake, you are just kidding yourself if you think sea salt is any better than table salt. Kelp, a giant edible seaweed, may well offer some dietary advantages. It is true that in Japan, where seaweed is commonly eaten, there is remarkably less breast cancer among women and this is attributable to the high selenium content of seaweed as well as a higher proportion of fish in the diet. Kelp has a relatively high selenium content, but it is also high in sodium. It is sold as a salt substitute, which it is not. Perhaps the biggest problem for many of us is sodium ascorbate. It is an excellent product with strong nutritional advantages, yet people trying to reduce their sodium intake must be wary of it. (For a full discussion, see the Sodium Ascorbate listing under VITAMIN C.) And the organically produced celery you will find in many health food stores contains just as much sodium as any other celery and is just as undesirable for anyone trying to reduce his sodium intake.

ZINC

There are many good reasons to want to increase your zinc intake, and there are very many people who are trying to do so and feeling bewildered because their zinc supplements don't seem to be doing anything for them. After you read about zinc herein, that situation will change and you will have an effective increase in your zinc intake, gaining whatever benefits you can realistically hope to derive from it.

What benefits can people expect to obtain from zinc? If you are a man, you have good reason to suppose that a higher intake of zinc will give valuable protection to your prostate gland, protecting it not only from the rather common cancer of the prostate but also from far more common "benign hypertrophy" or enlargement of the prostate. Pathological studies have shown that almost invariably the prostate that is diseased or enlarged contains less zinc than the prostate that is functioning normally. Though not generally accepted, this indication that zinc helps the prostate to

maintain normal health is widely accepted. Will a higher zinc intake help after symptoms of prostate problems have begun to show
themselves? Some physicians have experimented with zinc therapy
and seem to have gotten good results, but their findings are by no
means conclusive.

Microgram for microgram, in proportion to its size and weight,
the retina of the eye uses more zinc than any other organ in the
body. And there is really no doubt that zinc is a very important
nutrient in the maintenance of eye health and good vision. Eye
diseases, once under way, seem for the most part to be untreatable
by nutritional means and it is doubtful whether zinc can help any
existing forms of retinitis. But as a preventive, it is certainly of
value.

It has been established that zinc is important to the healing of
burns and wounds, a process that takes longer and is less effective
when the zinc in the body is insufficient. People getting older
frequently experience a diminution and sometimes nearly a total
loss of the sense of taste. That problem also derives from an insufficient supply of zinc and can frequently be neatly reversed by adding more zinc to the diet. These problems and others, however,
derive from the fact that zinc has two broad, general functions in
the body that must be carried on fully or ill health will manifest
itself in any of a number of ways.

The first of these functions is the activation of enzyme systems.
Like magnesium, zinc plays a key role in the body's production of
important enzymes, entering into some as one of their building
blocks, acting as a catalyst to others. In either case, the resulting
production of enzymes when needed is always essential to some
bodily function or other. Growth and healing after injuries are
among the functions most affected by zinc. This is probably because incredibly small traces of zinc enter into the production of
the nucleic acids, RNA and DNA—acids contained within the
nucleus of each cell of the body—which hold all the patterns and
instructions for the cell's development, how it is to function, how

and when it is to reproduce itself, and how long after coming to life it is to die. In order to properly govern all the activities and functions of the living being, the nucleic acids themselves must regularly reproduce themselves and, in doing so, must reproduce in perfect detail all their incredibly complex structures. In order to do this they must have zinc, and if they don't have enough, there will be flaws in their reproduction that manifest themselves as diseases, weaknesses, malformations, and similar undesirable changes that come over all of us from time to time.

So we all need zinc, and the sad fact is that few of us are likely to get enough of it from our food alone. Not that we need very much. Fifteen milligrams a day seems to be the best estimate of how much zinc we actually require. But where will we get even that small amount?

The best food source of zinc is shellfish. Oysters are the best of all, and the legendary reputation of oysters as an improver of male potency may well have some basis in fact because of the large amount of zinc that oysters can add to the diet. Today, though, oysters and clams (another excellent source of zinc) have become so scarce and expensive that they are completely beyond the reach of most of us. Seeds such as sunflower and sesame are also good zinc sources but have the disadvantage of being oily foods that are just packed with calories. Fine as snacks, they are just about impossible to eat in sufficient quantity to provide a good daily source of zinc. The zinc is milled away from the wheat berry in the milling of flour and what we are left with is a sure insufficiency of zinc unless we get it in some kind of daily supplement or other.

TYPES AND POTENCIES OF ZINC SUPPLEMENTS.

Protein-chelated zinc. Chelation is a process by which one material is chemically locked to another by a bonding in at least three points of attachment. The chemistry by which this is accomplished is quite complicated and the most desirable effects are sometimes impossible to achieve. It has been learned that the body tends to reject elemental minerals and will absorb and use such minerals much better when they are bonded to some other material that the body will accept more readily and permit to enter the bloodstream through the lining of the stomach and the intestines. Amino acid chelation, which bonds an element to one of the constituent acids that make up protein, has been quite successful with some of the elements, such as magnesium.

When it comes to zinc, however, manufacturers so far have found it impossible to make an amino acid chelate. What their attempts end up with is a molecular attachment at only a single point, which is less firm, and less efficient at conducting the mineral into the body. This is known as a complex rather than a chelate, which is what such zinc products should be called. However, the word "chelated" has captured the imagination of the buying public, few of whom actually understand what it means. Mineral products do sell better if they are called "chelated," so the makers go right ahead using the term and nobody seems interested enough to compel any greater accuracy. This is even truer of gluconates, which are chemical salts and not chelates at all, yet which are all too frequently called chelates in the advertising of their makers.

When you get a protein-chelated zinc product, it is actually a protein-complex product. The difference, to you, is that its efficiency ratio is lower and you will have to get a higher potency in order to get as much zinc as you wish into your system. Potencies will be stated from 10 milligrams to 100 milligrams per tablet. These will be weights of the full complex, which may or may not be stated, but a 60 milligram tablet of what is called protein-chelated zinc will actually contain about 15 milligrams of elemental zinc.

Since the absorption is less efficient than might be desired, take 30 milligrams of elemental zinc for each 15 you are trying to get into your bloodstream.

Zinc gluconate. This is another product that is called "chelated" but is actually not. It is a salt formed with glucose, which theoretically should be quite helpful in carrying zinc into the body, since the body certainly accepts glucose with no problem. In actuality, however, zinc gluconate has proven to be a big disappointment to everyone but the people who are profiting by its sale. A 100 milligram tablet of zinc gluconate will contain about 15 milligrams of elemental zinc, from which you will actually absorb no more than 2 or 3 milligrams. The rest is all waste. If you want 15 to 30 milligrams of absorbed elemental zinc, you are going to have to swallow a lot of tablets of this product.

Zinc sulfate. Actually, when it comes to zinc, the best absorption is provided by this sulfate product. If your doctor wants to give you supplemental zinc, he will prescribe zinc sulfate, and if you decide to take supplemental zinc for yourself and want to be sure the zinc is actually getting into your body, zinc sulfate is what you should use. For preventive and maintenance purposes, a daily dosage that will provide 15 milligrams of elemental zinc and no more is recommended. The label should read "15 milligrams elemental zinc from (or as) sulfate." A larger dose than that might set up some irritation in your stomach and turn out to be unpleasant. Stick to a 15 milligram tablet, and if you feel you need more zinc than that, eat some sunflower seeds every day or clams and oysters if you can get them. You may well find, though, that 15 milligrams is quite enough for your needs, provided it all gets into your bloodstream. As zinc sulfate, it will.

VITAMIN AND MINERAL COMBINATIONS

There are good reasons why various vitamins and minerals should be combined in differing ways, and some other reasons that are not so good but still make sense, at least commercially. The further nutrition advances as a scientific discipline, the more apparent it becomes that in the enormous complexity of our body chemistry nutrients do work together and work better together, and nutritional problems frequently—perhaps always—involve more than one nutrient.

For just a few examples: vitamins A and D occur together in nature and work together in human biochemistry. Doesn't it, therefore, make good sense to combine them in a single product so that the consumer will get both together in the proper proportions? Selenium has been found to increase the biological activity of vitamin E, and often the best value of desirable vitamin E activity in the body can be achieved by taking a lower potency of E combined with a little selenium. Or, since there are many people whose natural tastes lead them to that Mount Everest of dieticians' aspirations, the well-balanced diet, and who really require little or nothing in the way of supplementation, does it not make sense to offer them the minimal "insurance program" they wish in a single tablet that is taken only once a day with the least possible trouble?

There are these and many other valid reasons why there should be a variety of combinations of vitamins and minerals offered to the consumer. There is also an enormous commercial consideration. The manufacturer or packager prospers in direct relation to the number of products he is able to market successfully. By dreaming up new combinations of the nutrients he is already selling, he is able to augment his line and make more money as long as he is able to dream up some kind of rationale to justify each new product. A true impresario of nutrition can easily multiply by four or five the number of products he has to sell simply by combining them in various ways. And in nutrition, as in every other field, the public welfare is an excellent sales ploy, but the basic objective is to make money. As in all areas of trade, the profit motive is the source of much that is good, much that is new, and of continual improvement in what we already have, but we ourselves must be on guard against what is false and wasteful.

In this section there are listed the various types of combination formulas with guidelines to help you distinguish what may be of genuine value at a reasonable price from alternatives that are pointless or irrational.

MULTIVITAMINS

Many people do not like taking tablets and want as few as possible. Many others do not want to bother figuring out what potency of each of the vitamins they should take and still more simply feel incompetent to do so. For all these people, the supplement that comes to them as the only one they need because it gives them all their requirements in a single preparation—often a single tablet—is indeed welcome.

Indeed, the idea does make sense in many ways, including the fact that in order to get the full range of vitamins into a single tablet, or even three tablets a day, the potencies must be kept relatively low. Since most supplements these days are being packaged in far higher potencies than anyone realistically requires, it is both more economical and safer to stick to the supplement that is lower in its potency level. It is also comforting to assume that somebody with professional education and knowledge has worked out the proper proportions between the various vitamins and that if you take this complete multivitamin, all will be in balance.

There are pitfalls, however.

Check the ingredients table. It will be long and bewildering. Look, however, for the lesser B vitamins: biotin, choline, inositol, and pantothenic acid. If these are not among the ingredients, then you will know that the maker of this particular supplement has been skimping and is not actually providing you with a complete multivitamin. Since what you are buying is nutritional insurance, you do want it to be complete in every detail and should be careful to see that the product you get is complete.

Do not buy a multivitamin to which iron has been added. Vitamin E and iron are antagonists. If both occur in the same tablet, as soon as they are released in your digestive system, each will neutralize the other and you will derive no benefit from them.

As a general rule, it is better to get a multivitamin preparation to which no minerals have been added. Some of the essential minerals like calcium and magnesium are required in so much bulk that it would be impossible to add your actual daily requirements. Adding small quantities of these minerals to a vitamin tablet may give you psychological reassurance but it will not fill your nutritional needs. There is always something a little phony about a multivitamin plus minerals.

Avoid the type of multivitamin that offers you megavitamins. Exaggeratedly large doses of a couple of the B vitamins and vitamin C can throw the entire tablet out of balance as well as making it so big it is better suited to horses than people. The high potency (up to a gram) of vitamin C will be mostly excreted in your urine within five hours. Some of the B vitamins will suffer the same fate, while the remainder will be stored in the liver and can build up to a dangerous excess.

Multivitamin combinations can be bought as tablets, liquids, or powders. The powders are essentially the same as the tablets except that they have not been pressed into tablet form. This does permit some separation and the distribution of the various ingredients may become irregular. On the whole, tablets are to be preferred. The liquids are perfectly okay if you have some reason for preferring them. You will not enjoy the taste, and if you are able to swallow the tablet so that you don't taste it at all, that might well be better.

To sum up: Your best choice in multivitamin preparations will be a low-potency tablet that gives you the complete range of all vitamins but has no minerals added.

MULTIMINERALS

These combination products tend to be quite complete in their content of essential minerals. Because, in the case of many of the mineral nutrients, an excess can be seriously toxic, the makers of mineral supplements cannot engage in potency wars, but compete instead with the number of different minerals that their supplements offer. This is all to the good. Since you are trying to insure yourself against any possible deficiency, you want the entire range of minerals that have been found to be essential in human nutrition. It is not hard to find in multimineral supplements.

What is of greater concern in this type of combination is whether the minerals supplied will actually be absorbed by your body. The digestive system tends to resist absorbing what you might call "naked" minerals and to accept only minerals that occur in food where they are complexed with other food elements, in effect being carried into the body by the food to which they are attached. In preparing a mineral supplement it is not always easy or even possible to duplicate the molecular arrangements that bring minerals into our systems with the food that we eat. For example, iron in its most absorbable form is complexed with hemoglobin, but no chemist has yet found the way to put heme iron into a supplement that must have a long shelf life. Here are some tips that will help you select a multimineral supplement whose minerals will actually get into your system, where they can do you some good, and not just be excreted.

If many of the minerals are present as gluconates (zinc gluconate, iron gluconate, etc.), it is an indication that the supplement is inefficient. The gluconates have a low ratio of absorption while other ways of complexing the minerals as salts are far more efficient.

Zinc sulfate is the only form of zinc that you can be sure will actually be absorbed by you. Prefer a smaller quantity of zinc sulfate to double or triple the amount of any other type of zinc salt.

Chromium should be listed as GTF chromium, the initials standing for Glucose Tolerance Factor. Those initials indicate that the chromium is combined with the same protein elements that occur in yeast, that have been found to give the chromium its biological activity which is a protection against diabetes.

Some of the minerals, notably magnesium, should be listed as "protein chelated." This indicates an attachment to a protein element in a manner that is similar to complexing but with an even stronger bond. It cannot be done with all minerals but for those with which it can be done, protein chelation provides much greater absorption efficiency.

Given your mineral ingredients in forms that will promote absorption efficiency, all multimineral supplements are much alike in potencies and contents and all tend to be perfectly fine for your objectives. You can buy them with confidence that they will do you good and will not harm you.

ANTIOXIDANTS

During the past ten years or so there has emerged a great deal of suggestive scientific material indicating that oxidation taking place in the bloodstream is the cause of wide-ranging, basic health problems, and that the preservation of oxygen in its pure state until it reaches the individual cells, where it is used to produce energy is a fundamental key to health. There is no doubt that oxygen, which is the breath of life because of its ability to burn sugar to produce heat and energy, can also be highly destructive. It is oxygen that turns fats and oil rancid. It is oxygen that turns iron and steel into rust. In the bloodstream, oxygen is transported by the red blood cells and should be delivered as required to every cell of the body. Along the way, though, it can easily combine with other materials it may encounter in the bloodstream, particularly lipids. When this happens, one of the results is the formation of unstable molecules that are highly reactive, breaking away from the parent body and entering upon a short but violently active existence. These are called "free radicals" and are blamed, by some biochemists, for many of the ills of human existence, such as certain types of cancer, arthritis, certain types of cataracts and other eye diseases, senility, and so on through the catalogue of what are called the degenerative diseases.

If this theory is correct, and even if not proved it is widely held by a number of scientists of good repute, then it is apparent that anything that will prevent oxygen from combining with other materials in the bloodstream should be a valuable protector of health. Indeed, it should keep the entire body in a more youthful and healthy condition. That, in the minds of many, makes the antioxidants—those particular materials that have the special ability to interfere with the oxidation process—seem to be particularly desirable to have in their bodies in large quantities.

Antioxidants are not particularly scarce. There are numerous materials that have this particular property, including some that are used as preservatives in the processing of food, which of course would be shunned by any self-respecting health nut. Antioxidant nutrients are another matter, and products that offer combinations of antioxidants have proven very popular with the buying public.

TYPES AND POTENCIES OF ANTIOXIDANT COMBINATIONS.

Vitamin E with vitamin C. Both these vitamins have strong antioxidant activity and, fortunately, neither one has any important ill effects caused by taking too much. It is not uncommon to find such a combination in which a single tablet will contain as much as 800 IU of vitamin E and 1,000 milligrams of vitamin C. The two make strange bedfellows inasmuch as the vitamin E will be digested slowly in the intestines, whereas the vitamin C is absorbed almost immediately from the stomach and will normally leave the system within five hours. If the tablet is coated for slow release, less of the C will actually be absorbed. It is probably better to take each of these two vitamins separately under conditions more favorable to obtaining the full activity you are seeking. Vitamin C is best taken in low potencies throughout the day. Vitamin E is fine to take in a single dose, but unless you are under professional instructions and taking the vitamin for a specific therapeutic purpose, you should not take a potency of more than 400 IU a day.

This combination can be obtained in vitamin E potencies from 100 to 800 IU, vitamin C potencies of from 100 to 1,000 milligrams.

Vitamin E with vitamin C and selenium. Selenium is a trace mineral that functions as a powerful antioxidant. It also stands in a special relationship to vitamin E, strongly increasing the biological activity of the vitamin by its presence. It does make sense, if antioxidants are what you are looking for, to add selenium to the combination of vitamins E and C. The tablet should contain no less than 10 micrograms of selenium and no more than 100 micrograms. When this trace mineral is in the mix, the tablet should not contain more than 200 IU of vitamin E.

In actuality, combinations of the three nutrients still contain up to 800 IU of vitamin E, which is far too much for any reasonable purpose. There is no known harm that this will do you, but it will obviously cost you more while providing no additional benefit.

Antioxidants with additional vitamins and minerals. It has become rather commonplace for vitamins E and C and selenium, which are the true nutritional antioxidants, to be combined with additional ingredients which, for sales purposes, are also called antioxidants and do indeed show at least a relationship to antioxidant activity. Vitamin A, for example, which is commonly added, is involved with the health of the lungs, which bring the oxygen into the blood. The minerals magnesium and zinc, also commonly added and called "antioxidants" have no direct antioxidant activity, but are involved in enzyme systems that ultimately do exercise controls over oxidation.

Packing such additional nutrients into an antioxidant combination gives it greater sales appeal. The well-informed will not buy these more complicated combinations, however. There is a danger in using them, which is that of overdosing. All minerals are extremely sensitive in this regard and too much of any one of them will invariably have uncomfortable ill effects. Vitamin A, which accumulates in the liver, is easily overdone. In no case can an antioxidant combination be expected to fulfill all nutritional needs of an individual. It must be assumed, therefore, that you are also taking other supplements. This could make it very easy for you, even without knowing it, to take vitamin A and some of the minerals from two or more sources at the same time and wind up with an excess that would lead to serious side effects.

If you are going to add antioxidants to your nutritional program, it is seriously suggested that you stick to vitamins E and C, neither of which will do you any harm even when taken in excess.

GERIATRIC FORMULAS

For many years there has existed a widely promoted and widely believed myth to the effect that older people tend to become anemic and deficient in iron. Naturally, as people become older, they tend to feel tired more easily and can no longer accomplish as much physical work. This is not "tired blood," however, but simply the natural running down of the body. It is very conceivable that improved overall nutrition can do a great deal to slow down the aging process and help elderly people to feel and look younger. If this is so, however, it will not be through any kindergarten chemistry process like correcting tired blood. By shopping carefully and reading the labels on the bottles, we can find a geriatric formula that will offer you far more intricate and worthwhile values. The kinds of geriatric formulas that are available are:

MULTIVITAMINS WITH IRON. As noted above, the iron in such a formula has no value except as a sales argument. Unless you have been told so by your doctor, there is little or no reason to suppose that you are anemic. Besides, it is unlikely that more than 10 percent of the iron in such a preparation can even be absorbed. As multivitamin preparations go, these geriatric formulas tend to leave out some of the lesser known but more expensive B vitamins such as biotin, choline, and inositol. They will also contain little or no vitamin E and generally be a basic, low-potency, no-frills supplement. For what they are, they tend to be expensive, and you may be sure that they will not correct any health problems you may have that are the result of aging.

MULTIVITAMINS AND MULTIMINERALS. The idea, of course, is that if you're going to supplement your diet to insure better nutrition, you may as well do it with all the essential nutrients and eliminate all risk of deficiencies. It is an idea that makes sense in many ways. What this means in practice though is that the maker of a multivitamin, multimineral supplement is using that same supplement as his geriatric formula, changing nothing but the label on the bottle.

To find a good vitamin-mineral formula that has truly been designed for geriatric use and will best serve your purpose, read the listing of ingredients and look for the following signs:

There will be less vitamin A than in most multivitamins. No more than 5,000 units.

The formula should contain at least a full gram (1,000 milligrams) of calcium and may contain up to 1,200 milligrams. This is in accordance with the increasing need for calcium, particularly in women, as people grow older.

Small quantities of digestive enzymes should be included.

RNA (ribonucleic acid) should be one of the ingredients.

There should be some vitamin E in the tablet, but it should be low potency—not more than 90 IU and preferably about 60. This is because high blood pressure is one of the problems of older people, and if vitamin E is taken for the first time, anything more than 90 IU could increase the blood pressure.

One way of recognizing a better geriatric formula is that it will come in two bottles, one for vitamins and one for minerals. That is basically because putting them all in a single tablet would make that tablet too big to swallow, and also because there are a few antagonisms that make it better to keep the vitamins and minerals out of direct contact.

A specific geriatric formula is seldom actually required by anyone. If that is what you wish, however, select a complete one containing all vitamins and mineral nutrients and check it, as suggested above, to make certain you are actually getting a geriatric formula.

HAIR-IMPROVING SUPPLEMENTS

Over the years, many investigators have observed phenomena in connection with nutritional research that suggested that one nutrient or another might have some value in keeping hair from falling out, restoring lost hair, and/or restoring color to hair that has turned gray. For example, many years ago it was found that rats would turn gray when deficient in pantothenic acid, a lesser B vitamin, and that addition of the vitamin to their diets could often restore the color to their coats. Adelle Davis recommended pantothenic acid for that purpose for many years. But in every study that has ever been made to determine whether pantothenic acid would improve hair color in human beings, it has failed. It will not do for us what it will do for rats.

Other investigations have found that some of the essential minerals are stored in the hair, making hair analysis a pretty good determinant of how abundant or deficient body stores of any particular mineral are. It is often true that if a particular nutrient concentrates in one particular organ, further investigation will find that that nutrient is especially needed for the health and functioning of the organ involved. For example, zinc concentrates in the prostate gland and it has been found that zinc is required for the health and functioning of the prostate. Because of this, various people have proposed at various times that the minerals found abundantly in hair are required for healthy hair.

At different times, therefore, such minerals as iron, copper, zinc, and manganese have been recommended for hair health. Studies that have been made have not borne out any relationship. Time after time hopes have been shattered as it has been demonstrated that there is no particular nutrient that has any discernible effect on the color of the hair or the amount of hair on any particular head. General health may well reflect itself in the luster and attractiveness of the hair, just as it does in animals. But that is general health, and there is no particular nutrient that is always involved.

Nevertheless, one entrepreneur about ten years ago decided to put together a combination of the nutrients that had been recommended for healthy hair at various times and see if he could sell it. It was remarkably successful. The special nutrients involved were pantothenic acid, choline, inositol, and a few other of the lesser B vitamins, plus iron, copper, iodine, manganese, and zinc. It was a great success. Apparently the public was eager to believe that a vitamin-mineral supplement would restore or improve hair. What one man could do successfully, fifty others could imitate. By now, every supplement maker has a hair-improving product, and none of them does the least good.

How is it possible to claim that a supplement will benefit the hair if it has no value? Well, it should be understood that the Food and Drug Administration, which generally regulates this particular industry, has a great deal of control over everything relating to the questions of disease and health. Claim that your product can cure a disease and you had better be able to prove it. But hair is not a disease and the claim that a product can improve hair is not considered a health claim. Rather, it all falls in the realm of cosmetics over which the FDA has little control.

Thus, in this particular area, it is possible to get away with a great deal. The only government agency that has tried to exercise any control over vitamin and mineral combinations for the hair has been the Post Office, which has gone after a couple of people who have made such claims through the mails. When it comes to products sold in the health food store, though, no agency seems to have any particular control and they will go on being sold.

You can be sure such products will not do your hair any good, however. Don't waste your money.

PET VITAMINS

If you feed your dog or cat regular commercial pet food, that food will probably have added to it all supplemental vitamins and minerals your pet may require. It is really only in unusual circumstances that there is any reason at all to give your pet supplemental vitamins or minerals. There are such circumstances, however.

If your cat is a tuna fish freak and refuses all other food, it could develop a vitamin E deficiency and should get a little supplemental vitamin E. If your dog won't eat dry dog foods but will only eat canned or fresh meats, it probably needs a regular daily source of calcium and some other minerals that are found in the bone meal that is contained in dry dog food. If your pet's coat is dry and lacks luster, the need could be for more oil or vitamin A in the diet. But these are all unusual cases. If you have a healthy, happy pet, why bother the animal with vitamin supplements it doesn't need?

Most pet supplements are obtainable as tablets in a base of desiccated liver, the flavor of which is attractive to many dogs and cats. They do not provide nearly as much calcium as your dog may need, nor as much oil as your cat may require. Otherwise, they are satisfactory as a supplement for the animal that will not eat commercial pet food.

Liquid supplements for pets are polyunsaturated oils of various types, all of equal value. They are fine for the animal with a dry coat if you can get the animal to take it. It isn't easy.

STRESS FORMULAS

Stress is a vague term with little actual meaning but great power to persuade the consuming public that it is suffering from this particular problem. It might be said that if you are alive at all you are going to encounter stress. Anything that calls for a little extra effort or coping with some unusual circumstance or other can be called stress. Polluted air is stress. So is driving a car, trying to make a living, having a romance, not having a romance, or stubbing your toe on the curbstone. Somehow, millions of us have been persuaded that stress is dangerous and that we need help to maintain our health in a stressful situation. Hence, stress formulas.

The heart of any stress formula is vitamin C, inasmuch as this vitamin is concentrated in the adrenal glands and relates both to the health of the adrenals themselves and to their ability to produce their hormones. Since the production of adrenal hormones is basic to our ability to meet demands for any kind of extra effort, it is reasoned that whatever is good for the adrenal glands is helpful in a stress situation. Such reasoning leads to the following kinds of formulation:

VITAMIN C WITH B COMPLEX. This is the simplest type of stress formula. Its formulation arises from two established bits of knowledge. Vitamin C promotes adrenal health and function and a number of the B vitamins promote the health and function of the nervous system. On the assumption that stress is a psychological phenomenon, this combination is presumed to be good medicine.

Potencies run high. Obviously, if you feel that you're under special stress and need help to cope with it, you're going to feel that the more help the better and be far more likely to buy a high-potency aid. Realistically, a stress formulation should give you perhaps 100 milligrams of vitamin C and a low-potency B complex, to be taken every three hours or so. You can find this stress combination in such low numbers, but you'll really have to hunt for it. More commonly, the vitamin C potency ranges from 250 milligrams to a full gram (1,000 milligrams); and the B complex potency will be one of those unbalanced "balanced" formulas in which you get from 25 to 100 milligrams of every one of the important B vitamins.

Taking such a high potency formula may not do much for your stress, but it will give you some of the most nutritious urine the mind of man has ever conceived. There is no way that the body can use such an enormous potency of vitamin C within the five hours or so that is its maximum survival time in the bloodstream before the kidneys filter it out. The B vitamins are also lost into the urine to some extent, but some of them are stored in the liver, where a big surplus can become toxic under certain conditions. So you could even be doing yourself more harm than good with this kind of stress formula.

VITAMIN C WITH B COMPLEX COATED FOR SLOW RELEASE. This product attempts to face up to the information in the paragraphs immediately above. Its aim is to gradually feed lower potencies of the vitamins into the bloodstream, both protracting the time that the vitamins are biologically active in the body and reducing the amount that is excreted and lost. This is done by use of a coating on the tablet, part of which dissolves in the stomach while most of the tablet's contents are preserved intact from the stomach's digestive juices. What it overlooks is that the stomach is the natural location to absorb both of the vitamins involved, while those that pass through into the duodenum are entering an alkaline climate that neutralizes the acid vitamins and nullifies their effectiveness as vitamins. In such a product, the potency may be 1,000 milligrams of vitamin C but no more than 200 milligrams or so will get into your bloodstream as actual vitamin C.

This product, in effect, makes promises it is unable to keep. It is not recommended.

VITAMIN C AS MINERAL ASCORBATES WITH B COMPLEX. By providing a form of vitamin C that is only slightly acid, this product provides a vitamin that will remain in the bloodstream longer, simply because it is the acidity that prompts the kidneys to filter the vitamin C out of the blood. Calcium ascorbate is the actual type that the product will contain, while any other minerals that the fancy of the maker may decide to add will be added simply as minerals which you may or may not feel that you require. Even though you obtain more efficient use of the vitamins in this formulation, the lower potencies are still to be preferred. As stress formulas go, however, those that contain ascorbates are preferable if they are not too expensive. You can expect them to cost a little more, but if the higher cost amounts to more than 20 percent, they are overpriced and you should do some shopping around.

VITAMIN C WITH SELECTED B VITAMINS. In order to reduce the cost and the retail price, some manufacturers have taken the trouble to produce a stress formula containing, in addition to its vitamin C, just those B vitamins that actually have something to do with the nervous system and its health. These are: thiamine (B_1), riboflavin (B_2), niacin (B_3), pyridoxine (B_6), choline, and B_{12}. If you can find this limited range of B vitamins in a stress formula that costs sufficiently less to make a difference, then this is the one to buy. It is really all that you might conceivably need and again, very high potencies will not do you any more good than low potencies.

MISCELLANEOUS STRESS PREPARATIONS. Stress is a word that has never been satisfactorily defined. It is not a disease certainly, and to say that something is good for stress does not constitute a health claim. This means, in effect, that one can call nearly anything a stress product and there is no legal way that any government agency can interfere or hold that the labeling is deceptive. For example, if a restaurant wanted to advertise its liver and onions as a "stress special" rather than a "blue plate special" it would be permissible. A bottle of aspirin tablets could easily be promoted as alleviating stress. In fact, when you start buying stress preparations, let the buyer beware.

Thus it is that a number of products that are simply multivitamins or vitamin and mineral formulations are also offered as "stress" formulas. The commercial logic should be obvious. If you make a multivitamin tablet, you sell as many of them as you can. Then you take the same product and put a different label on the bottle calling it a stress formula, and you sell a great many more. It's legal and it's profitable.

If you see any stress preparations containing any ingredients other than vitamin C and B vitamins, you can be pretty sure that is exactly what has been done. If you buy one, you are not getting what you are looking for and paying for.

VITAMIN COMBINATIONS FOR CHILDREN

Notoriously, children have limited tastes in food and insist on eating too much of the few things they like best, and simply cannot be compelled to eat anything resembling a balanced, nutritious diet. This being so, many parents believe quite correctly that their children would benefit by vitamin supplementation. The big problem, like that of food, is to find some way to persuade the children to take the supplements after the parents have bought them. It is done, generally, by giving them a flavor that children will enjoy. This, in turn, creates the reverse problem of keeping the children from overdosing with a supplement because they like its taste. Since this can be a serious problem, it is suggested that any pleasant-tasting vitamin supplements be kept out of sight and out of reach, just like medicines.

Although there are other types produced by pharmaceutical companies and available in drugstores, within the health food industry there are only two types of children's vitamins. They are:

CHEWABLE VITAMINS FOR CHILDREN. Because all manufacturers are aware that children are delicate and can easily be harmed by overdosing with anything, including vitamins, there are no potency wars between makers in this area. To determine a proper dosage for children, what the makers do is take their lowest-potency adult formula and reduce the potency of each ingredient by 50 percent. It is then produced with an attractive flavor—usually fruit—and sweetener.

Since most adherents of health foods consider sugar one of the dangerous drugs, the sweetener is sometimes a synthetic like saccharine or sorbitol (both more dangerous than sugar) or it may be fructose, honey, or molasses. For the amount of sweetener required for one tablet a day, it might just as well be sugar.

The tendency in children's vitamin supplements is to leave out anything that tastes bad. Thus yeast is not used as a source of B vitamins because children would dislike the flavor and refuse it. For the same reason, the essential minerals are not included in supplements for children. The one exception is iron, because some children do actually require an iron supplement. However, iron also gives the tablet an unpleasant taste and children tend to refuse it.

LIQUID VITAMINS FOR CHILDREN. A good many children will not swallow anything like a pill and decide they hate the taste of all chewable vitamin supplements. For them there remains only a liquid that can be added in drops to their fruit juice or milk or disguised in other ways so that they will still get the supplementation their parents feel they require. The liquid is water, with flavor and sweetener added, and the vitamin content per so many drops or per teaspoonful will be identical to that of the chewable tablet. It is easier to overdose with a liquid. Be careful not to do so. The effect on children of too much vitamin A or vitamin D can be severe.

SECTION 2:
HERBS

HERBS

All plants that are not foods are potentially herbs, and you may be sure that all of them have been tried for herbal purposes at one time or another. Roots, stems, bark, flowers, fruits, and seeds may all be considered herbs if they are not eaten as food. All have been tried as medicines to treat disease, poisons to destroy enemies, love potions, charms to ward off evil spirits, charms to bring success in hunting or victory in battle, and so on through a wide range of human desires and needs that people have believed could be affected by herbs.

In the minds of many people, long use makes materials natural. For instance, many people consider plastic containers synthetic, artificial, and unnatural since man's ability to synthesize plastics is no more than fifty or sixty years old. But glass containers, which man learned to synthesize a couple of thousand years ago, are considered entirely natural. In the same way, herbs that have been used for thousands of years by witch doctors and witches, as well as by everybody's great-great grandmother, are considered by some to be desirable, natural materials. For others it is hard to conceive that swallowing something that tastes unpleasant and has a foul odor and strong effect on the person using it can be considered natural. However, each to his own taste.

For whatever reason, there has developed a large group of people who believe that the medicines their doctor may prescribe for them or the patent medicines available in a drugstore are all dangerous and sure to induce undesirable and perhaps lethal side effects. And there is much to be said for this point of view. The medicines in use today are often dangerous drugs, and there is a certain wisdom in avoiding them if you are able to do so. When people choose the alternative of medicating themselves with herbs, however, are they doing any better? Actually, they are increasing the risks that they run. The belief that because herbs are plant material rather than pure chemicals, they are necessarily milder and safer, is totally erroneous. As a matter of fact, some herbs like belladonna (deadly nightshade) were used by Lucrezia Borgia and the Roman Agrippina to give undesirables a quick exit from this world. So if you don't know what you are doing and swallow the wrong herb at the wrong time, the results are liable to be quite serious.

There are, of course, many, many, herbs that are or could be perfectly valid medicines. In fact, a great deal of the modern pharmacopeia is made up of products that are extracted from herbs or whose chemical principle is based on herbal medicine. The bark of the willow tree was used for hundreds of years as a painkiller and it contains precisely the same chemical, acetylsalicylic acid, that makes up present-day aspirin. The foxglove plant was the original source of digitalis. It is still possible today to use the original herbs rather than the medicine, if that is the way you want to go. But— do not assume that the herbal version will be either milder or safer. When you make an infusion of willow bark, how much do you use? Do all varieties of willow contain the same amount of painkiller? Is the infusion that you swallow going to be more or less powerful than the standard 10 grain dose of aspirin? You don't know and you really have no way of finding out. That's one of the big problems.

Under good conditions, herbs should be quite useful medicinally. Let's say that what you want is a very mild sedative, milder than any of the tranquilizing or sleep-promoting drugs you can get in the drugstore. There is an herb called valerian that has an extremely mild and gentle sedative effect. But how much should you use? There, it's very hard to get information. Your health food dealer will probably be able to sell you the valerian, but he cannot tell you how to use it because that would be practicing medicine and he could go to jail for doing so. The most he can do is suggest that you buy a book which lists medicinal herbs and tells you what they are supposed to be good for and how to use them.

But how reliable is the author of the book? In most cases—perhaps all cases—such books are produced by people who are professional writers rather than health professionals. Their objective in producing the book was to sell books and make money and they may or may not have tried to be scrupulously accurate. It is possible that the information in such a book is everything that it ought to be; but it is also possible that it is entirely, dangerously wrong. If so, who's ever going to know?

There are some health professionals whose business it is to know all about herbal remedies and how and when they should be used. They are called naturopathic physicians. If one of them prescribes a particular herb for you it will be with instructions as to just how to use it and just how much of it to use, and you can probably do so in perfect safety and possibly much benefit to your health. Numerous other health professionals—doctors of medicine, osteopaths, and chiropractors—have become devoted to what is known as holistic medicine, which is the attempt to treat the entire person and correct the causes of illness, rather than just treating the group of symptoms that have been given the name of a particular disease. In the practice of holistic medicine, herbs seem to be playing an increasingly important role. And more and more people who have health problems they do not want to take to a doctor are buying books about herbal medicine and then treating themselves with the plant materials they can buy at a health food store.

In fact, even though throughout history people have been treated with teas made from herbs, known as decoctions or infusions, some entrepreneurs have now gone to the trouble of drying and powdering the herbs and selling them as tablets, because it is well known that people would rather buy tablets they can swallow without effort and without tasting what they are swallowing. It is certainly less trouble than boiling an herb for fifteen minutes to half an hour, then straining and cooling the resulting tea, and taking it by the teaspoon. But who can tell you how many tablets of what weight are equal to one teaspoon of a decoction of the herb you are using?

If you ask the manager of your health food store, he will assure you that he sells herbs only to make teas that are more wholesome substitutes for coffee, cocoa, etc. In fact, he does and there are dozens of blends of herbs with a pleasant flavor that are enjoyable to drink and contain no caffeine or other stimulants. There are many, many other herbs, however, that people are buying to treat various problems. Most of them, surely, are harmless and even if they don't do what you expect them to, at least will not hurt you. But some are very dangerous and how are you going to know which is which? We do not recommend self-medication with herbs any more than with patent medicines from the drugstore. Regardless of our recommendation, though, many people want to buy and try herbs and want to know what they can get. What follows is as complete a list as could be mustered with a description of what people believe the herbs will do for them and any dangers in their use that are known. In many cases herbs are believed to be treatments for an unreasonably wide variety of ailments. That the many uses for which an herb is supposed to be good are listed here does not mean that it actually has such value, or any value at all.

What follows, then, is simply a listing of the various herbs that may be found and purchased in health food stores, and what purpose they are said to serve. Their medicinal use is not recommended except on the advice of a knowledgeable health professional, such as a naturopathic physician.

One additional warning. Recently herbal combinations imported from Hong Kong have appeared on the market. They purport to be specific remedies for particular ailments and many people are tempted to try them. They are very dangerous. Apparently there is little or no supervision of labeling in Hong Kong and it has been found that the packagers have been including powerful and dangerous pharmaceutical drugs in their combinations without mentioning it on their labels. People have been killed by taking such concoctions. The reader should be warned that if it comes from Hong Kong he cannot trust the label listing of ingredients and is using something completely unknown that could easily be injurious.

ABSINTHE

Also known as wormwood, this herb was used to flavor the French liqueur absinthe until it was found to be habit forming and to cause deterioration of the brain. Its most common use has been to kill parasitic worms in pets and sometimes in humans. It may cause convulsions and is generally considered too dangerous to use.

AGRIMONY

This is commonly combined with licorice and brewed as a tea. The tea is used as a spring tonic to end the winter doldrums. Combined with mugwort and vinegar, it can be made into a poultice that is claimed to remove old scars.

ALFALFA LEAF

This is often used as a tea that has a flavor some people find pleasant. It is considered a good source of vitamins C and K and of such nutritional minerals as are deep in the soil where the alfalfa was grown. Vitamin K promotes coagulation of the blood and too much of it can be dangerously toxic. If this tea is used, it should be sparingly.

ALFALFA SEED

This can be brewed into a tea with a flavor resembling that of sweet peas. It possesses the same nutritional characteristics as alfalfa leaf, listed above.

ALOE VERA

This is widely used as a cosmetic that is believed to smooth and moisturize the skin. It is considered to promote healing. As a decoction, it is claimed to be good for abrasions, acne, athlete's foot, burns, constipation, indigestion, eczema, ear infections, fever blisters, hemorrhoids, mouth sores, poison ivy, poison oak, psoriasis, stomach ulcers, and ulcerated sores and to promote hair growth. Obviously, it cannot have such a wide range of medicinal values and one should be skeptical about many of the claims for aloe vera. It is widely believed in as a cosmetic preparation, however, and probably of value for this purpose.

ANGELICA

It can be used for a pleasant-tasting tea. This herb is also used commercially as a flavoring for candies and liqueurs. It is sweet and has a high sugar content. It has been used medicinally as a general tonic, as a stimulant, as a digestive, and as an expectorant. It is said to promote perspiration and urination and has even been claimed to be a successful treatment for alcoholism, inducing an aversion to alcohol.

ANISE SEED

It makes a pleasant tasting tea with a flavor resembling licorice. It is considered to be a digestive aid and said to soothe coughs and headaches and relieve congestion of the respiratory system. By some it is believed to increase the flow of breast milk in nursing mothers. Used as a flavoring in cakes and candy, it is pleasant to the taste and apparently harmless.

ARBOR VITAE

This is a highly aromatic herb, infusions of which have been used since ancient times as an ingredient in soothing ointments.

ARNICA

It has in the past been widely used as an ingredient of ointments intended to relieve muscular aches and pains. It apparently has been fairly successful as a counterirritant but is strong enough and irritating enough so that warnings have been issued against using it in home remedies. As a carefully measured dose in an ointment it may be fine, but if you make your own ointment and get too much arnica in it, you could cause yourself serious trouble. It is not to be used internally. It is a poison.

ASAFOETIDA

It was widely used in the nineteenth century as a remedy against respiratory diseases and was the bane of millions of children on whom it was used because of its foul odor. It is sold as a root gum or as a powder and is taken internally. It is reputed to be a sedative, a digestive aid, and a laxative.

ASH TREE LEAVES

They can be made into poultices that are claimed to remove warts. The claim is dubious.

BALM OF GILEAD

It has been known since the writing of the Old Testament. It is a decoction that is used to soothe irritated skin and is considered to be of cosmetic value.

BARBERRY

This has such a wide variety of claims made for it that it resembles a nineteenth-century patent medicine. It is said to be a blood purifier; to rectify anemia; to treat bladder infections; to cure boils, constipation, diarrhea, indigestion, and gallstones; and to improve the condition of the gall bladder. It is also claimed to be good for the gums and the heart, to relieve heartburn, to reduce high blood pressure, to cure infected kidneys, and so on. The claims for this herb seem to be endless.

BASIL

This leaf, dried and powdered, makes an infusion that has a reputation, probably undeserved, as an aphrodisiac. It is said to have antiseptic properties and to have a tonic effect on the human system. It is sometimes used to relieve nausea and to settle an upset stomach. It is also sometimes used as a snuff and its users apparently enjoy it.

BAYBERRY

Another cure-all that is said to be good for canker, chills, colds, cuts, diarrhea and dysentery, the eyes, hay fever, hemorrhage, vaginal infections, menstruation, miscarriage, the lungs, lumbago, and so on through just about the entire catalogue of human disease. It is a bitter bark that is made into a decoction claimed to be a good gargle for a sore throat. It will cause vomiting if taken in too large a dose.

BEE POLLEN

It is rather widely used as a remedy for an enlarged prostate gland. It would not appear to differ in any way from pollen that is not gathered by bees. Since what is gathered by a bee cannot be differentiated and the flowers from which it comes may not all be known, there is a distinct possibility that people allergic to specific pollens may unwittingly stir up an allergy attack when using bee pollen.

BELLADONNA

Also known as deadly nightshade, this is a killer and only to be avoided. It is often used to dilate the eyes when that is desired and sometimes as a sedative. It is much too dangerous to be used except under careful professional supervision.

BERGAMOT

It makes a pleasant tea that closely resembles in flavor the Chinese teas, yet does not contain any stimulants. Therefore, it is a good tea substitute.

BILBERRY LEAF

It has a basic astringent quality that is believed to be of value for intestinal and digestive disorders. It has been used for nausea and for diarrhea and as a tonic.

BISTORT

This herb, also known as dragonwart, is strongly astringent and in decoction is considered a good antiseptic gargle and mouthwash that will also treat infections of the gums. Taken internally it is used to treat digestive disorders. It has been given to children as a cure for bed-wetting and may even have succeeded in frightening the kids into continence because it tastes so bad.

BLACKBERRY LEAF

Sometimes used as one of the ingredients in an herb tea blend. In infusion it is used as a rinse for oily hair and skin and as a pleasant additive to the bath water.

BLACK COHOSH

One of the more popular herbs, it is believed to be a source of estrogen and is used to treat female problems that may be due to insufficient estrogen production. It is also considered good for bee stings, asthma, arthritis, insect bites, bronchitis, diabetes, snake-bite, Saint Vitus's dance, thyroid disorders, and so on through just about the entire catalogue of things that can go wrong with the human body. It can cause headaches, and users are warned to discontinue if headaches begin.

BLACK WALNUT BARK

It is used as a treatment for various skin disorders such as poison ivy, ringworm, eczema, herpes, boils, and cold sores. It is used as a poultice or a tincture and is sometimes taken internally. At various times it has also been considered a treatment for syphilis and for one type of vaginal discharge.

BLACK WILLOW BARK

It comes from the plant that we commonly know as pussy willow. It is astringent with a very bitter taste and has been tried as a possible cure for numerous incurables such as baldness, arthritis, and dandruff, and also for bed-wetting, convulsions, bursitis, burns, gallstones, fever, gout, hemorrhage, and sexual desires that a person may find troublesome and wish to repress.

BLADDER WRACK

This is a seaweed and consequently high in iodine. It has been used to treat goiter. It is brewed into a tea.

BLESSED THISTLE

It has the reputation of increasing the flow of mother's milk and is given to mothers whose milk is inadequate. It has also been used without much justification for a wide variety of problems, particularly those of women. It may be a source of plant estrogens, though this is not positively known. Estrogens taken daily for months will cause the blood pressure to rise.

BLOODROOT

This was used as a war paint by some Indian tribes, which is fine. It has, however, come to be recommended sometimes for medicinal purposes, which is extremely dangerous. It is a violent emetic that can cause serious illness and even death.

BLUE COHOSH

This herb is also known as squawroot. Taken as a tea, it has the reputation of making childbirth faster and easier and also easing menstrual cramps. It is also recommended at times for a variety of other diseases for which it is probably not effective.

BOLDO

This is a shrub that grows in the mountains of Chile. It is used as a tea that has a refreshing, slightly lemony flavor.

BONESET

An herb that was widely used by the Indians, it makes a bitter tea that is considered to be good for fever and a tonic that will also relieve indigestion. Large doses are emetic in their effect, however, and it should be used with caution if at all.

BORAGE

It is used either as a tea or as a savory that is added to salads, etc. The ancient Greeks used to put it in their wine. It has the reputation of dispelling melancholy and improving the spirits. It is also used as an eyewash and considered a good blood cleanser.

BRIGHAM TEA

Also known as Mormon tea, it is sniffed up the nose to treat nose bleeds and sinus congestion. It is apparently a nerve stimulant that will increase restlessness when used. Like many other herbs, it is also recommended for an unreasonably wide variety of diseases for which it is probably of little or no use.

BROOM TOPS

Used as an infusion, it is known to have a narcotic effect and should not be taken internally. It has been used for more than a thousand years in the practice of witchcraft.

BUCHU

This is used as an aromatic tea reported to be invigorating as well. It is used to treat venereal disease, bladder infections, bed-wetting, and enlarged prostate.

BUCKTHORN BARK

Also known as black dogwood, it is brewed into a tea. It is used as a cathartic but has often proved too powerful and has caused severe diarrhea.

BURDOCK ROOT

It is brewed into a tea that is primarily considered a regulator of the kidneys and an aid for swollen joints. It is known to cause hallucinations and bizarre behavior and may be deliberately used for this purpose by some. It is reputed to be good for the usual unreasonably long catalogue of physical ills.

BUTTON SNAKEROOT

Also known as backache root, it is brewed into a stimulating tea. Apparently some believe it helps a backache.

CALAMUS ROOT

This is also known as sweet flag. It is sometimes candied and is recommended to be chewed in very small quantities daily. It is considered a cause of cancer and should be avoided.

CARAWAY SEED

A popular savory used to flavor rye and other breads, it is also used as an ingredient in an herbal tea that is considered good for the digestion and also believed by some to improve the memory. For those who believe in love potions, caraway has been used as such for a thousand years.

CAROB

Also called St. John's bread, this seed pod is ground into a powder and used as a confection to substitute for chocolate. It has a somewhat binding effect and is considered a good treatment for diarrhea as well as for basic digestive problems, such as colitis, that induce diarrhea.

CASCARA

This bark in decoction is considered to be a soother and relaxant of the digestive system and a treatment for constipation. It is widely used in laxative preparations.

CATNIP

This is brewed into a tea which is used in an enema in order to treat a fever. By those who believe in it, it is considered to be good for practically everything, but this is doubtful. But if catnip does not improve what is wrong with you, at least your cat will enjoy it.

CAYENNE

This very strong red pepper is used as a seasoning in many spicy foods and is also reputed to be good for a wide range of ailments. It is considered an improver of the digestive system and of the blood circulation as well. It is believed to strengthen the heart and also to help stop internal bleeding and to ease the effects of shock. Some also consider it a catalyst for the action of other herbs.

CELANDINE

This herb is brewed into an astringent that, applied to the skin, is believed to stop itching. It has also been used as a wart remover.

CENTUARY

This bitter herb is included in lotions that are supposed to remove freckles and other skin blemishes.

CHAMOMILE (sometimes spelled CAMOMILE)

A fragrant herb that makes one of the most popular of all herb teas; its flavor resembles that of dried apples. It is recommended as a cleanser and purifier of the blood and is said to have been used successfully to assist drug withdrawal. Chamomile is widely used as a hair rinse and as a complexion steam and as a tea it is among the most popular of all. Alas, it is also a known allergen and will stir up some of the most common allergies, such as sensitivity to ragweed. Use with great care.

CHAPPARAL

Also known as creosote, this is a very strong material that had been used as an antiseptic, but given up because it injured tissue as well as killing bacteria. It is an Indian remedy once used internally for a number of diseases, but it is really too strong and can easily cause great pain, if not injury. Confined to external use it might be of value in treating infections but again, one must be extremely careful not to use it in too much strength for fear of burns.

CHERRY BARK, CHERRY STEMS, AND CHERRY PITS

These all brew into bitter, astringent teas that are believed to be a good tonic and blood purifier. They contain an element, however, that while not poisonous in itself, can be converted by the body into poisonous cyanide. Please do not use.

CHERVIL

Also known as french parsley, it is a food seasoning that has been used in the past as a cure for hiccoughs. It is an early spring herb considered a cleanser of the blood. An infusion is reputed to lower the blood pressure and to increase perspiration.

CHIA

This is a seed from one variety of sage that can be used in poultices and is also believed, as a food, to have general health-restorative properties.

CHICKWEED

It can be used as a food or brewed into a tea or an infusion. It is believed to be a remedy for overweight. It is a mild laxative that is also believed to have tonic properties and to be good for coughs. Externally, it is used as a scrub for acne and inflammations of the skin and is believed to help sore eyes.

CLEAVERS

Chiefly used externally, it is incorporated into a salve that is used for sunburn and is also supposed to remove freckles.

CLOVE

This popular aromatic spice also has mild anesthetic properties and is used to ease toothache. It is also used in mouthwashes and is considered a digestant and an antiseptic.

CLOVER BLOSSOM (RED)

This is made into a tea that is considered a treatment for scarlet fever and a purifier of the blood. It is also quite popular as a tea.

COLA NUTS

Known to us chiefly as an ingredient of cola drinks; they are also crushed and brewed into teas. They contain large quantities of caffeine and their chief effect is to stimulate the heart.

COLTSFOOT

Brewed into a tea, it is used to treat coughs, catarrh, and asthma. It is also used as one of the ingredients of an herbal tobacco that is considered a treatment for bronchitis.

COMFREY

Comfrey is one of the most popular of all herbs. Applied to the skin as a poultice, it is believed to reduce wrinkles and make the skin look more youthful. Brewed into a tea, it is considered a purifier of the blood that will be of some benefit to practically any ailment. As a wash or a poultice it is considered a good treatment for inflammations and various skin disorders. There is some question, however, about possible toxicity of comfrey taken as a tea. If it is to be used at all, it would probably be best to limit its use to external application.

CORNFLOWERS

They can be made into an infusion that is considered good for tired eyes.

COUCH GRASS

Made into a decoction or tea, it is used as a general tonic or as a treatment for bladder complaints.

DAISY FLOWER

Brewed into teas or used for ointments or poultices, it is believed to be good for skin inflammations.

DAMIANA

Either smoked or used as a tea, it is considered both an aphrodisiac for women and a treatment for various female problems.

DANDELION

It is both eaten as a food and made into a tea. It is considered a builder of the health of the liver and as a tonic that cleanses the blood. It has diuretic properties and is believed to improve the bladder by increasing urination.

DEVIL'S-CLAW

Taken as a decoction, this is widely used because of its reputation as a treatment for arthritis and rheumatism. It has been found, however, to cause miscarriage in pregnant women and should not be used by anyone who is pregnant.

DILL

The popular flavoring of chicken soup and pickles, dill is an ancient herb that is a mild sedative that has been used to calm babies with colic. It is believed to relieve flatulence and otherwise improve the digestive system. It used to be considered an effective remedy for hiccoughs. It is also said to stimulate the appetite and to encourage milk production in nursing mothers.

DONG QUAI

A root imported from Korea, it is often used in conjunction with ginseng when the intention is to create a female aphrodisiac. Its effectiveness is dubious.

ECHINACEA

It is considered to be of value in the treatment of gangrene. It is reputed to be a cleanser of the lymphatic system and glands. It is used in bladder infections and boils as well as gangrene.

ELDERBERRY BARK

This is not safe to take internally, since it has a violent purgative action. The juice of the bark and leaves, squeezed out, has been found to be cooling, soothing, and healing. It has been used for the skin for more than a thousand years.

ELDERBERRY FLOWERS

They can be made into a tea that is said to relieve headaches and infections of the throat. It is also used externally as a compress for the eyes and a wash for the complexion.

ELECAMPANE

A pungent root, its decoction is often used as a tonic. It is astringent and antiseptic and is used as a treatment for coughs and bronchitis. It is sometimes candied and used as a cough lozenge. It is also used as a wash for acne.

EUCALYPTUS

It can be made into a tea, not very pleasant to the taste, but claimed to be useful for colds and infections of the respiratory tract. The oil is used commercially in cough drops and might have some value in that regard. It is also rubbed on the chest for treatment of respiratory disease.

EYEBRIGHT

Brewed into a tea, it is used as an eyewash and has a strong reputation as being good for all kinds of eye problems. It can also be taken internally, in which form it is claimed to be good for allergies of various sorts.

FALSE UNICORN

This is reputed to strengthen the muscles of the uterus and to be of value in all kinds of female problems and complaints.

FENNEL

Brewed into a tea, it is considered to curb the appetite when one is attempting to lose weight. It is also said to promote the flow of milk in nursing mothers. A decoction of fennel seeds is considered of value for tired and inflamed eyes. Fennel was also widely used in witchcraft.

FENUGREEK

Unlike most herbs, fenugreek makes a tea that is actually tasty. It is considered a treatment for intestinal ulcers and a general intestinal lubricant. It is also considered to be of value for the mucous membranes and a treatment for migraine.

FLAX SEED

It is considered dangerous to take internally because it is essentially an irritant that induces a warming sensation. It seems to be of value, however, as a poultice for the same purpose.

FOXGLOVE

This herb contains digitalis and other elements that stimulate the heart. It has been used as a cardiac medication and probably still is, but it is much too dangerous and actually poisonous if taken in quantities that are not carefully regulated. Do not use it.

GALANGAL

It is generally considered an herbal flavoring and is used to improve the flavor of herb teas generally. It is also used, however, to treat flatulence and is considered to be stimulating in its effect.

GARLIC

It has been considered to have medicinal properties for thousands of years. It is a prime treatment for dysentery and the juice has been shown to have antibiotic properties. It is also believed to lower blood pressure and has at times been put to many other purposes, including the warding off of vampires.

GENTIAN

This has been used for thousands of years as an antiseptic, and indeed, gentian violet was used for this purpose by the medical profession until just a few years ago. It is very bitter in flavor and is used as a tonic to stimulate the appetite. It has also been used to help people stop smoking.

GINGER

It is added to bath water as an aid to weight loss on the theory that it opens the pores and promotes sweating. Teas made from ginger are believed to improve digestion and to have antibiotic properties. It is also used as a spice and is sometimes candied and eaten as a confection.

GINSENG

This is perhaps the best known of all herbs, having a fabled value as a potent aphrodisiac. In actuality it does contain estrogen and might conceivably be aphrodisiac for some estrogen-deficient women, though it has the opposite reputation as a male aphrodisiac. Believed to be a mysterious herb from Korea, ginseng is actually grown in West Virginia and exported to the Orient. The herb is considered a universal panacea by those who subscribe to such things. Because of its estrogen content, if used excessively it can produce high blood pressure, insomnia, nervousness and agitation, and swollen and painful breasts. Because of its popularity it is available in many forms and may be bought as capsules, as chips for chewing, as a powder, or as a liquid extract already prepared for use, as well as the whole root.

GOAT'S RUE

This is used as an infusion with the reputation of being an antidote to poison. Since the type of poison is never specified, it may not be very effective.

GOLDENROD

This is one of the most common of allergy-stimulating plants. It is sometimes used as an herb and taken as a tea or infusion, but it is extremely dangerous to those who have any of the allergies known as hay fever, even if they are not known to be specifically allergic to goldenrod. The reaction can kill. This herb should be definitely avoided.

GOLDENSEAL

One of the most popular of today's herbs, perhaps because it is believed to eliminate signs of drug use from the urine and therefore is widely used by people who want to hide their drug addiction from the police. Many put goldenseal to more ordinary uses, though. It is considered a treatment for diabetes and is said to lower the blood sugar level in the same way that insulin does. It is also used as a treatment for kidney problems and for cardiac difficulties and is believed to correct digestive disorders. In fact, whatever it is that ails you, some book or so-called expert is sure to recommend goldenseal to you. Be careful how you use it, however. It is known to be toxic when taken too frequently or in large quantity. If it actually does lower the blood sugar, that, of course, in itself is dangerous to most people.

GOTU COLA

This Oriental herb is considered an antidote to aging. It is said to promote longevity, to eliminate pigment spots, to ease the menopause, and to improve the memory. It is also considered a treatment for high blood pressure. It is taken as a tea.

HAWTHORN BERRY

Made into a tea or crushed and added to wine or brandy, it is considered a treatment for low blood pressure and for low blood sugar. It is supposed to stimulate the activity of the adrenal glands and in that way to be a heart stimulant. It was a popular cardiac treatment in the nineteenth century. Overuse may produce dizziness and a fast heartbeat. Do not use it except under the supervision of a health professional.

HEMLOCK

It is still used occasionally as a sedative and antispasmodic. This is the poison that killed Socrates and it is just as poisonous today. It is far too dangerous to use, even though it does have medicinal properties.

HENBANE

This has been used in the past as a remedy for toothache. Its use frequently lead to convulsions, however, and sometimes to death. People who are knowledgeable about herbs do not use this one anymore.

HI JOHN THE CONQUEROR

Also known as jalap, this is an excessively powerful cathartic that can easily cause severe pain and discomfort. If one wants a cathartic, there are effective ones that are far gentler.

HIBISCUS FLOWERS

When dried, they can be used to make a tea that many consider refreshing.

HONEYSUCKLE FLOWERS

They are added to tea blends for their well-known fragrance. Their aroma seems to be their only value.

HOPS

They are used not only to flavor beer, but also as a soothing herbal tea. They are said to have a general sedative action and to promote sleep even when dried and kept under a pillow as a sachet. They are also said to soothe earaches. Generally, hops are used as a mild tranquilizer.

HOREHOUND

Considered a remedy for coughs and respiratory infections, it is used as a tea and is also an ingredient of cough drops.

HORSERADISH

It has a powerful aroma that is used to clear stuffed nasal passages. A decoction of horseradish is said to be diuretic in its effect but one must be careful not to take too much, for it becomes a strong laxative. It has antiseptic properties and has been used to expel parasitic worms.

HORSETAIL

This is brewed into a tea that can be used as an astringent lotion to tighten the skin. It is said to strengthen the fingernails and improve the hair. It is also used as a treatment for anemia and for certain bladder complaints. Horsetail is used as a decoction or a tea.

HYSSOP

Brewed into a tea considered refreshing by many, it can be applied to bruises and discolorations as a poultice and also used as an antiseptic gargle. The tea is supposed to improve digestion and its antiseptic properties are said to be of value for coughs and colds.

IRISH MOSS

Also known as carrageen, it is an edible seaweed used commercially as a thickener. The water in which it is cooked is considered to have medicinal value for bad breath, jaundice, obesity, and the thyroid. It is also said to soften the skin when applied topically.

JABORANDI LEAF

A Brazilian herb used as an infusion, it is said to promote hair growth when applied to the scalp.

JEWELWEED

This is used to make a rinse for the hair that imparts a lasting sweet fragrance.

JOJOBA

An oily seed, its oil was thought by the Indians to be a remedy for dandruff and hair loss. It is also used as an ingredient for face creams and is believed to have definite moisturizing properties.

JUNIPER BERRIES

They are one of the flavor ingredients of gin. Juniper-berry tea is used to treat insect bites and stings. It is considered a regulator of the blood sugar and of adrenal activity. This herb may be irritating to the gastrointestinal tract and should be used with care, if at all.

KELP

This seaweed is dried and pulverized to be used as a seasoning that provides relatively large amounts of dietary iodine. It contains the full range of sea minerals and is used for treatment of the adrenal gland and in the treatment of anemia, it is said to be good for leg cramps, elevated blood sugar, goiter, and eczema. Kelp is used to treat hot flashes in menopause.

LADY'S MANTLE

An herb of the rose family, it is used as an astringent to improve oily skin. It is thought to be able to draw poison from boils and other inflammations and is considered a general herb for the control of female problems. It is also thought to be an aphrodisiac for women.

LADY'S SLIPPER

This is the American variety of valerian, a very popular mild sedative.

LAVENDER

It is used as an ingredient in herbal tea blends to lend its delicate and delightful fragrance. Lavender oil, which concentrates the fragrance, is considered a treatment for headache and is said to have antiseptic properties valuable in the treatment of insect bites and small wounds.

LEMON BALM

Also known as melissa, this is a favorite among herb teas for its flavor and has been used as a tea for thousands of years. It promotes perspiration and is recommended for fevers, headaches, and colds. Added to bath water it is claimed to bring on menstrual periods.

LEMON GRASS

Used as an herbal tea, it is also a good source of vitamin A. The flavor is considered highly enjoyable, particularly when a few cloves are added to the tea.

LEMON VERBENA

This is used for a tea that has a gentle sedative effect. It is fragrant and enjoyable. It is said to settle the stomach and to soothe nasal and bronchial congestion. The herb is also used as an aromatic scent for soaps and perfumes.

LICORICE ROOT

Used as a tea, it is said to be a valuable aid for those who want to stop smoking. It is considered a treatment for female complaints, Addison's disease, and hypoglycemia. It has a delicious flavor and has been widely used in candies and cough drops. However, used in large quantities it can cause heart failure as well as lesser cardiac difficulties. Be very, very careful in using licorice.

LIFE EVERLASTING

It makes an astringent tea that is recommended as a gargle for sore throats.

LILY OF THE VALLEY

This is a well-known poisonous plant that can easily sicken or kill you. The flowers can be used pharmaceutically to produce a drug used in the treatment of heart disease. Do not, however, fool around with this easily grown and beautifully fragrant plant. Keep it out of your mouth and keep children away from it.

LINDEN TEA

A soothing tea that is used widely in Europe, it is said to act as a gentle sedative, to improve digestion, and to soothe the nerves. It promotes perspiration and is reputed to be a treatment for respiratory disease. Added to bath water, it is believed to relieve freckles.

LOBELIA

In an overdose this can cause severe vomiting, sweating, pain, paralysis, and even death. The herb also induces hallucinations and bizarre behavior. Obviously, it is one of the most dangerous of herbs, despite which it continues to be used as a treatment for earaches, contagious diseases, convulsions, hyperactivity, hypoglycemia, tetanus, pneumonia, ringworm, and other health problems. Use with extreme care or preferably not at all.

LOVAGE ROOT

It is used cosmetically to remove freckles. When the root is boiled, the water is said to have antiseptic properties and to be a deodorant. It is also used as a digestive and relieves flatulence. The leaves and seeds are eaten in salads.

LUNGWORT

Made into an infusion, it is reputed to be particularly good for pulmonary complaints of all types. The leaves are sometimes eaten in salads.

MAIDENHAIR

The fern is brewed into an herbal tea that is said to have especially soothing properties.

MALVA

This is the base for a number of popular herbal teas. When its flowers are used for this purpose, the teas become blue or lavender in hue. This is prized in Italy and in the Orient.

MANDRAKE

This legendary root, said to grow only where a man has died, has anesthetic properties that have caused it to be recommended for painful ailments such as colitis and gallstones; it is used for fever and rheumatism. The herb contains powerful narcotics, however, and if the dose is large enough, can easily be fatal.

MARIGOLD

The flowers are used for a delicate tea that many find enjoyable. It could unexpectedly trigger an allergy, however, and might be very dangerous to the allergy-prone user, even if he is not aware of any previous allergy to marigolds.

MARSHMALLOW ROOT

It is considered a treatment for the kidneys and for problems of the bladder. It is said to be soothing and healing for bronchitis and similar respiratory inflammations. A poultice is believed valuable for sprains and aching muscles. Marshmallow is also said to improve the flow of milk in nursing mothers.

MISTLETOE

Even the most ardent of herbalists suggests that you use mistletoe only if no other treatment is available and the need is dire. This is a highly poisonous plant whose effect on the body has been compared to that of cobra venom. It was formerly used for the treatment of convulsions and some other severe problems. It was also favored by poisoners.

MORNING GLORY SEEDS

They have been used for cathartic purposes, but they have been found to contain hallucinogenic ingredients and to constitute a dangerous drug.

MULLEIN

The herb is used to make an herbal tea. The leaves are made into a poultice for the treatment of boils and other skin infections. The dried leaves may be smoked as a treatment for consumption and in powdered form, are rubbed on rough warts to eliminate them.

MUSTARD SEED

This is, of course, used as a condiment and is also used in a poultice as a counterirritant to relieve aches and pains. Swallowed whole the seed has an emetic effect. The seed in hot water is supposed to make a good bath for tired feet.

MYRRH

Used primarily as an incense, this aromatic gum is also powdered and used to make a mouthwash that is believed to have antiseptic properties. It is used externally in poultices to treat canker sores and herpes infections. It is also a breath improver when used as a gargle.

NETTLE

Made into a tea or used in soups, it is considered good for internal cleansing, just as are most astringents. It is very high in iron and is used to treat anemia. A strong infusion is supposed to eliminate dandruff and encourage hair growth. The leaves, which irritate or sting, are sometimes used as a rub that is believed to relieve rheumatic pain.

OATSTRAW

Considered a good treatment for bed-wetting and poor appetite, oatstraw is also used to treat the kidneys and to relieve lumbago.

ORANGE FLOWERS (ORANGE BLOSSOMS)

Their delicate fragrance makes one of the most pleasant herbal teas.

OREGANO

The basic seasoning of all Italian cooking, oregano is also used herbally in mouthwashes, salves, and liniments. It is brewed into a tea by those who enjoy its distinctive flavor. The oil of the plant is believed able to induce menstruation and an infusion is considered a fine soother of an upset stomach and a treatment for morning sickness. Stuffed into a pillow, the fragrant herb is supposed to aid sleep.

PAPAYA

This tropical fruit contains an enzyme that assists digestion and thus is something of a treatment for any ill of the digestive system. It is considered a treatment for diverticulitis and to be of value for some allergies.

PARSLEY

It is said to dry up a woman's milk when she wants to stop nursing. It contains iron and is rich in vitamins and other minerals and is said to be good for anemia. It is supposed to relieve menstrual pain and to stimulate the kidneys and the digestive system. Crushed parsley leaves make a soothing antiseptic dressing for bites and minor wounds. Parsley seed contains a strong oil that is considered unsafe for internal use.

PASSIONFLOWER

It is used for a soothing tea that seems to help alcoholics and is claimed to reduce a fever. It is sometimes used to treat headaches and high blood pressure and is also considered a good sleep inducer in cases of insomnia.

PEACH

The leaves can be made into a tea that is considered to be good for the bladder and also to be a mild laxative. It is used as a treatment for morning sickness and also to treat edema. Some medical authorities warn that peach leaves contain a chemical that the body can convert into poisonous cyanide.

PENNYROYAL

This popular herb is used to ease childbirth, but it is known to induce abortion in the early stages of pregnancy. The oil will cause gastrointestinal upset and, in severe cases, for instance, when a great deal is used in a deliberate abortion attempt, it has been known to cause severe shock and even death. Externally the oil will soothe insect bites. This is a dangerous herb that is best avoided.

PEONY ROOT

It has long been used by the Chinese as a remedy for mental illness, but there is no record of its success.

PEPPERMINT

It makes a pleasant tea that is probably the best liked and the most used of all the herbal teas. It can be applied to relieve itching skin. Chewing the leaves is believed to relieve toothache. Peppermint oil has anesthetic properties. Peppermint tea is said to be excellent for indigestion and cramps. It is a stimulant strong enough to interfere with sleep if you drink it too late in the day. Taken as a hot, stimulating drink it will temporarily relieve a cold.

PERIWINKLE

This herb is commonly brewed into an herbal tea that is not as safe as it seems. The plant contains alkaloids that can be highly toxic and is considered poisonous.

PLANTAIN

The leaves are used to make ointments to treat bites, burns, and bleeding wounds. In infusion or decoction, it is claimed to reduce body temperature and is used to treat fevers. It is astringent and in a compress it is purported to soothe the eyes and cleanse the skin.

PLEURISY ROOT

This is brewed into a tea that is reputed to improve circulation by relaxing and dilating the capillaries. This particular preparation is also considered a treatment for such contagious diseases as chicken pox and measles. It is also said to relieve water retention and bring the tissues back to normal.

POKEWEED

It is considered toxic not only by ingestion, but also when it enters the body through open wounds that the herb is used to treat. It is brewed as a spring tonic and also used in poultices and ointments but has a dangerous narcotic effect. It is used as a purgative.

POPPY FLOWERS

They are brewed into a tea that many people find delightful. The seeds, which are used in baking, impart an exotic and enjoyable flavor to the tea.

PRICKLY ASH

The root, bark, and berries are all used as herbs. It is recommended as a treatment for toothache and has a bitter flavor that makes it an appetite stimulant.

PSYLLIUM

This seed is mucilaginous and acquires bulk as it travels through the digestive tract. It is considered a soothing agent for an upset colon and also a treatment for constipation, which it improves by adding bulk and moisture. Psyllium is sometimes included in laxative preparations.

QUEEN OF THE MEADOW

It is available either as a powder or in the whole leaf. It is said to lower the blood sugar and thus to be of value to diabetics. It is also supposed to be good for the enlarged prostate and to reduce water retention by treating the kidneys.

QUININE BARK

This is the source of the drug that treats malaria. Teas brewed from the bark have been used for the same purpose for a thousand years. Quinine teas are also used as an ingredient of hair tonics.

RASPBERRY LEAVES

The leaves of the red raspberry are made into a tea that for hundreds of years has been considered of particular value to pregnant women. It is used to treat morning sickness and to ease childbirth and is considered a good tonic after delivery.

RED ROOT

It is brewed into a tea that can be drunk or used as a mouthwash and gargle.

RHUBARB ROOT

Imported from China, dried and powdered, it is considered to be an astringent medicine that is good for stomach and bowel disorders. In China it is used as a purgative. It is highly acidic and its use may be dangerous.

ROSE HIPS

They can be brewed into a tasty tea or used as an ingredient in combination herbal teas. They are vastly overrated as a source of vitamin C, practically all of which has vanished by the time the rose hips are dried and crushed or shredded. The flavor, however, is very pleasant, and it is a favorite among herbal teas.

ROSEMARY

This aromatic herb is used widely in cooking. As an infusion, it is considered a treatment for headache and migraines. It is said to soothe nerves, stimulate digestion, and strengthen the heart and the head. It is considered to have a benign effect on blood pressure and the prostate. Rosemary oil is used as a treatment for baldness.

RUE

An aromatic herb that is used in cooking, it can also be brewed into an invigorating tea. It is considered a good insect repellent when rubbed on the skin. Herbalists warn against its use during pregnancy, because it can cause abortion. An infusion was formerly used as an eye bath and a few people still use it today in that manner. It is also considered to be an antidote for poisons. It is said to be of value to the nervous systems of menopausal women.

SAFFLOWER

Brewed into an infusion, it is recommended as a treatment for hypoglycemia. It has a laxative effect and is said to induce perspiration and reduce fevers. It is considered a treatment for gas and heartburn and the digestive system generally.

SAFFRON

The pollen of a crocus, saffron is very expensive, probably too much so for herbal use. It is claimed, however, that it will bring on menstruation when a period has been skipped. An infusion is supposed to be a digestive.

SAGE

It is an aromatic herb widely used in cooking that is also considered one of the most valuable of medicinal plants. Sage tea is an astringent that is claimed to have tonic properties and to cleanse the blood. An infusion is said to treat headaches and nervous tension and to promote menstruation. It is considered an antiseptic gargle and mouthwash and a rinse of it is claimed to revitalize and darken graying hair.

SAINT JOHN'S WORT

It is brewed into a tea. At one time it was considered a prime remedy for melancholia. Oil expressed from it is claimed to have a soothing effect on sore joints, cuts, and sprains. The tea is supposed to be useful for insomnia. This herb is a photosensitizer, which means that if you have it in your system and go into strong sunlight, your skin will have a decidedly toxic reaction, becoming painfully sensitive and perhaps puffing up as well.

SARSAPARILLA ROOT

Not only a popular flavoring for sodas, it is widely used as an herbal tea. It is believed to contain both male and female hormones and is recommended by some herbalists for the treatment of acne in boys. Claims are made for it with regard to such problems as ringworm and psoriasis, as well as the usual general claims for improvement of the digestive system.

SASSAFRAS

Formerly one of the ingredients in root beer, sassafras is no longer used since it was discovered to contain a chemical that will induce cancer in test animals. Herbally, sassafras tea was considered to be a warming tonic. It is also a very pleasant flavor for a tea, but there is a definite risk in using it.

SAW PALMETTO BERRIES

This pleasant, aromatic herb tea is reputed to help people gain weight and also to enlarge the breasts of women. Some herbalists claim that it will rectify sexual frigidity in women and increase prostate activity in men.

SENNA

It is usually used in combination with other herbs to make a tea that is laxative in effect. Used alone it may cause griping pains. It is supposed to be good for the liver and as a treatment for jaundice, as well as a treatment for various types of internal parasites.

SHEPHERD'S PURSE

Brewed into a tea it has the reputation of being decidedly unpleasant to the taste. It is a constrictor that raises the blood pressure by narrowing blood vessels and that treats constipation by constricting the intestines. It is believed of value to stop internal hemorrhages of the respiratory system.

SKULLCAP

It is usually combined with valerian or similar herbs to make a soothing tea that is considered good for insomnia, convulsions, and epilepsy. Its mildly sedative effect is claimed to lower high blood pressure and to be of value for emotional disturbances.

SLIPPERY ELM

It can be brewed into a tea or ground up into a powder that is then made into lozenges. It is used to relieve sore throats and is taken internally to soothe an irritated stomach or bowel. It is sometimes used as a douche for its mucilaginous quality and in ointments or as a poultice to soothe skin irritations.

SOAPWORT

In decoction, it is used as a wash for poison ivy and for acne. It is not to be taken internally.

SOLOMON'S SEAL

It is believed to remove black and blue discolorations of bruises when it is used as a poultice. It is not to be taken internally.

SOURWOOD

It is brewed into a tea that is considered to have a pleasantly acid flavor.

SOUTHERNWOOD

A member of the wormwood family, it has an oil that is considered to be a good vermifuge. Its ashes are used in ointments to encourage the growth of hair, particularly the early beards of young men.

SPEARMINT

It makes an herbal tea with a pleasantly brisk and invigorating flavor that is enjoyed by many. It is used as an appetizer and a digestive and is also thought to have antiseptic properties. It is also recommended by some herbalists for colic and cramps and, when served very hot, has been found to bring temporary relief of colds.

SPIKENARD

Combined with ginger into a salve, this herb is reputed to be a treatment for pimples.

SQUAW VINE

An old Indian remedy for female problems, its tea is considered good for easing childbirth and menstruation. It is also reputed to be a good eyewash.

STRAWBERRY LEAVES

Brewed into an infusion or tea, they are considered useful to ease the pains of childbirth. They are also given for flu and in some cases for nausea.

SUMAC ROOT BARK

Its tea is not very pleasant to the taste but is considered a good tonic. Being astringent, it may also be used as a wash for the skin.

TAG ALDER BARK

It makes a decoction that is claimed to be a good foot wash, soothing and resting the feet. It can also be used as a poultice for scrapes and bruises.

TANSY

It was once popular as a spring tonic and considered a purifier of the blood and the internal organs generally. Now, however, it is considered dangerous to use internally and we are advised to use it only in infusion as a wash to improve the complexion. As a poultice, it is said to be good for aching joints and varicose veins.

THYME

It may be brewed into a strong, aromatic tea that is enjoyed by some people. Thought to be a digestant that is generally beneficial to the digestive system, it is considered a treatment for diarrhea. It has also been used as a mouthwash and gargle and as a scalp rub.

UVA-URSI (BEARBERRY)

Brewed into a tea, it is considered a pleasant douche to promote vaginal cleanliness. It is believed to be a treatment for bladder infections, bed-wetting, and venereal disease.

VALERIAN

It makes a very soothing herbal tea that is quite popular because of its calming effect on the nerves. It has definite sedative and anesthetic properties but should be used with caution. Large doses can produce headaches and palsy. Valerian is also used externally as a wash for skin sores.

VERVAIN

Its slightly astringent tea is used to treat headaches. It is also used as a gargle and as a cleansing wash for wounds. It is supposed to be of value as a treatment for gallstones.

VIOLET LEAVES

They may be brewed into a tea or added whole to the bath. As a tea or infusion, they have a laxative effect and are considered good for insomnia and nervous ailments. They have also been used to treat skin inflammations in poultice form.

WAHOO BARK

It can be brewed into a laxative tea that has been found sometimes to have a poisonous effect. It is probably better not used.

WATERCRESS

This is usually used as food in salads but can also be brewed into an infusion that is taken as a tonic and is considered good for rickets. It is also claimed to be of value for a weak heart and the eyesight, to improve an anemic condition, and to increase the flow of mother's milk. It is also claimed to remove spots and blemishes when applied to the skin.

WATER ERYNGO ROOT

Also known as sea holly, this herb is steeped in wine to make a drink claimed to be of special value to women in restoring vitality and sexual appetite. It has been found to have an emetic effect at times. It is also used as an expectorant.

WHITE OAK BARK

Brewed into a decoction, it is considered a valuable application to the skin to clear away complexion blemishes. Used as a gargle, it is believed to heal sores in the mouth and to tighten up loose teeth. A cloth soaked in the decoction and applied to varicose veins is thought to be helpful in reducing their size. Used as a douche, it is considered of value for leucorrhea.

WHITE SNAKEROOT

A poisonous plant that should be avoided if you happen to encounter it in a store.

WHITE WILLOW BARK

It is considered of value for external use for a variety of applications from hair rinse to eyewash and deodorant. It is also taken internally and considered to have the wide-ranging tonic effects that are claimed for nearly all herbs. It has, of course, the analgesic properties of aspirin.

WILD ALUMROOT

It is frequently combined with goldenseal to make a tea that is strongly astringent in flavor. Like other astringents, it is claimed to be a blood purifier and good for the kidneys and bladder infections.

WILD CHERRY BARK

This has been widely used as a flavoring for cough drops and for similar purposes. We are warned by the FDA, however, that like many other fruit-bearing trees it contains a chemical that the human body can convert into cyanide. It should therefore be avoided.

WILD YAM ROOT

Made into a decoction, it is said to relieve gas pains and is particularly recommended for the stomach. It is considered good for ulcers and is also used for menstrual pains, nausea, and morning sickness.

WINTERGREEN

It makes a pleasant and refreshing herbal tea that can be drunk iced in summer as well as hot in winter. The tea is astringent and stimulating in its effect. Applied warm in a poultice, it is considered good for boils and similar skin infections. It is used as a douche for venereal disease and is gargled as mouthwash and for sore throats.

WITCH HAZEL

This is the base of the well-known astringent lotion that is used after shaving by many men. It is used externally as a treatment for bruises, swellings, and sprains. It is used in poultices and ointments, as well as in facial lotions.

WOOD BETONY

Brewed into a slightly bitter tea, it is used for a wide variety of purposes. An infusion of the dried leaf is considered a tonic and a cure for headaches. We are warned not to ingest the fresh leaf, however, which contains a toxic material that is destroyed in drying. The dried leaf has been used as a medicinal snuff and its smoke is also inhaled as a treatment for bronchitis. The fresh leaves contain an astringent oil that is used in poultices and is considered good for insect stings and bites.

WOODRUFF

This brews into a tea that is considered especially relaxing and pleasant to use. The fresh leaves are sometimes crushed and the juice is applied to wounds.

YARROW

This astringent herb is considered useful for healing. The leaves, when chewed, are believed to stop toothache. Brewed into an infusion, it is used in shampoos and is supposed to be a cure for baldness. The tea can also be boiled and the steam used as a treatment for oily skin. The tea is used to bathe wounds and is believed to promote healing. It is considered the tonic that restores a lost appetite. It promotes perspiration when taken internally and is used for fevers. In people with hay fever, it can unexpectedly trigger severe allergic reactions. Such people should avoid this herb.

YELLOW DOCK

It is brewed into a slightly bitter herbal tea. Taken internally, it is supposed to relieve itching anywhere in the body. A paste made of it is considered a good treatment for poison ivy and poison oak. The tea or infusion is considered good for the liver and the spleen.

YERBA MATÉ

This herb is high in caffeine and is drunk as a substitute stimulant instead of coffee or tea. It is very popular in South America.

YERBA SANTA

It is chewed or smoked as a tobacco substitute. It also brews into an enjoyable tea, which is considered a blood purifier.

YOHIMBÉ

Infusions of this herb have been used as an aphrodisiac. It contains a toxic alkaloid, however, and is dangerous to use.

* * *

There are also a number of herbal combinations that are packaged for flavor, to be used strictly as teas and neither intended nor claimed to have any medicinal value. These can make very pleasant and wholesome alternatives to coffee or tea and they keep growing in popularity. Although new combinations are continually being formulated and introduced on the market, and it is impossible to list every one, those that are available at this writing are:

BRAZILIAN BREAKFAST

Roasted maté, green maté, orange peel, lemon grass, orange blossoms, orange leaves, cloves, ginger, star anise.

BREAKFAST BLEND

Rose hips, hibiscus, orange peel, cloves.

CINNAMON ROSE

Cinnamon, rose hips, hibiscus, blackberry, chicory root, orange peel, blackberry leaves, crystal malt, cloves, natural oils and flavors.

COUNTRY APPLE

Rose hips, apples, hibiscus flowers, chamomile, roasted chicory root, cinnamon, crystal malt, nutmeg.

EMPEROR'S CHOICE

Black tea, cassia bark, Eleuthera ginseng, orange peel, rose hips, ginger, lovage root, peony root, licorice root, cassia oil, panax ginseng.

FEELING FREE

Hibiscus flowers, rose hips, lemon grass, peppermint leaves, orange blossoms, lemon verbena, orange peel, cinnamon.

GEMINI MINT

Spearmint and peppermint leaves.

GENTLE ORANGE

Orange peel, alfalfa, roasted chicory root, fennel seeds, orange petals, cloves, natural orange flavor.

GINSENG BLEND

Peppermint leaves, alfalfa, maté, anise seed, ginseng root, rose hips, huckleberry.

GOLDEN LEMON TWIST

Lemon grass, blueberry leaf (huckleberry).

HERB BLEND

Peppermint leaves, alfalfa leaves, maté, rose hips, anise.

LEMON MIST

Lemon grass, lemon verbena, spearmint, blackberry leaves, rose hips, comfrey leaves, alfalfa, red clover tops, orange peel, lemon peel, orange blossoms, eucalyptus leaves, bergamot oil.

LICORICE TWIST

Whole anise seed, licorice root, roasted chicory root.

MANDARIN ORANGE SPICE

Rose hips, hibiscus flowers, orange peel, blackberry leaves, natural mandarin orange, orange juice flavors.

MELLOW MINT

Alfalfa, peppermint leaves, papaya leaves, comfrey leaves, a dash of licorice.

MINT MEDLEY

Peppermint leaves, spearmint leaves, rose hips, lemon peel, alfalfa leaves, hibiscus flowers.

MORNING THUNDER

Black tea, green maté, roasted maté.

MO'S 24

Spearmint, hibiscus flowers, comfrey, chamomile, alfalfa, blackberry leaves, rose hips, peppermint, nettles, papaya, eucalyptus, blueberry, rosemary, elder flowers, red clover, catnip, yarrow.

MU TEA

Mandarin orange peel, hoelen, onicus, attractyllis, herbaceous peony root, Japanese parsley root, cinnamon, ginger root, licorice, peach kernel, rehmannia, Japanese ginseng, cloves, coptis, moutan.

ORANGE SPICE

Decaffeinated orange pekoe and black cut tea, orange peel, spices, orange extract.

ORIENTAL SPICE

Peppermint, strawberry leaf, ginger.

PELICAN PUNCH

Crystal malt, peppermint leaves, chamomile blossoms, carob, fenugreek seeds, fennel, vanilla extract.

QUIETLY CHAMOMILE

Chamomile flowers, orange peel, orange petals, lemon grass, peppermint leaves.

RED HIBISCUS

Hibiscus flowers, orange peel, lemon grass, orange petals.

RED LIGHTNING

Hibiscus, rose hips, orange peel, peppermint leaves, lemon grass, wintergreen, wild cherry bark.

RED ZINGER

Hibiscus flowers, rose hips, lemon grass, peppermint, orange peel, wild cherry bark.

ROASTAROMA

Crystal malt, roasted barley, roasted carob, chicory root, cassia bark, star anise, allspice.

SLEEPYTIME

Chamomile flowers, spearmint, tilia flowers, passionflowers, lemon grass, blackberry leaves, orange blossoms, hawthorn berries, skullcap, rosebuds.

SWEET ALMOND

Roasted barley, maté, almond flowers, cinnamon, fennel.

SWEET CINNAMON SPICE

Rose hips, lemon grass, verbena, cinnamon, hibiscus.

SWEET DREAMS

Chamomile flowers, hibiscus flowers, peppermint leaves, spearmint leaves, rose blossoms, cinnamon, orange flowers.

SWEET ORANGE SPICE

Wood betony, sweet orange peel, dandelion, cloves.

TAKE-A-BREAK

Roasted carob, roasted barley, roasted chicory root, cinnamon, anise seed, roasted wheat.

TANGY AUTUMN

Spearmint, hibiscus, lemon grass.

TOASTY SPICE

Malted barley, roasted malted barley, roast chicory root, cinnamon bark, roasted carob, fennel seed, allspice, cinnamon.

TRI-BLEND

Peppermint, chamomile, alfalfa.

WINTERBERRY

Raspberry leaves, wintergreen, ginger, cloves.

SECTION 3:

FOODS AND
FOOD PRODUCTS

FOODS AND
FOOD PRODUCTS

WHAT MAKES A FOOD A HEALTH FOOD?

These days there are very few food products that you can get in a health food store that cannot also be obtained at your nearest chain supermarket. Whether it be dairy products made from raw milk, whole-grain breads, candies made without any chocolate or white sugar, or vitamin tablets that are promoted as "natural," the wares of the two kinds of stores have come to overlap more and more and are frequently identical. Often the only difference is price. The large chain markets operate on the turnover principle. They try to stock only those items that can be sold fast, and their competitive price mark-up may be as little as 5 percent of the selling price. But, if they invest one dollar in item X and sell it for $1.06, after apportioning overhead, they may find that their profit on item X is as low as two cents per sale. If they sell 80 a year, however, in a year's time they are making a $1.60 profit on a $1.00 invest-ment.

The health food store, on the other hand, gets less traffic and has less turnover and in most such stores, the owner marks up his merchandise by 40 percent of the selling price. The item that costs him $1.00 is priced at approximately $1.65 on his shelves. It should be obvious, then, that identical items will often sell for considerably less at the chain supermarket.

Then what keeps customers flowing into the health food stores, and what keeps those customers satisfied?

Perhaps the greatest single attraction of the health food store is that nebulous attitude we call "confidence." The customer has a close-to-religious faith that the health food store owner is part of a popular movement in which integrity and the observance of dietary principles are far more important than making a buck. Sometimes this is even true. There are a good many owners of small stores who in their own lives have treated illness by following rigorous dietary principles, regained their health, and become apostles of the health food creed. Their customers are inspired by faith which, within the framework of their nutritional principles, is fully justified, and they keep coming back.

What are these nutritional principles?

Briefly stated, it is believed by millions of health food devotees that one should never eat table sugar (sucrose), though substitute forms of sugar may be all right; one should never add salt to anything and all foods eaten should have a low sodium content; food should be processed as little as possible because processing removes or destroys some of the vitamin and mineral content; foods should be whole, for instance, the whole wheat berry should not be fractionated into just the portion that makes good flour for baking; and food should be "organic," which means that it should be grown without benefit of pesticides and with only animal manures and plant compost as fertilizers. The customer who has faith in the store he patronizes has confidence that whatever he buys there will conform to these principles, so that he does not have to read labels and exercise great care to avoid buying something that has salt added for flavor or that is contaminated by forbidden sugar.

The customer will also tend to bring his health problems to the health food store, consulting with the store clerks, manager, or owner about what might be good to correct constipation or headaches or body odor or excessive sweating or a skipped menstrual period. Whether or not the store personnel are free to give such advice will vary from one state to another. In some places it is considered practicing medicine without a license and is severely punished when detected. In others the giving of such advice is protected by the First Amendment guarantee of freedom of speech and may be freely carried on as long as no fee is charged for the advice. Even where the rendering of health advice is firmly prohibited, however, ways have been developed to do it within the parameters of what is legally permissible. The store may have a large variety of health articles reprinted from health magazines, one or more of which can simply be handed to the customer. The magazines are also for sale, as are a wide variety of books and pamphlets, any of which may be recommended to the customer without violating a prohibition on the dispensing of health advice. So one way or another, the customer does get advised, whether correctly or erroneously, on what to eat or take for any particular illness, and this assurance that any particular product is good for what ails him is an important factor in what makes a health food a health food and what makes a customer prefer to buy it at a health food store.

Of all the attractions of the health food store, however, the chief one is its claim that everything purchased in the store is a natural food product that has been produced organically, thus assuring the customer that he is not inadvertently poisoning himself, that his purchases are giving him the highest possible nutrition, and that buying at a health food store is somehow putting him into greater harmony with nature. It is worthwhile to take a closer look at what is meant by "organic" and how well these beliefs and this faith of health food devotees are borne out by the facts.

ORGANIC PRODUCE

Although several Americans have attempted to claim credit for inventing the methods and principles of organic food production, the movement actually was brought to the United States in the late nineteenth century by Christian Socialists from northern and central Europe. The method was old even then, being essentially the way people had learned to farm before modern science had produced efficient new fertilizers and pesticides that were able to save crops from the ravages of insects. Like many other old things that have been discarded for the new, organic food production has much to be said in its favor.

The basic principle is one of frugality. An effort was made to return to the land as much as possible of what had been taken out of it. Animal and human manure were used as fertilizer. The leaves that fell from trees, the stalks and leaves of food plants, and all garbage were piled neatly and allowed to stand until the compost heap rotted into a nitrogen-rich mixture that was then spread on the farmlands and plowed into them. Animal bones, the unusable portions of skin, everything the farmer could get his hands on was returned to his farmland. Such practice is very good farming because it not only adds fertilizer to the soil but also keeps adding the very kind of material that turns into topsoil over time, topsoil being earth that has a crumbly texture to absorb and hold water and is also rich with fertilizing matter.

Unless farmland is treated with this kind of respect, it tends to erode and lose its topsoil over a matter of decades. In the 1930s, millions of acres of farmland in the United States turned out to be farmed out and no longer productive enough to support a hardworking farmer. Enormous acreage was abandoned at that time. Since then, however, new farming methods have worked a revolution. Chemicals have been found that will keep even the poorest land from caking and shedding water, so that previously unusable farmland has been reclaimed. Nitrogen is extracted from the air and combined with minerals in different proportions favorable for the growth of different kinds of crops. New pesticides have just about ended the loss of any substantial portion of a food crop to insect predators. Most farmers have eagerly adopted these new methods and have prospered with them.

A social price has been exacted, however. Insects are hardy creatures and any pesticide powerful enough to kill them is going to be powerful enough to sicken or even kill humans as well. Foods sometimes accumulate too much nitrate from the high-powered fertilizers that are used to produce bountiful crops, and too much nitrate eaten by anyone can lead to serious consequences. In recent decades there has developed a serious disparity between the interests of the commercial farmer and the interests of the people he is feeding. We want big crops and lower prices for food, but how deeply we wish we could be sure that our food supply is in all ways completely safe.

Out of this quandary has emerged the organic gardener or farmer. He uses the food growing methods of a French peasant of fifty years ago. He is pledged to use no pesticides whatsoever but tries to protect his crops with predatory insects, such as the ladybug, that live by attacking and eating other insects. He is a small producer who has a steady, assured market in the health food stores and therefore is able to follow his more costly methods because the customer will pay a handsome premium for his uncontaminated food.

At least, that's how it works in theory. The practice is somewhat different.

Several organizations at different times have decided that it might be a good idea to set up an inspection program that would periodically inspect the plants of people claiming to be organic growers so that their produce could then be certified as being what the public expects organic produce to be. When warned in advance, the growers could all show their mouldering compost heaps and discuss how they controlled insects by releasing praying mantises and ladybugs. But if the inspectors looked hard, they could sometimes find bags of pesticides hidden out of sight in the back of the barn. When an agency of the New York City government decided to make a comparison between "organic" produce from the health food stores and commercial produce from the markets, it was found that there was more pesticide residue on the produce that had been obtained from the health food stores.

The reason is not hard to find. Insect predators do not do that good a protective job, and it is very hard indeed for a grower to see insects devour the crop over which he has labored long hours and in which his money is invested. The commercial grower knows that he must live by certain Department of Agriculture regulations, which compel him to stop using pesticides so many days before harvesting and perhaps to use certain other cleansing procedures to eliminate residues of the pesticides. But the organic grower who does his spraying secretly is assumed not to be using pesticides and therefore does not have to follow the procedures to get rid of them. The crops of the secret sprayer might therefore be expected to show more pesticide residue at the point of sale, and they do.

On the other hand, it cannot be denied that there are many completely sincere and honorable organic growers who would rather lose their entire crops than allow them to be contaminated by chemical sprays. If you're lucky, you might well get such absolutely pure foods when you buy them at a health food store. How can you tell? There is no way. The store manager has no way to tell and neither does the distributor from whom he buys.

But there are many types of produce, such as melons and bananas, for which it doesn't matter whether pesticides have been used or not because they cannot get into the edible portion of the plant. And if you buy what is sold as organic, even if it is not truly organic, it has probably been grown by a smaller grower who has given his crops more personal care and kept them growing until they were ripe before harvesting them and speeding them to the market. This means that the produce you buy at your health food store will probably taste better than what you can get at a supermarket, and, having been left to grow to maturity, will also have higher vitamin values and be generally somewhat more nutritious. So it might well be worth the premium you pay in any case. Do not, though, let yourself be taken in by the myth that if a food has been fertilized by compost rather than by a commercial fertilizer it will contain a wide range of trace minerals that are not found in the same food grown commercially. Growing plants take from the soil those minerals that they require for their own growth and health. That is true no matter how they are grown, and if the minerals they need are not present in the soil, the plants simply will not grow. If there are other nonessential minerals in their soil, the plants may also take minerals they do not require but can accept. Fertilizing with compost in no way guarantees that the compost has provided such minerals or that the plant was able to absorb them. Organic foods are probably somewhat higher in mineral content in most cases, but if you happen to believe that the fact they have been grown organically makes them a treasure trove of mineral nutrition, disabuse yourself. It just doesn't work that way. No matter how they are grown, ripe, tasty plant foods are nutritious and good for you.

Vitamin content, however, is a somewhat different matter. But that is not so much a matter of fertilization with compost as it is of the variety that is being grown. As a good example, large scale gardeners grow tomatoes of varieties that are selected for their firmness, so that they can be picked and packed without bruising, and their ability to keep for many weeks without spoiling, but not for their vitamin content. Small organic growers, on the other hand, whose tomatoes appear in the store bins within a few days of being picked, tend to concentrate on those varieties that contain more vitamin C. This is a common difference and the produce you can buy in a health food store does definitely tend to have a higher vitamin content.

There is much more to be said about the special qualities, oddities, and differences of the foods and food products that are obtainable in a health food store. These matters, though, are better explained in relation to the particular products involved and that is how we are doing it. The listing that follows is comprehensive and by referring to it as you consider your purchases, you will find yourself making wiser selections that will come closer to giving you the value you are seeking, and you may save yourself some money as well.

ACIDOPHILUS CULTURE

Generally sold in individual envelopes that are usually packed several dozen to a box, this looks like nothing more than a grayish white powder, but actually is a measured amount of dormant bacteria. Their scientific name is *Lactobacillus acidophilus,* a variety of bacteria that is found in the air and in cow milk as it comes from the cow. These are one of the several varieties of lactobacilli that cause milk to turn sour, which they do by converting milk sugar (lactose) into lactic acid. In the course of souring milk, they also cause it to thicken, and this variety of bacteria may be used as a yogurt starter or to make buttermilk or sour cream.

When milk is pasteurized, the acidophilus bacteria are killed by the heat process, which keeps them from souring the milk as it stands on the market shelves. Many people consider this undesirable because the acidophilus bacteria, when alive, have the special property of being able to colonize in the human intestine. They do not live long there—perhaps just for a matter of three days or so— but if one were to take some live acidophilus bacteria daily in milk or otherwise, it would provide a continuous and substantial population of these bacteria deep in our digestive system.

These bacteria have particular value. In the first place, as they die they enter into the stools, providing a great deal of extra bulk that softens the stools and tends to reduce any problem of constipation. While they are alive in the intestine, these bacteria war for food and living space against other types of bacteria that are sometimes harmful and undesirable. It is, for example, very difficult for the infectious salmonella bacteria to survive among large numbers of acidophilus, and if you happen to be well supplied with acidophilus, it is extremely unlikely that you will ever contract dysentery.

The acidophilus bacteria themselves will not harm you in any way.

People, therefore, will add a packet of *Lactobacillus acidophilus* to the milk they are drinking, in which medium the bacteria resume active life and, as soon as they are swallowed, are on their way to colonize in the intestines. The bacteria may also be added to other types of fluids but they do not survive as well as they do in milk. If you are bothered by odorous intestinal gas, constipation, or a tendency toward diarrhea, you may well find *Lactobacillus acidophilus* helpful and free from any distressing side effects.

ACIDOPHILUS MILK

This is one of the oldest of health foods. Sixty years ago physicians were recommending it for children with intestinal problems. It is simply milk that has been pasteurized, because unpasteurized milk might contain the bacteria of tuberculosis, undulant fever, and other diseases as well as those that sour the milk, and then after pasteurization has had an acidophilus culture added to it. Such milk sours quickly, for which reason many stores do not like to carry it. However, it is obtainable at some health food stores.

For a discussion of why people would buy acidophilus milk, see ACIDOPHILUS CULTURE above.

ALFALFA

You will not find alfalfa in any type of market except a health food store. The reason is not hard to find. Its taste is unpleasant. It is raised as a cattle feed and is an excellent one, especially relished

by rabbits. The plant has a special property of sinking phenome-
nally deep roots, which are able to tap the mineral nutrients that
lie far below the surface and cannot be reached by most plants.
The alfalfa leaf is thus mineral rich and some people, who do not
care how their food tastes as long as it is nutritious, do buy and
eat alfalfa leaves.

ALFALFA SEED

Like alfalfa leaves, alfalfa seed has little in the way of flavor to
recommend it. People do buy it and sprinkle a little on salads. It
is also used in herbal teas. But far and away the major use of alfalfa
seed is for sprouting. If you learn the technique, which is really
very simple, a handful of alfalfa seed can be converted in a few
days into a far greater quantity of alfalfa sprouts, which are a truly
delicious addition to any salad. It is characteristic of sprouts that
they contain in condensed form all the nutritional values of the
parent plant. When they are delightful to eat as well, that is a real
bonus.

ALFALFA SPROUTS

These delightful salad vegetables are obtainable today not only in
health food stores but in practically all supermarket produce de-
partments. They are very popular and with good cause. If you have
never tasted them, we urge you to do so. They are good in many
types of sandwiches, as well as a salad ingredient. There is absolutely no difference between the alfalfa sprouts you can buy at a
health food store and those at your neighborhood market. Select
those that are freshest and cost the least.

ALGAE

If you happen to have a swimming pool, you are familiar with
algae. They are the organisms that seem to appear from nowhere

and thrive in water, colonizing on the surface in large patches that resemble small oil spills or attaching themselves to anything solid on or near the surface. Although most people's normal relationship to algae has been to try to get rid of them, scientific thinkers have long pointed to algae as a possible source of food for the future, if and when shortages should grow far more acute than they are at the present time. Nobody has ever claimed that they taste good, but the organisms have high protein values and those that live in seawater contain all the minerals that are normally found in the sea.

Recently there have appeared, under a variety of trade names, jars and packages of seawater algae being sold as a new way to lose weight. The claim is that the algae are a very low-calorie yet complete food on which the dieter can subsist in good health and with high energy while losing weight at a fast clip. It is true to the extent that the amount of algae a normal person can stomach without vomiting provides very few calories, and if you eat nothing else in the course of a day, you are certainly going to lose with astonishing rapidity. Starvation has the same effect. Eating as few calories as the algae can provide, you are certainly going to feel hungry and weak and will find your energy resources low, regardless of what the promotional literature may claim.

Algae, in themselves, will not do you any harm and we can see nothing dangerous in them, other than the associated promotional claims that might induce you to eat far less than is safe for anyone. If you can muster faith in the algae preparations as a reducing aid, they will work just as well as any of the dozen other weight loss methods in which you have faith.

APPLE JUICE

Sold in both cans and bottles, apple juice has a bland yet sweet flavor that makes it a big favorite, particularly of small children. It is probably because it is so well liked and therefore so fully consumed by youngsters, rather than any special properties of apple juice as contrasted with other fruit juices, that has caused it to be singled out by the dental profession for warnings about its use. Like all fruit juices, apple juice is acidic. Held in the mouth for long periods of time during the day, as when drunk from a nursing bottle by a small child, the juice is able to erode delicate little teeth and has often done so.

The apple juice you can get in a health food store will contain no preservatives and will have no sugar added. The same is true of the apple juice you can buy in any market. The apple juice you can buy in a health food store may not be pasteurized, in which case it will have a tendency to ferment quickly and provide you with an alcoholic beverage that is sometimes known as hard cider. Since the variety of yeast that does the dirty work is neither selected nor controlled but simply a random element, the resulting drink may taste terrible. Because spoilage is a nuisance and sometimes a costly one, commercial markets do like to have their apple juice pasteurized. That is about the only true difference between one brand and another.

Nutritionally, this juice is not nearly as good a drink as might be supposed. Most of the vitamin and mineral content of the apple is in the pulp just beneath the skin. Its chief nutritional value is in the pectin it contains. Both are eliminated from apple juice. What remains is a sugary drink that is bad for the teeth, whether pasteurized or unpasteurized, but does have a pleasant and enjoyable flavor.

APRICOTS

This fruit is especially vulnerable to crop-destroying fruit flies and some other insect pests. Therefore it is sprayed numerous times during the growing season by commercial growers. If pesticides are used, there will be residues. If you are sure that the organic foods in your health food store are truly organic and have not been sprayed, your liver may be grateful for the differences. For additional information on apricots, see APRICOTS, DRIED.

APRICOTS, DRIED

This is among the most popular of dried fruits because of its flavor, which most people find delicious, and because it will not spoil over long periods of time without refrigeration or any special care. It is rich in carotene, the yellow pigment that converts in the body into vitamin A. Unlike those found in ordinary markets, the kind you can buy in a health food store will not have had any sulfur added to preserve them. That is because it is one of the tenets of the health food religion that sulfur is bad for you and must be avoided. In actuality, it is one of the essential minerals, a component of some of the most important amino acids, and perfectly safe if not eaten to excess. The tiny amount used to preserve dried fruits is anything but an excess and adds a flavor that many people find quite pleasant.

There does not seem to be any particular need to sulfur-dry apricots, however, and when it is done it is usually simply in compliance with Department of Agriculture regulations for interstate commerce. Those who grow apricots in the same state as the health food store do not have to comply and their fruit is not sulfured. It may also be sun dried, which is a slow process, rather than dried quickly in an oven. Some think that sun drying improves the flavor.

Dried apricots are justly a favorite among hikers and campers who like to be able to carry a food supply into wilderness areas where they cannot buy food. The dried apricot keeps well and is a high-calorie food for its weight, providing some important dietary minerals as well as vitamin A.

Apricots are one of the chief foods of Hunza, an Asiatic mountain principality, which is one of the regions of the world where the life span is appreciably longer than it is in most places. Because of this, the apricot has been invested with mythical health-giving properties in the minds of many people. This is reinforced by the fact that Laetrile, the controversial treatment for cancer, is made from the kernels of apricot pits. It is unlikely that apricots contain any special virtue other than that of being a pure and wholesome fruit with good nutritional value.

APRICOT KERNELS

The apricot kernel is unpleasantly bitter and there is no way to prepare it that will make it taste any better. Why, then, do people eat it? Because it contains substances called amygdalin and nitrilosides, which are present in many fruit seeds but apparently are richest in the apricot kernels. It is these substances that are made into Laetrile, which some people believe is an active treatment for many types of cancer and which many others consider at least an effective palliative. There has been a great deal written and stated from the lecture platform to the effect that eating a few apricot kernels every day will keep a person from ever contracting cancer. And there are enough people who take this seriously to make it worthwhile for many health food stores to sell apricot kernels.

Most doctors will warn you that these special chemicals in apricot kernels are converted into cyanide inside the human body and could easily poison or even kill you. The advocates of Laetrile firmly believe that the particular form of cyanide is nontoxic except to malignant cells and that is why it is a protection against cancer. People have become very sick from eating apricot kernels but this may have been because they ate too many. Those who claim to know advocate eating no more than five or six kernels a day.

In the principality of Hunza, deep in the Himalaya Mountains, the people are very poor and very frugal and prefer to eat the kernels of the major crop, apricots, rather than let them be wasted. The kernels are dried and pulverized and then added to bread and other foods before cooking. It does not seem to harm anybody, which may indicate that the kernels are harmless, as the Laetrile advocates say, or that the cooking detoxifies what would otherwise be poisonous, or there may be some other, unknown explanation. In any case, there is little cancer in Hunza and the Laetrile advocates are convinced it is because the Hunzakuts eat apricot kernels. It should be mentioned that in other longevity regions of the world such as Vilcabamba in Peru, there is also very little cancer and they never heard of an apricot kernel.

APRICOT TABLETS

These are offered as an energy booster and consist of powdered and dried apricots mixed with powdered whey. It is true that apricots, particularly when dried, supply a good number of energy calories in desirably nutritious form in proportion to the weight that is involved. That makes them not very different from raisins or prunes. The tablets are not particularly desirable because they are simply too small to really offer you much in the way of energy, which obviously is what you are seeking when you buy a package of energy tablets. The ingredients are fine, but if you really want to benefit from them, it is suggested that you eat real apricots and use more powdered whey than you will ever get in a tablet.

AVOCADO

This oily fruit is much prized by the nutrition conscious. Its oil is polyunsaturated and therefore attractive to those who believe that this type of oil reduces the levels of cholesterol in the blood. The avocado contains vitamin C and provitamin A and also is rather rich in vitamin E, quite unusual among fruits. Its tough, inedible skin is not penetrated by any pesticide that may be used to protect the tree, and therefore there is no danger even in heavily sprayed avocados. Do not pay a premium price for organic avocados unless you have the mystical faith that organic produce is necessarily better. Rationally there is no difference between the commercially produced and the organic avocado.

AVOCADO OIL

The oil, pressed out of avocados, is one that you will find only in a health food store. It is too thick in texture and too expensive to be attractive to commercial markets. In the health food store it is a popular item, however. Containing a good quantity of vitamin E, which is an antioxidant and preservative, avocado oil has less tendency to become rancid and therefore has a longer shelf life than other vegetable oils. Although it is not good for cooking it is used as a salad oil by many people who consider it more nutritious, even though it is comparatively thick and sticky. Some women and some professional beauty advisers consider it to be a valuable cosmetic oil, used as a moisturizer and as a skin softener. There is also a mayonnaise made with avocado oil.

BANANA CHIPS

If what you are looking for is a crispy munch that will provide a salt-free substitute for potato or corn chips, banana chips may well be the answer. They are faintly sweet in flavor, like the banana, and very pleasant. They possess the virtues of all bananas, which are simply a high potassium content, valuable to those using diuretics, and a very easy digestibility that makes bananas one of the first foods given to infants.

Banana chips are fried, however, and the addition of cooking oil to what is already a high-calorie food makes banana chips very high calorie indeed.

BEE POLLEN

Bees crawl into flowers searching for nectar, and in the course of this search their legs, bodies, and wings accumulate a debris of pollen which then may fertilize another flower as the bee crawls into it. When the bee returns to its hive, pollen is dropped on the floor of the hive. This pollen, packed into capsules or made into tablets, is bee pollen. It is in no way different from any other pollen but there are those who believe that because it has been touched by a bee, it has somehow been mysteriously transformed into something better for health.

Each type of flower has its own kind of pollen. They differ from one another as much as, say, duck eggs differ from chicken eggs and both differ from goose eggs. Possessing similar characteristics, the pollen types still differ one from another even in their nutritional values. They probably should only be discussed singly, yet pollen is sold as just pollen and written about and treated as though all pollens were identical. If you buy pollen and use it, the simple fact that there is no way whatsoever to identify what kind of flower the pollen came from could be fatal. You might be allergic to ragweed, goldenrod, and timothy hay. You could swallow pollen tablets five hundred times with no ill effects, yet on the five hundred first time get a tablet that has some ragweed pollen in it and go into a severe allergic reaction. It is because such things can and do happen that the Mayo Clinic has issued special warnings against bee pollen.

Not all people are allergy prone, however, and most are able to take pollen till the cows come home with nary an ill effect. It is even claimed that in some cases, by swallowing small quantities of the pollen to which they were allergic, people have been able to overcome their allergies. This would be a process parallel to that sometimes used by allergists, when they inject small and then increasingly larger doses of the pollen into a patient. The difference, of course, is that the allergist knows exactly what pollen he is using and how much of it, whereas there is absolutely no way of telling about the pollen you buy in tablets or capsules.

Considered as a food, pollen would rank very high on the nutritional scale. Even accounting for the individual differences between varieties, most pollens are high in protein content and possess a favorable distribution of the amino acids that make up the protein, so that it could be easily converted into body protein. The pollens also tend to have a relatively high content of zinc and magnesium, two minerals that tend to be insufficient in the ordinary diet and both of major importance to human health. Because both these minerals have been used, sometimes quite successfully, as a treatment for benign enlargement of the prostate gland, some experimental trials were conducted about twenty-five years ago, feeding capsules of pollen to middle-aged and elderly men whose prostates were causing trouble. The results were inconclusive, showing that about 40 percent of the people tested seemed to show some improvement in the condition of their prostates. From these experiments, though, there has arisen a widespread belief that pollen has a strong therapeutic value for the prostate gland. It is only a belief with no evidence to confirm it. If you are sure you will have no allergic reaction to the pollen, there is nothing to stop you from trying it in the hope of being able to empty your bladder more completely so you will not have to get up during the night and go to the bathroom, but it is unlikely that you will actually receive any help.

The mystique of the honeybee is widespread, which is why pollen is usually known as bee pollen in the health food store. Even though it has just been carried around for a while on a bee's legs and has not been changed in any way, the very fact of association with a bee gives it a magical quality in the minds of many people. They expect all kinds of miracle cures for a wide assortment of ailments and, faith being sometimes of great importance in healing, they sometimes get those cures and will swear by pollen forever after.

The bee products do have special virtues that should be taken seriously, but in truth, bee pollen is not a bee product at all.

BEE PROPOLIS

Propolis is a product that is manufactured by bees in the construction of a hive. It consists of tree resins to which the bees add other materials to make a kind of glue that is used to seal up all cracks and chinks in the hive and to close the hive entrance to a dimension that will not admit anything larger than a bee and through which the bees must squeeze.

Propolis has been tested in France where there is great interest in bee products, and it has been found to have strongly antiseptic properties. Beekeepers believe that hives stay free of contagious and infectious diseases because when bees return to the hive from outside, their wings and bodies are rubbed against the propolis-bearing hive entrance and any bacteria on them are killed.

Be that as it may, the product has become very popular in Europe and is rapidly growing in popularity in America. In Germany it is sold in small paper-wrapped chunks, which people chew. (This is also available in some American health food stores.) It can be chewed for hours or simply held in the mouth to dissolve slowly, or it can also be swallowed at any time. Thousands of people have found that all kinds of sore throats can be cured almost instantly by chewing propolis for twenty to thirty minutes. It has also been found good for sore gums. Since its effect on the mouth is decidedly beneficial, probably the best way to take propolis is in a chewable form and to chew it before swallowing. It is also available from a Danish company in flakes that can be chewed and in granules that come packed into capsules. Taken internally, propolis is considered a valid treatment for any kind of bacterial infection of the digestive tract. This would include such problems as dysentery, colitis, diverticulitis, gastroenteritis, and others. It should also treat or protect against salmonella infection.

Propolis from American beehives is also available in many health food stores. The chief difference seems to be price, the American product being much cheaper. Distributors of imported propolis claim that their products are purer, more carefully prepared, and of better quality. They have to claim something when they are charging three or four times as much for what they sell. There is no reason to believe that any of these claims of superiority are true. Propolis is propolis, whether it is manufactured by American, French, German, or Scandinavian bees.

BEEF JERKY

Actually an Indian food, jerky has been used on this continent as far back as history goes. It was not beef jerky, of course, until the importation of beef cattle, but before then essentially the same food was made from venison, buffalo meat, and other types of animal flesh. It consists simply of thin strips of lean meat that are dehydrated, in the sun or by more modern methods, until what remains is a hard, tough, and fibrous strip that looks as if it might be wood and can keep for many months without spoiling and without requiring refrigeration. The Indians and early settlers used it because it was light to carry on a trip and one could not be sure of finding game for fresh meat and because it was a way of preserving meat through the long winter when hunting was difficult even at home. Today hikers and campers use it in exactly the same way, when going into a wilderness area where fresh meat will not be available.

The way to use beef jerky is to break off a small piece from the strip, just as one would take a plug of chewing tobacco. In the mouth it slowly absorbs saliva and softens enough to be chewed. One can then chew it for anywhere from thirty minutes to an hour, softening and expanding it all the time, and finally swallow it. Hikers like to chew it while they're walking and believe that it provides them with a steady source of energy. The flavor is indifferent, but many nature enthusiasts claim to love it. It is certainly a valuable lightweight addition to the food that can be transported and used while one is going through rugged and wild terrain.

For the best flavor, jerky should be smoked while it is drying. The eating of smoked foods is forbidden in health food lore, however, and many health food stores will not carry the smoked variety. The nutritional value is simply that of beef—a fairly high quality protein that also contains some minerals and practically no vitamins.

BEEF TEA

This is an old English favorite that has recently been gaining in popularity in the United States. It consists of defatted beef that is boiled until it disintegrates, forming a thick soup, with the water continuing to cook off until what remains is the consistency of a paste. With a few flavor additives, it makes a tasty broth that can be made just as strong as you choose to make it. It is especially enjoyable in cold weather. For those who have difficulty in chewing meat, beef tea provides a pleasant and easy-to-swallow high-protein drink. Some beef teas in their preparations also included added beef blood—you can tell by reading the label—and if so, the tea then makes a valuable treatment for iron deficiency anemia.

BIOFLAVONOIDS, CITRUS

Sometimes known as vitamin P, the bioflavonoids are not recognized as a vitamin at all in the United States or Canada. They are biologically active substances found in a number of fruits and vegetables, the most active of which are taken from the white pulp of oranges, lemons, and grapefruit. These are the citrus bioflavonoids, among which the type known as hesperidin is far and away the most active of all. They seem to have two major roles within the human body. Primarily, they strengthen the walls of the capillaries, the smallest and most fragile of our blood vessels, which our bodies possess by the tens of thousands.

Capillary hemorrhage initiates bruise formation on the surface of the skin and can have similar unpleasant results internally. Capillary seepage through the walls also involves some dangers, particularly in the region of very delicate organs such as the eyes and the nasal sinuses. Whether or not the bioflavonoids are recognized as a vitamin, having them in our system in adequate supply to maintain the integrity of our tiny blood-conducting vessels is certainly desirable to everyone.

The second role of the bioflavonoids is a synergistic interplay between them and vitamin C. Closely associated with vitamin C in nature—they are found most richly in citrus fruits, bell peppers, and paprika, all rich sources of vitamin C—the bioflavonoids seem in ways that are not yet fully understood to improve and amplify the biological activity of vitamin C. They work together and many people consider it best to take them at the same time or even in a single tablet.

Most people, though, do not actually have any need to buy supplemental bioflavonoids, since they get quite enough in their daily diets. In fact, that is the reason that they are not recognized as a vitamin. In our country, nobody has yet identified any disease that is caused by a deficiency of bioflavonoids. The probability is not that there is no such disease, but that there simply is no bioflavonoid deficiency. It is different in Eastern Europe, where the bioflavonoids were first discovered by one of the world's leading nutritional biochemists, who has always maintained that vitamin P is a true vitamin.

You can probably get along fine without any supplement of bioflavonoids, but it will do you no harm to take one if you are so inclined. If you do, your choice should be the citrus bioflavonoids, making sure that they contain a high proportion of hesperidin.

BIOFLAVONOIDS, MIXED

The desire to have not only the most active bioflavonoids, but to include in the diet all types, whether active or not, is part of the mystique of the health food enthusiast. There is no rational explanation why this is preferred. It is simply part and parcel of the same conviction that holds that the entire wheat berry, bran and all, is preferable to any fractionated portion of it and so on through the roster of foods. Since this approach has often earned the derision of scientists, only to be proven quite correct in the long run, perhaps it should not be dismissed in relation to the bioflavonoids.

In any case, a supplement of mixed bioflavonoids will include the citrus bioflavonoids (see above) plus one other important one, rutin, which is derived from buckwheat. It is the particular virtue of rutin that it has been used successfully to remove an excess of copper from the blood. Inasmuch as too much copper is highly toxic, this is a desirable property. A copper excess does not occur often, but it does happen, especially in people whose homes have expensive copper plumbing. Rutin, like hesperidin and the other bioflavonoids, strengthens the walls of capillaries and can be a decided help to people who bruise easily or who suffer from any of the numerous effects of internal seepage from the capillaries.

In selecting a type of mixed bioflavonoids, it is worth your while to read the label and make certain that it contains good amounts of both hesperidin and rutin.

BONE MEAL

Widely advocated and used as a source of supplemental calcium to the diet, bone meal is seldom the best choice for this purpose. The reason is that it contains about half as much phosphorus as it does calcium and in our systems, a surplus of phosphorus will bind calcium to it and carry the calcium right out of our bodies. Since the meat-rich American diet normally contains more phosphorus than we can use, adding to that quantity with the phosphorus in bone meal defeats the purpose of a calcium supplement. Instead of increasing the amount of calcium in our bones, blood, and tissues, it decreases it.

That is not to say that bone meal is always bad. If you are a vegetarian, by the very fact of not eating meat you are probably avoiding a surplus of phosphorus and for you the combination of calcium and phosphorus may well be the most advantageous form of calcium supplementation.

Bone meal is made from the bones of cattle, which are pulverized, sterilized, and then tableted or packed as a powder in jars. It is usually supplemented with a small amount of vitamin D, which has the property of facilitating the deposition of calcium into bone. If you are already getting supplemental vitamin D from another source, as for example a vitamin A and D supplement, then a toxic excess of vitamin D might be the result of taking bone meal with the vitamin, and you should choose a brand that is pure bone and nothing else.

Bone meal also frequently includes the marrow of the original bone or even has marrow added to it. The only reason for this is the doctrine of wholeness, which holds that if there is marrow in bone then when you eat bones you should also eat the marrow along with it.

Bones, ground up to facilitate spreading, have been used as an agricultural fertilizer for many centuries. Such fertilizer has proven itself especially valuable for flower bulbs. And it was out of the concept that anything that is good food for plants ought to be good food for people as well that bone meal was first introduced as a human dietary supplement. It has enthusiastic advocates all over the world and may, in fact, be a perfectly satisfactory calcium supplement for the majority, who really do not require any large extra amount of calcium and might easily accumulate an excess of this mineral if they took a more efficient calcium source. It should be noted, however, that bone meal will also contain contaminants, possibly poisonous, that are stored in the bones of cattle while they are alive. These include lead, fluorine, sometimes arsenic and even, on occasion, radioactive strontium 90.

For a discussion of why people take calcium supplements, including bone meal and of the relative efficiency of various calcium supplements, see CALCIUM in Section 1: Vitamins and Minerals.

BRAN

Although there are other kinds, when people refer to bran they mean, by universal agreement, wheat bran—the outer shell of the wheat berry that is milled away before the wheat is ground into flour. For about a hundred years this bran, which is indigestible and provides no nutrition, has been both staunchly advocated as an aid to health and just as bitterly condemned. There is no doubt that, in passing through the digestive system unassimilated, bran accumulates fluid and adds bulk to the stool, thus sometimes increasing the ease and frequency of bowel movements. To many people this has constituted a desirable cleansing of the bowel. At times it has been advocated by the medical profession and at other times it has been condemned as dangerous roughage that might irritate the intestines or even scrape or puncture the intestinal wall.

Although there are many breakfast cereals that contain varying percentages of bran, all of which are treated to add some flavor, if you buy bran in a health food store it will not be flavored in any way nor will it have undergone any cooking process. It will be plain, raw wheat bran with the lack of anything pleasant about its taste or texture that many health food devotees find reassuring.

About ten years ago a world-famous British surgeon, Dr. Denis Burkitt, reported on widespread observations and records he had made in Africa to the effect that a large quantity of nondigestible fiber in the diet provided positive health benefits to the Africans who ate that way, including an almost total absence of cancer of the colon and far lower levels of cholesterol in the blood, which translated into fewer heart attacks. This was immediately seized upon as meaning that an increase in the amount of bran consumed would bring about these results. Bran became very popular and has remained so to this day.

In actuality, the nondigestible fiber that Dr. Burkitt was referring to, he has pointed out, was the kind that is found chiefly in root vegetables such as turnips, rutabagas, parsnips, carrots, and beets. Using such root vegetables as a major element in the diet, Burkitt says, can be expected to bring the benefits he has written about. Bran would be just about useless for the purpose.

In truth, recent studies have shown that while corn bran does have a substantial cholesterol-lowering effect, wheat bran does not. Nevertheless, when indigestible fiber is advocated by anyone, it is wheat bran that leaps to the mind of most people and it is wheat bran that they buy and use. You need not be afraid of it. The medical profession has admitted that it was wrong in its condemnation. But all that you can reasonably expect from bran is that it will improve your elimination processes.

BREAD

It is to the credit of the devotees of health food and the industry that supplies them that both the variety and the quality of bread in the American diet have improved vastly in recent years. Today there is a wide overlap, with the supermarket offering most of the types of bread you can get at a health food store, and the health food store, conversely, going in for most of the more wholesome types of bread that are now available everywhere. There are some differences that may not always be pertinent. Bread is not a national but a local product, which is always produced locally, even if it is the most repellent brand of flavorless and nutritionless white bread. Thus it is impossible to describe it in complete accuracy. In one region the health food stores carry whole-grain breads that are baked entirely without any salt, while in another region such breads may be unobtainable and the stores do the best they can with what they can get. It would be pointless to attempt to describe the various varieties in which choice is just a matter of taste preference. There are, however, some special breads worth considering, which you can get at a health food store and perhaps nowhere else.

Bread, far from being the staff of life, had turned for a while into an inferior food lacking vitamin, mineral, or usable protein content and offering only too many calories plus a host of more or less toxic preservatives, moisturizers, bleaching agents, and other assorted chemicals. Today, though, you can buy breads that are a genuine, highly nutritious food. That you can get them in places other than the health food store is a tribute to the health food industry, which introduced and promoted them first.

SPROUTED-GRAIN BREAD. All grains are seeds and any seed can be sprouted. Characteristically the sprouting adds a better flavor and during the sprouting the vitamin content of the seed increases to its highest point. The mineral content, of course, does not change. Thus, if you want a bread with the highest possible nutritional values, the thing to use is sprouted grain. It also should taste fine. The baker will probably choose a less refined sweetener like molasses or honey in preference to sugar. This has little or no nutritional significance but some people find it reassuring and it does lend the bread a more interesting flavor. Salt may be used or omitted, depending on the baker. It will taste better with salt. It will be better for you without.

Sprouted breads are sometimes made entirely of whole grain wheat and more often of mixed grains. The mixed grains should be preferred because soybeans are usually used as well. The soybean contains a great deal of the amino acid lysine, which is the one amino acid that is in very short supply in wheat and keeps wheat protein from having any great protein value. When wheat and soy are mixed together, however, the protein value soars and the bread becomes a more complete and better food.

If you have never tried a bread made of sprouted whole grains, you will probably be very pleased by the flavor and texture and you can eat it as though it were real food, which it is.

WHOLE-GRAIN BREAD. In order to make bread, you must first make flour. In the dough for the whole-grain bread, a few un-milled kernels of whatever grains are being used are added to the dough to give the impression of entire grains. They do not change the flavor nor do they add to the nutritional quality of the bread. With or without them, however, a good whole-grain bread will include the most nutritious elements of the grains being used, which are ordinarily removed in order to make a finer-textured flour. Whole-grain bread does not spoil easily because the oily elements, which can become rancid, have been separated from the starchy components of the grain.

Whole-grain breads may feature as many as seven different grains, including oats, barley, corn, millet, soybeans, and, of course, wheat. The addition of most of these grains is meaningless in nutritional terms, though the combination of soy and wheat in a proportion of about one to six provides a bread with high-quality protein.

No matter what grains are used additionally, all breads that rise and have the favored light texture that is provided by air pockets in the bread are fundamentally wheat breads. It is gluten, a special element found only in wheat, that when mixed with water forms a sticky, somewhat rubbery mixture (sometimes known as library paste) that traps air bubbles when the flour is being kneaded and thus creates the desirable light texture. As a nutrient gluten has no particular value. While gluten breads are sometimes promoted as being high-protein breads, which is true, the protein is not usable in human metabolism and is of no significance.

Thus the chief advantage of a many-grained whole-grain bread is its flavor, if you happen to like that flavor. The most nutritious whole-grain bread would be one that is 85 percent whole-wheat flour and 15 percent soy.

MISCELLANEOUS BREADS. It would be a rare health food store that does not have at least half a dozen types of breads, and some of the larger stores may carry as many as twenty. Most of these breads are identical to what you can get in any market. There are some special types for special needs, however, that you can find in some health food stores and perhaps nowhere else. One is the salt-free bread, which is of value to the many people whose blood pressure is high and who must, therefore, eliminate as much salt as possible from their diets. The lack of salt seriously dulls the flavor of such breads, but that is a problem that people face with all foods when salt must be eliminated. Another type is the gluten-free bread, usually made with potato starch, that is very helpful to the parents of children who have celiac disease, an inability to tolerate gluten that seriously restricts the foods that may be fed to such a child. Adults, also, sometimes suffer from what is known as gluten malabsorption syndrome and may not eat any wheat. A Scandinavian-type whole-grain rye bread that is very solid and flat because, having no gluten, it does not rise is also available as a gluten-free bread. These breads, however, are often heavily salted simply because the combination of rye and salt provides a very enjoyable flavor, and rye without salt is quite flat. Some health food stores will not carry such breads for this reason. Breads may be called whole wheat whether or not they contain any wheat germ or wheat bran. Therefore you must read the label carefully if you want a whole-wheat bread containing those portions of the wheat berry. Most of the breads you can buy in a health food store will contain no preservatives. They will therefore grow stale quickly, which makes them more suitable for a family than for a single individual.

BUCKWHEAT

This grain deserves greater popularity than it enjoys. It is sold in one-pound cardboard boxes that contain either the whole grain including its shell, or the whole grain that has been lightly milled to remove only the shell, leaving the rest of the grain intact. Buckwheat's chief nutritional claim to fame is that it is the major source of rutin, one of the more important bioflavonoids that has a strengthening effect on the walls of the capillaries, improves the biological activity of vitamin C, and will also remove an excess of copper from the bloodstream.

Buckwheat cooks into a grain dish called kasha loved by many people. It is added to potted and stewed meats in the same way that potatoes might be or served separately with the gravy from such dishes. It is also used as a filling for a pastry known as a knish.

BULGUR

This is simply entire grains of wheat with the husks milled away. It is of a special strain that originated in Bulgaria and thus benefits from the widespread conviction that foods of Bulgarian origin are better for health than other foods. This conviction probably arose in the nineteenth century when Metchnikoff, a leading scientist of his time, advocated drinking sour milk to prolong life because the long-lived Bulgarians did it. Today the Bulgarians still drink sour milk but their longevity is no greater than anyone else's, nor is their health. So much for the mystique of Bulgarian health, but bulgur wheat can still make a delicious substitute for the more common starchy foods such as potatoes and rice. Even after boiling it has a firm, chewy texture that is very pleasant. It is a good stuffing for fowl and goes well with many meat dishes. Nutritionally, it has the virtues of whole-grain wheat. It contains most of the B vitamins, some vitamin E, and some of the mineral nutrients, including zinc and magnesium.

BUTTERMILK, POWDERED

Buttermilk, in its original form, was the soured, fat-free milk that was left as a residue after the churning of butter. It was quite different from the buttermilk you can buy in your market today, which is whole milk to which a culture of lactobacillus has been added to sour it. When it has reached the desired degree of sourness, it is pasteurized to kill the bacilli, and what remains is a very pleasant sour-tasting form of milk with no live lactobacilli, considered the most desirable and healthful element in true buttermilk. In a few states, where it is still possible to obtain raw (unpasteurized) milk, one can also obtain real buttermilk made from the raw milk. It tastes awful. Yet there are many people who would love to have raw buttermilk available but cannot get it because most states require that all milk must be pasteurized. The answer, for them, is powdered raw buttermilk. You can simply add the proper amount of water to it and have a reconstituted buttermilk that contains no butterfat and in which the dormant lactobacilli will resume their life and activity. You probably will not enjoy drinking it, but it is one way to give yourself a daily supply of the live lactobacilli, which do help to avoid or overcome intestinal infections, and also promote bowel regularity.

CANDY BARS

It is a tribute to the power of money that every health food store stocks a variety of candy bars, usually near the cash register where you will be tempted to buy one on your way out and be less likely to steal one and put it in your pocket. One of the firm principles of every guru of health foods and natural living is the avoidance of sweets, which have the effect of causing a swift rise in the blood sugar level and a demand on the pancreas to produce more insulin. This can result in plunging the blood sugar excessively low, a condition known as hypoglycemia that causes sluggishness, nervous irritability, depression, and when it is chronic, can even induce suicidal tendencies. A more common result is that the pancreas, chronically overburdened, loses its efficiency at producing insulin and the candy eater becomes diabetic. It is preached vigorously and believed devoutly that sugar is bad and should be completely avoided.

Yet every health food store sells candy bars, and the only reason for it is that they are a high profit item.

They are different, of course, from the candy bars you might buy anywhere else. Instead of being coated with chocolate, forbidden because it contains a stimulant similar to caffeine, these candies will be coated with carob, which is in itself a fairly wholesome food that many people believe to resemble chocolate in flavor. Instead of being sweetened with sugar, they will be sweetened with honey or molasses or maple syrup, all of which are essentially different forms of sugar and create exactly the same problems as sugar in the bloodstream. They may be filled with raisins or peanuts like any other candy bar, and they may also have added for the pretense of healthfulness such exotic items as wheat germ and lecithin. The amount of such health food type ingredients is insubstantial and the nutritional value they add to a candy bar is practically nil. They are simply a pretense that permits the customer to think that in satisfying his craving for sweets he is buying something good for his health. All he is actually getting is a candy bar, no better for him than any other candy bar, but costing about three times as much.

CAROB

This is a rather innocuous product that is strongly promoted for use as a substitute for chocolate. It is sold powdered as a substitute for cocoa, used as a covering for candy bars, and made into a syrup to be used wherever chocolate syrup would normally be used. Carob in its natural state is a long flat seed pod that grows on the carob tree. It is also known as St. John's bread. The entire pod can be chewed and it is often used this way. The outer skin is tough but otherwise it is rather soft, moist, and sweet. Its virtues are negative. Unlike chocolate, it contains no stimulants; and since it is naturally sweet, it does not need to have sugar added to it. It takes a strong imagination to believe that the flavor actually resembles chocolate, but it is pleasant and acceptable in itself and helpful to those who need some kind of substitute in order to avoid chocolate.

CARROT CHIPS

Since people do a great deal of snacking, and the popular potato chips and corn chips require a great deal of forbidden salt for their flavor, it was to be expected that someone would create other varieties of chips that can be left unsalted and are still enjoyable to eat. Carrot chips have recently been made available. The trouble with them is that like all chips, they have been fried to their crisp and enjoyable texture. This makes them a high-calorie food and if you eat them in any quantity, they are going to put pounds on you just as potato and corn chips do. They are salt-free, however, and rich in provitamin A and nonnutritive fiber. You might enjoy them more than you expect.

CHARCOAL TABLETS

Charcoal has the unique quality of being able to absorb many times its own volume of gas, and to absorb practically any type of gas. These tablets are sold, therefore, as an aid to people who have too much gas anywhere in the digestive system from the stomach to the bowel. The charcoal will do what it is supposed to do—reduce the amount of gas that the body releases. You should be cautioned, though, that charcoal tablets are possibly as dangerous as charcoal broiling your meats, and for the same reason. The charcoal is believed by some to be carcinogenic and to stimulate the development of stomach cancer. There is no hard evidence either pro or con, but if you believe in being very cautious about what you put into your stomach, charcoal tablets are something to be very cautious about.

CHIA SEED

This is a seed of a desert plant that was believed by the Indians to have magical properties. In Indian lore the seed was used as an emergency ration and it was said that people could survive in the desert for weeks with no other food. Analysis, however, reveals no special properties in the chia seed. Its protein content is incomplete, its vitamin and mineral content unimpressive. It is sometimes used as an herb and a good many people do buy and use it. We couldn't say why.

CHLOROPHYLL

Chlorophyll is the blood of plants, the circulating green fluid that gives leaves their color. Chlorophyll contains a number of minerals, depending on the type of plant and the soil in which it stands, but iron and magnesium are always among them. It is probably the magnesium content of the chlorophyll that gives it its very special property. It is a deodorizer. If you suck on a chlorophyll lozenge or chew a chlorophyll-containing chewing gum, it will neutralize any odors in your mouth. If you swallow chlorophyll tablets, the odor of your stools and any gaseous discharges will be much reduced. Over a period of time chlorophyll will even reduce or neutralize persistent body odor. It does work as a deodorizer, but you have to be careful in using it. Because of the mineral content, if you take too much chlorophyll into your system, you might find yourself suffering from an excess of iron, magnesium, or one of the other minerals that chlorophyll may contain. Chlorophyll mouthwashes and chewing gum will work well for you as a breath sweetener and freshener. Chlorophyll tablets should be used only occasionally and their regular use is not recommended.

CIDER

Cider is just about the same beverage as apple juice, with the exception that apple juice is always strained and while cider may be strained, it need not be, and it may contain small particles of the fruit. It is a pleasant drink, sweet and rather bland in flavor. It contains some of the apple's vitamin C and minerals. Like all fruit juices, cider is acidic in nature and should not be held in the mouth for too long a time since it can erode teeth and its sugar content encourages cavity formation. That makes it a bad drink to be given to children from a nursing bottle, as is commonly done. It is a pleasant and wholesome drink, however, when taken from a glass and swallowed.

CIDER, SPARKLING

This is strained cider charged with carbon dioxide, which has recently appeared in fancy bottles and is apparently being offered as a substitute for champagne as a celebratory drink. It is too sweet to resemble champagne in anything but appearance. But again, it is a pleasant nonalcoholic drink that may well lend a festive quality to meals where no alcohol is permitted.

COCONUT OIL

The oil of the coconut is one of the two vegetable oils that are monounsaturated rather than polyunsaturated. That means chemically that each molecule has only one open bond to which an atom of hydrogen or oxygen might attach itself, rather than several. As a cholesterol-reducing agent, it is virtually without value. In its effect on the liver and ultimately the bloodstream it is far more like an animal fat than like such oils as corn, sunflower, etc. This does not mean that there is anything very bad about coconut oil, but simply that a lot of people are using it for the wrong purpose and are mistaken in thinking it is like any other vegetable oil.

In flavor coconut oil is very pleasant. It is faintly sweet and both smells and tastes like coconut. It tends to be a bit thicker and more viscous than most vegetable oils and therefore does not make a very good salad oil. But if you go in for frying chicken or veal cutlets, coconut oil is without a peer for this purpose.

This particular oil is also widely used for cosmetic purposes. Since it has little tendency to become rancid, it mixes well with pigments to create various cosmetics to tint the skin and lips. When an oil is to be used for massage, coconut oil again has excellent qualities for the purpose and its light fragrance has nothing repellent about it.

There is no particular reason why coconut oil should be considered a health food, but neither is there anything in it to be afraid of or to avoid.

COFFEE, DECAFFEINATED

It would be a rare health food store in which you could find natural coffee such as you can buy in any market, since caffeine is a rather powerful stimulant and is considered to be an enemy of health. But you may well find as many as half a dozen different brands of coffee that has been treated to remove the caffeine, leaving some of the coffee flavor and none of the stimulation. On its face this seems to be a good idea. However, there is good reason to believe that decaffeinated coffee is more dangerous to drink than the stimulating beverage it replaces. It is not easy to remove caffeine from coffee, and the chemicals that do it have shown evidence of inducing cancer of the stomach.

Use of a food that really has no food value and that has been processed with chemicals that add a new danger to the food is not what one expects of the stock of a health food store. To their credit, many of the health food stores will not carry this product. Too many others do.

COFFEE SUBSTITUTES

There are various roots and grains which, if roasted until they are nearly burned, have a bitter flavor and can be brewed into a drink that an active imagination can interpret as tasting like coffee. They are free of caffeine and will not do you any harm. Though they are sometimes promoted as helping you to fall asleep, the only way they actually do so is by giving you no caffeine that might prevent you from falling asleep. Such drinks are not particularly nutritious nor will they do anything for your health. Neither will they hurt you in any way. If you happen to like them, fine. If you don't like them and are just trying to avoid coffee, you will probably do better with one of the dozens of pleasant-tasting herb teas or even a powdered carob drink.

COLD-PRESSED OILS

The normal and most efficient way to obtain oil from a plant is by heat extraction, which involves both heating and using chemical solvents to separate the oil from the rest of the plant. Because, in the minds of many health food devotees, any processing with chemicals makes food a hazard, there arose the practice of producing edible oils for the health food market by the original method that has been used since biblical times. Pressure is applied to the fruit or vegetable and out comes the oil. It contains residues of pulp and will also be mixed with other fluids, so that an additional process of slow separation must be pursued. The end result is a smaller amount of oil from any given weight of plant food, which is necessarily more expensive. But the oil is cold pressed.

The ultimate difference between the two types of oil is somewhat in favor of the cold-pressed oil. Plant oils naturally carry a content of vitamin E which protects them against becoming rancid. The heat extraction method destroys all or most of the vitamin E in an oil, and it must then be replaced by other preservatives to prevent rancidity. Similarly, the oils will have a small content of dissolved minerals, some of which, like magnesium, will be destroyed by the heat extraction method. No effort is made to replace such minerals.

Cold-pressed oils are thus somewhat more nutritious than their heat extracted counterparts. You may also find that the flavor is pleasanter to your taste. Their shelf life is shorter, however, because their preservative content is so much smaller. Once the bottle has been opened, rancidity may easily occur and that can have very serious results to your digestive system and your general health. If you use cold-pressed oils, therefore, buy them in small quantities and once you have opened the bottle, keep it refrigerated and try to use it up quickly. With such minimal care you will get no problems from cold-pressed oil but only satisfaction at its high quality.

CORN BRAN

When corn is made into corn meal, the outer shell of the corn kernel is milled away. These indigestible millings are the corn bran. Until very recently, it has not received any particular advocacy or consideration. However, there has recently appeared a great deal of medical information about the value of indigestible fiber in the diet, not the least of which is that the free cholesterol circulating in the bloodstream is significantly reduced and carried out of the body by such fiber. Although many people involved with health foods immediately leaped to the conclusion that wheat bran would be fine for this purpose, actual testing under reliable, controlled conditions has found that corn bran is far more effective among brans. For a consistent cholesterol reducing effect you would probably do better to eat more sweet potatoes, turnips, beans, and rutabaga, but if it's bran that you want, corn bran is the one type that will truly give you the effect you are looking for.

CORN CHIPS

They have been around for a long time and have long been a snacking favorite. They are available everywhere as a heavily salted chip that is very enjoyable if you don't mind the heavy salt content and the quantity of high-calorie oil they absorb in the process of being fried. Health food stores have their own version, which is manufactured without any salt and, consequently, does not taste nearly as good. It contains just as much oil and will put just as much weight on you if you keep nibbling them while watching TV. But it is somewhat better for you than the original because it will not raise your blood pressure and will not cause your tissues to accumulate fluid.

CORN GERM

As is characteristic of all grains, at the heart of each kernel of corn there lies a small plant organism known as the germ. This is the true seed which, if fertile, will sprout and grow into a new corn plant, while the surrounding kernel is mostly starch that is food for the seed. The germ contains a lot of oil, which is undesirable in the corn meal and is therefore removed in the milling process. The germ is available as a health food. It can be eaten as a cereal or added to other cereals or sprinkled on salads and such foods. It has a very high content of vitamin E, a good amount of vitamin A, and some of the B-complex vitamins. It also has a pleasant flavor. It is packaged and sold raw, however, which leaves it vulnerable to quickly becoming rancid. To protect yourself against rancidity, which is very dangerous in any food, buy your corn germ in the smallest possible package, keep it refrigerated, and use it up quickly.

CORN MEAL

Throughout the south, corn meal has long been a dietary staple. Because it is just about devoid of vitamin B_3 (niacin) and vitamin B_6 (pyridoxine), people who lived almost totally on corn meal developed a deficiency disease, pellagra. Skimpy diet was at fault, but corn meal got the blame and it has been unjustly avoided by many. It is a perfectly good, rather bland-tasting grain that can be used as a cereal or to bake nonrising types of bread like taco shells and tamales. If you bake your own bread, adding a little corn meal to your normal flour will give you a bread that is heavier and more moist in texture, which some people find very enjoyable. In nutritional terms, there is not much to be said about corn meal except that you can obtain it in a fairly natural state, produced with a bare minimum of processing.

COUGH DROPS

It seems that people have always been troubled with coughs, and over the years there have been dozens or perhaps even hundreds of folk medicine cough remedies, none of which seem to have much actual effect on a cough other than to stimulate salivation and thus moisten the throat, easing any irritation or tickling sensation that may cause coughing. Cough drops, in effect, are little more than candy, and in fact, in health food stores and drugstores alike, they are usually sold in the candy sections. In health food stores cough drops tend to contain all the old folk remedies for coughs, including various pungent oils such as menthol, eucalyptol, and such, plus wild cherry syrup and other ingredients essentially herbal in nature. The only thing different about the health food products is that some of them contain no sugar at all and, devoid of sweet flavoring, taste pretty awful. You may find that reassuring. Some people do. No one type of cough drop is to be recommended over the others, because they all do pretty much the same thing. They keep the mouth and throat moist and thus temporarily relieve some types of coughs.

Health food store cough drops are all free of the modern drugs that do suppress the tendency to cough, but which sometimes have a sickening effect and even cause nausea. They will do you less harm.

CYSTINE

Usually designated as 1-cystine, which is a technical indication that this is the natural form, it is one of the four amino acids (the building blocks of protein tissue) that contain sulfur. The other three are synthesized within the body, making cystine the only one that we must obtain dietarily if we are to have it at all.

That is not so easily accomplished. The only food that will give us this amino acid and the sulfur it contains in substantial quantity is eggs. Since egg yolk is rich in cholesterol and warnings are periodically issued against eating too many eggs, people tend to be deficient both in cystine and in sulfur. That can have unfortunate effects. The sulfur, which is an essential mineral, will not be found in any mineral supplements because health food devotees and pundits have a prejudice against it, based primarily on the fact that whenever there have been killer fogs the sulfur content of the air has been high and that the sulfur in fireplaces was thought to cause cancer of the scrotum in chimney sweeps. But dietary sulfur in reasonable quantities, which would be obtained primarily from cystine, is important to healthy skin, hair, and fingernails. Deficiency of sulfur is believed involved in psoriasis and perhaps in the development of rheumatoid arthritis as well.

If you avoid eggs in your diet, you probably lack cystine and are deficient in the sulfur that it contains. You can make up for the lack by getting pure cystine, either in tablet or capsule form, at your health food store. On the whole, however, unless you have a severe cholesterol problem, you might do better to eat a couple of eggs three times a week and get it that way. There is good evidence that the lecithin in the egg yolk keeps the cholesterol from hardening and clumping in the blood and that a reasonable amount of egg in the diet will really do no harm.

DESICCATED LIVER

The more the liver is studied and the more that is learned about it, the more apparent it is that this organ is truly fantastic in the variety and importance of its function. It purifies the blood, removing and detoxifying a wide variety of inimical materials. It transforms carotene into vitamin A and vitamin D into the hormone-like structure that the body can actually use to build and replenish the bones. It converts surplus sugar into a storage form that does no harm but is held as a reserve against future needs. It stores a large number of minerals and feeds them into the blood as they are required. And these functions only scratch the surface of the many things the liver does.

Liver is best known to most people because it stores iron, vitamin B_{12}, and folic acid, and therefore is a sovereign remedy for many types of anemia. It also stores all the vitamins of the B complex and has long been promoted as a source of B vitamins. It is a very good one, which will supply all the B vitamins in reasonable potencies as well as a wide assortment of related and important food elements. In fact, if any food can truly be said to be a powerhouse of nutrition, liver is that food. And since it would be distasteful to many and actually impossible for most to eat liver every day, desiccated liver, which is liver dehydrated to about one fourth its original weight and either pressed into tablets or sold as a powder, came into being many, many years ago.

Peculiarly, it is not possible for the manufacturer to offer desiccated liver as a B-complex supplement, or, indeed, as a supplement offering any of its many nutritional values. That is because, while the vitamins, minerals, and even enzymes are always there, their potencies will vary somewhat from one liver to another. Since the law requires that potencies must be stated precisely on the label of a product, which the manufacturer cannot do, his only recourse is to sell the product as simply desiccated liver without any claim at all for its ingredients. Nevertheless, you can be sure that if you take 3 or 4 grams of desiccated liver daily, you are adding good amounts of all the B-complex vitamins, of iron and other important minerals, of vitamins A and D, and probably vitamin E as well.

In fact, over the past thirty years or so, billions of people have been steady users of desiccated liver supplements and most of them have felt that they were benefiting by the use.

However, desiccated liver has also been used by many in the belief that it has special qualities to provide one with extra energy. This began long ago in the laboratory of a nutritional biochemist who was running a series of experiments on the endurance and survival ability of rats. It was a simple experiment. He gave a group of rats a controlled diet for a week or two, then threw them in a tank of water to see how long they could swim before they drowned. He was rather stunned by the difference in rats given intravenous injections of liver extracts. The survival time far outdistanced what had been accomplished on any other type of food, and in some cases, it proved just about impossible to drown the rats at all. They just kept swimming and swimming.

A leading magazine dealing in popular nutrition seized on the information and played it up. Its editor assumed, without much justification, that if you could get that kind of an effect by injecting liver extract, you could get just the same effect by eating desiccated liver. Desiccated liver, which unlike liver extract, could be sold by advertisers for public use, was vigorously advocated as an energy-providing supplement. The biochemist objected, particularly when he checked on his own results and found that more often than not he was unable to repeat them. He never did find out what factor it was in the liver extract that apparently gave his rats superrodent endurance, but might have been missing in the extract that did not work on the rats. His objections were ignored, however, as advertising for desiccated liver brought in profits for the magazine that was pushing it.

Since then, and that was a long time ago, desiccated liver has been sold by the billions of tablets to people who believed it would increase their energy. Some manufacturers, having found that their customers actually did not gain any added quanta of vigor, started adding other ingredients that they felt might step up the energy potential. Today there are a number of such combination products, calling themselves energy tablets or antifatigue tablets, or other words to that effect. Desiccated liver has remained the base, combined with other ingredients such as kelp, vitamin A, yeast, pollen, and vitamin E.

Of them all, those that combine desiccated liver with kelp seem to produce the most satisfied customers who believe that their energy is being increased, even though there is no scientific evidence to prove it. The original researcher has long speculated that the presence or absence of iodine in the liver extract he used might be the unknown factor that sometimes made the liver extract a high-energy source. If so, the kelp combination, which is high in iodine, would be a valid improvement on desiccated liver alone.

Otherwise, there is no way that it can be said that any particular combination product does or does not increase the energy of the user. If you are curious, you can try a couple for yourself. But do not expect too much.

Desiccated liver alone remains a superb food supplement.

DOLOMITE

This product, like several others, had its origin in its use as an agricultural fertilizer. It is simply limestone that comes from areas that once lay beneath the oceans and which therefore absorbed a high content of magnesium from the ocean water. In very rough terms, its mineral content is something like 40 percent magnesium and 60 percent calcium. It is offered and used as a magnesium supplement, the chief virtue of which is that it is "natural." One simply has to quarry the stone and pulverize it. It makes a good fertilizer for crops, like tomatoes, that thrive on a lot of magnesium. With human users it is not so successful.

The trouble would seem to be that while plants will absorb essential, inorganic minerals without trouble, the human being will reject such essential minerals and will absorb them only when they are coupled or chelated with other organic materials that the body normally accepts easily. Thus, if you eat a brazil nut, which has a high magnesium content, you will absorb and utilize the magnesium, which will enter your bloodstream attached to some of the protein of the nut. But if you swallow a dolomite tablet, it is very unlikely that you will actually absorb any of the appreciable magnesium content of that tablet. In fact, in all too many cases, it has been found that the tablets pass through the entire digestive system without even breaking down in shape and are excreted as tablets.

That is unfortunate. Magnesium is one of the most important of mineral nutrients, being necessary for so many enzyme systems that it has been said to enter into the functioning of every single cell of the body. It is estimated that the average diet falls short of a person's magnesium needs by about 200 milligrams a day, so some form of supplementation is desirable. And there are forms that are readily absorbed and used by the body. See MAGNESIUM in Section 1: Vitamins and Minerals.

When it is possible to manufacture a magnesium supplement

that will be readily absorbed and will fulfill all the roles of magnesium in the body, why would anybody choose to manufacture and sell dolomite tablets? That is a hard question to answer. In any case, if it is magnesium you want there is no doubt that you can do better than taking dolomite.

EGGS, FERTILE

One of the tenets of health food enthusiasts is that there is supernutritional value in those foods that contain that mysterious force we know as "life." In other words, a nut that can grow into a new nut tree or a seed that can grow into a new sunflower or pumpkin is considered to be one of the super foods. Carrying that principle a step further, it is believed that the wheat germ, which is the portion of the wheat that actually grows into a new plant, is superior to the rest of the wheat berry, which merely feeds the developing germ. And in the same way, it has been assumed that a hen's egg that has actually been fertilized by a rooster is a better food than the same egg that has not been fertilized, with the additional nutritional value lying in the speck of rooster sperm that touches the egg yolk to fertilize it. This has been believed by many people for many years, and health food stores carry in their regular stock a good supply of fertile eggs.

Professor Roger Williams of the University of Texas is a nutritional biochemist who decided some years ago to eliminate a great deal of speculation and theorizing by actually testing, one by one, an enormous range of foods to see which had the greater nutritional value. The test he applied was a simple one. If laboratory animals can be fed entirely on one particular food and can stay alive and in fairly good health on that food alone, it is a good, nutritious food. Otherwise, it is obviously less nutritious. He has testified before Congress and the National Academy of Science and has published his results. Packaged white bread will not sustain life, whereas whole-wheat bread will. Most packaged breakfast cereals will not.

Whole-grain cooked cereals will. And sad to say and a shock to thousands, ordinary eggs will sustain life but fertile eggs will not.

So do not believe that fertile eggs offer you anything but a nutritional disadvantage. It was a plausible theory, but in practice it just doesn't work. Needless to say, those theoreticians of the health food movement who have vigorously advised their followers to eat fertile eggs have simply ignored the evidence produced by Dr. Williams.

EGGS, ORGANIC

A great deal has been written in criticism of what are called "factory eggs." In commercial production, hens are kept in crowded henhouses where they have no room to move around and barely enough room to perch and lay an egg daily. They are fed, sometimes from conveyor belts, a commercial mash designed to encourage egg production that may sometimes contain antibiotics to prevent or cure disease. They never receive the services of a rooster and if they could talk, they would certainly complain about their treatment. It is claimed that this is reflected in a lower nutritional quality of the egg.

Organic eggs are more generally known as "free-range" eggs. The hens are kept in a yard where they are free to scratch for worms and beetles and pick up their daily chicken feed from the ground. There will usually be one or two roosters in the yard and the hens will deposit their eggs in nests and try to sit on them. The eggs are believed to be more nutritious. No analysis, however, has ever been able to show any difference at all between the eggs, though the free-range eggs do seem to have more flavor.

It is obviously more expensive to produce free-range eggs and they are sure to cost more wherever you buy them. Sentiment or a belief in the mystique of the natural may cause you to want the free-range eggs anyway, and there is nothing wrong with that. They are perfectly good eggs. Remember, though, that there is absolutely no way you can tell by examining the egg whether it comes from an egg factory or is free-range. They look identical and if the store owner chooses to buy commercially produced eggs and sell them at inflated prices, there is no way anyone can tell. It comes down to a question of how much faith you have in the store where you shop.

EGGSHELL CALCIUM

Many people can use extra calcium in their diets, but its effect will be negated if it is taken along with the phosphorus with which it is usually associated in nature. If these people prefer their calcium to come from a natural food rather than a mineral source, eggshell calcium is one good way to get it. The eggshell is practically pure calcium, and it is powdered and then pressed into tablets. For a more complete discussion of why this might be a preferable product, see CALCIUM in Section 1: Vitamins and Minerals.

FRUCTOSE

This is the sugar of most fruits, the big exception being grapes, whose sugar is glucose. Fructose, as a sugar, may be used to some extent in diabetic diets because, if it is not overdone, it can be metabolized without insulin. Glucose, on the other hand, is forbidden to diabetics unless they are actually using insulin, and then only as a doctor may recommend. Fructose is available as a powder or in tablets that can be added to foods.

Recently a popular reducing diet claimed to stimulate the fat-burning process by using a controlled amount of fructose and completely avoiding glucose, or table sugar. The use of relatively large amounts of fructose involves certain hazards. This particular sugar stimulates the formation of dental cavities at a faster rate than does table sugar. It is also believed by some doctors to stimulate the formation of fatty deposits in the arteries. Thus it might be prudent to try a different reducing diet.

GARLIC

For thousands of years garlic has occupied a special place in folk medicine and in witchcraft. It has been used as a sovereign remedy for dozens of diseases, on most of which it has no effect. However, in some respects it has strong health value. It contains a chemical element named allicin that has valuable antibiotic properties, of particular use in the digestive tract. Long known as a prime treatment for dysentery, it was used by the German armies during World War I for this purpose, with conspicuous success. (During later wars it was no longer possible to get soldiers to eat garlic every day.) Many people who travel to foreign countries and want to protect themselves against dysentery have succeeded in doing so by eating a clove or two of garlic every day. Garlic is also known to have a benign effect on the blood pressure and in countries where it is a regular part of the diet, such as Spain and Italy, there is very little high blood pressure compared to northern Europe and the United States.

Except, perhaps, by implication, nobody bothers to make any claims for organic production of garlic. It is easy to grow and in fact grows wild in the spring just about everywhere. Insects find its strong odor as repellent as many people do and avoid it, so no one ever has to bother to spray a garlic crop. And it will grow well in poor soil and so requires no fertilizers. You can assume that garlic is organic no matter where you buy it. While not many people will chew a whole clove of garlic, it is a fine flavor additive to a wide variety of foods and has definite health benefits if used in this way.

GARLIC OIL

For those who want the benefits of garlic but do not want the strong odor on their breath, there are available tiny capsules of garlic oil. This oil contains all the health virtues of the garlic bulb, but the capsule can simply be swallowed, leaving neither taste nor odor in the mouth.

GINSENG CIGARETTES

Ever since it was first recognized that cigarettes can and do kill people, promoters have been bringing out various substitutes that contain no tobacco but will permit the person trying to break his smoking habit to puff on something that looks the same. One of the newest of such substitutes is ginseng cigarettes. It is doubtful they will do any more to help anyone give up cigarettes than have the predecessors. Containing ginseng, which the Chinese have believed for many centuries to be an aphrodisiac, these cigarettes may be smoked by people who hope to be sexually stimulated. It is unlikely. Ginseng does contain plant estrogens, which might be aphrodisiac to women in special circumstances, but they would be lost in burning and not enter the body anyway.

About these and all substitute cigarettes—it should be noted that smoke, any kind of smoke, entering the lungs is injurious. It does not have to be tobacco smoke in order to do you harm. No conscientious health adviser would ever recommend any type of cigarette.

GLANDULAR TISSUE, DRIED

Ever since those far-off times when a warrior would eat the heart of a brave opponent to increase his own courage, there has been a belief that a person can strengthen the functioning of any particular organ by eating that organ from another source. Insofar as the glands are concerned, there might be some value in the practice inasmuch as the hormones one's own glands should be producing and feeding into the bloodstream may also be contained in the glands that are being eaten. We know that this is true of both the thyroid and adrenal glands, both of which are used to stimulate glandular activity but which are so powerful in their effects that neither may be sold without a prescription.

There are physicians who are unorthodox in their belief that particular glands should be stimulated for holistic improvement of a patient's health and that whole glandular material is exactly what will do the job. Thus, there are now available carefully made preparations that in effect are whole glands, dried to prevent spoilage and extend their life, but always at very low temperatures that do not in any way damage the hormonal content or the enzymes that are contained within the gland. Tableted and neatly put up in pharmaceutical-looking packages, one can find desiccated whole thymus, spleen, pituitary, and others. Desiccated liver, of course, is well known and widely used and will probably be found in a different section of the store.

Perhaps it should be repeated that those glands known to have a definite effect, which include ovaries and testicles, as well as thyroid and adrenal, may not be sold except on prescription and will not be found on the shelves of the health food store. Those that are there are permitted because they are not recognized to have any specific effect. If your doctor has recommended that you get and take them, by all means do so. Otherwise, please be aware that these desiccated glands may have definite if unknown effects that may not be at all desirable. It is recommended that you use them only on the advice of a physician.

GLUTAMINE

This is a nonessential amino acid. That means that in ordinary circumstances our bodies produce as much as we require of it, and we should not have to eat any more in order to have a sufficiency. We do get more from various dietary sources, however, including soybeans, in which this amino acid is abundant. Every time you eat soy sauce, you obtain a lot of glutamine as monosodium glutamate (MSG) which is also used as a flavor enhancer and has become common in the American diet. It has now been pretty well established that glutamine is a brain food and, particularly in the case of retarded children, that it has a favorable influence on intelligence. It is available in tablets for people who believe they can improve their mental abilities by taking it, even though such effects on people of normal intelligence are very doubtful. It is also incorporated in what are coming to be known as "smart pills," which combine glutamine with other nutritional factors.

By and large, glutamine may not be all that effective but it is probably harmless in most cases. It should be remembered, though, that some people have an allergic reaction to monosodium glutamate known as Chinese restaurant syndrome. They get headaches and become flushed and suffer general distress that does not wear off for two or three hours. No one knows for sure, but it could well be the glutamine in MSG that has this effect. If you take it at all, and there is probably no reason why you should, be careful how much you use.

GOAT'S MILK

In regions that are too rocky or too cold for much pasture grass to be found, it is hard to keep cows but goats get along fine. In such regions the children are given goat's milk and they thrive on it. In our country not much of it is used and that only as an alternative to cow's milk for children who, for one reason or another, are unable to digest cow's milk properly. That is usually because the protein molecule of cow's milk is unusually large and sometimes makes trouble for immature digestive equipment. Goat's milk is so little in demand, however, that you will find it only in health food stores and not in all of them.

Nutritionally, goat's milk is somewhat closer to human milk than is a cow's. It contains less protein in smaller molecules, as is also true of milk from the female breast. Its fat content is higher than cow's milk and it contains more sugar, giving it a very sweet taste that children may love but that adults tend to dislike. Its greatest peculiarity is that, no matter what the mother goat is fed, the milk will contain virtually no iron. Thus, nursing children, fed nothing but goat's milk, have frequently become anemic. It is a problem that is easily remedied if you are aware that it exists. A little infant food containing liver will do the trick, or if nothing but liquids can be taken by the child, a little beef tea or heme iron mixed into the milk will give it plenty of iron for the infant's needs.

For more convenient storage without fear of spoiling, goat's milk is also available evaporated and canned to be reconstituted by adding water.

GRANOLA

There are dozens of types of granolas and no purpose would be served by listing them separately. Except for flavor, they all tend to divide themselves into two chief types. They are either sweetened or they are not. Your neighborhood market will carry only sweetened granolas whereas the health food store will also sell them with no sweeteners added.

Without sweetening, granolas are highly nutritious dry breakfast cereals. They usually contain dried apples and other dried fruits, nuts and seeds, and a variety of grains, almost always including oats. Wheat germ is a frequent ingredient. Since all the foods that can be enjoyed raw will be included in their raw state, the granola is an only lightly processed melange of natural whole foods with a high vitamin and mineral content and good protein quality, which is especially important in a breakfast food. The only problem is that some of the ingredients may go rancid quickly. To avoid this, eschew the giant bargain size package and buy your unsweetened granola in the smallest package obtainable. Once you have opened it, keep it stored in the refrigerator and use it quickly.

The sweetened granolas contain natural sweeteners such as brown sugar, molasses, and honey. The fact that they are natural does not improve their nutritional quality. The granolas are so sweet that if you eat a normal portion for breakfast, you can be sure you are eating too much sugar, which, far from being a health builder, is generally destructive to health. Immediately, it will cause a steeplechase effect in the levels of your blood sugar and in the long run, it can induce diabetes or hypoglycemia. Sugar is bad for your teeth and bad for your blood vessels and bad for your health overall, and that is true whether it is refined table sugar or the crudest of molasses.

HALVAH

This is candy. It is loaded with sugar and if, like most customers of health food stores, you are seeking a more nutritious and health-giving diet, you should not eat halvah, at least not very much of it. It is a borderline product, which the store can justify selling because, aside from sugar, it contains wholesome and desirable, if very rich, ingredients. Essentially halvah is a mixture of sesame seeds with some type of nut, formerly almonds, now usually peanuts. To this is added sugar and vanilla and/or chocolate flavoring. It is a delicious confection, but don't kid yourself that it's good for you just because you can buy it in a health food store. The calorie count is astronomical.

HONEY

Honey is certainly a completely natural food. Does that mean it is good for you? Certainly not. Gathered from flowers as nectar and processed by bees into the thick and viscous liquid that we know, honey is even sweeter and higher in calories than table sugar, spoonful for spoonful. That is possible because the sugar in honey is fructose. To a limited extent, it does not require insulin to be metabolized and therefore may be of interest to a diabetic. But some people feel that fructose causes atherosclerosis and it certainly causes tooth decay even faster than table sugar.

People who avoid sugar for the sake of their health are only kidding themselves if they think that honey is any better for them. Honey does contain some minerals but since it is cloyingly sweet and you cannot eat much of it, the mineral content is of no nutritional importance. Contrary to the belief of many, the minerals do not in any way improve your ability to metabolize the sugar content. Much has also been made of the antiseptic properties of honey, but this is simply a property of its sugar content. All sugar kills germs, which is why sugar is a good preservative.

If you like its flavor, you can certainly eat some honey without its doing you any appreciable harm, and you can enjoy it. But it offers you no health advantage whatsoever.

HONEY, RAW

There are some health food enthusiasts who recognize that ordinary honey is simply a high-calorie food that is loaded with sugar, of no particular value to health, but who believe that raw honey is a different matter with special health-giving properties. They are mistaken. Raw honey is only very little different. It is not strained, so it usually contains a little pollen and perhaps a grain or two of propolis. Neither is it pasteurized, so any enzymes in the honey are not destroyed by heating. However, it has never been shown that the enzymes in honey accomplish anything in particular except accelerate the deterioration of the honey itself. And it contains too little pollen or any other foreign matter for any nutritional significance whatsoever. Raw honey is simply honey that has not been strained or pasteurized. It is still just honey, and while it may taste terrific, this is fundamentally just concentrated sugar.

KEFIR

In those few states where it is permissible to sell raw milk, one of the products of the raw milk dairies to be found in the refrigerated section of the health food store is kefir. There is nothing sensational about this product and no claims are made for it. It is simply raw milk, to which a sweet fruit flavoring is added in exactly the same way as it is to the more familiar fruit-flavored yogurts. It makes a very pleasant drink equivalent in value to raw milk but with nutritionally undesirable sugar added.

KELP

Since mammalian life originated in the sea and developed on the nutrition available in the sea, it is not too surprising that the minerals in seawater are precisely those minerals that are essential to man. Thus, in one sense, kelp, which is simply an edible variety of seaweed, ought to be a good prepackaged mineral supplement. There are a couple of problems, though. The biggest is sodium chloride, which we know better as salt. Over the eons the seas have become much saltier than they were when amphibious life crawled onto dry land. As a consequence, there is far more sodium in the seaweed known as kelp than is good for us. No one with high blood pressure can afford to use kelp at all, and because of its high sodium content, no one should use very much of it.

The iodine content of seawater, like the sodium, has kept increasing as the actual amount of water on earth slowly diminished. That, today, makes kelp a good source of iodine for those who are actually deficient in this mineral, but perhaps too much of a good thing for people who have no thyroid problems.

Kelp is the whole seaweed, dried and then pulverized for ease of use. It is usually packed in bottles that resemble salt shakers and from which the pulverized kelp can be shaken. It can be put on top of a salad or a meat though it actually has little flavor. It will give you a wide distribution of essential minerals, but be careful not to use so much that you take in too much sodium and iodine.

LACTASE

There are millions of adults and not a few children who are better off not drinking cow's milk because their bodies fail to produce the enzyme lactase, which splits milk sugar (lactose) and makes it digestible. Failing to digest milk sugar, those who still drink milk suffer diarrhea and sometimes severe intestinal pains along with it. The avoidance of milk does not present any particular problem to an adult, but there are a good number of children who ought to have milk but cannot handle it digestively. The enzyme lactase is the answer. It is obtainable as a powder packed in a small envelope containing exactly enough to split the sugar of a quart of milk. All you do is add a packet of lactase to a bottle of milk and put it in the refrigerator for twelve hours. After twelve hours the milk sugar is split and you can drink the milk and digest it with no problem at all. It makes the milk taste a little sweeter and you may not like it. But kids like sweet things and the children will have no objection.

LACTOBACILLUS ACIDOPHILUS

See ACIDOPHILUS in this section.

LACTOBACILLUS BIFIDA

There are various strains of the bacteria known as lactobacilli that turn milk sour, each imparting its own special flavor and texture to the resulting yogurt, buttermilk, or sour cream. These lactobacilli have the special quality, if alive, of colonizing in the gut where they war against such inimical bacteria as coliform and salmonella. The net effect is to create bulkier stools that are more easily eliminated and to reduce intestinal upsets and gases.

Most lactobacilli do not reproduce indefinitely in the gut. They live there for about three days and then vanish unless they are replenished. *Lactobacillus bifida* is the one exception. This strain is the same that is found in mother's milk and once it is established in the gut, it will continue to thrive and reproduce indefinitely. If used, therefore, for the purpose of correcting intestinal disorders and protecting against bad food or water, bifida might well be the lactobacillus of choice. Unfortunately, it is produced and packaged only in West Germany and is not available everywhere. Many of the health food stores do carry it, however, and if you really want it, you can probably find it.

LACTOBACILLUS BULGARICUS

This strain of lactobacilli is the original strain with which yogurt was first developed in Bulgaria. It has just about the same properties as acidophilus but gives milk a flavor that connoisseurs consider superior to that of any other strain. It makes a thicker and creamier yogurt or buttermilk.

LECITHIN

Lecithin was originally discovered as a constituent of egg yolk, although today practically all the lecithin that is used is derived from the soybean. It is an emulsifier, which means that it has the special property of breaking up fat globules into very small fractions that will distribute themselves equally throughout a liquid instead of clumping. Since the tendency of the fat cholesterol to clump and attach in large globs to the walls of arteries is a major cause of heart disease, it is thought by many that a bloodstream content of the emulsifier lecithin is a valuable protection. It very likely is, though the appropriate studies that would prove or disprove this concept have never been made. Lecithin is available in granules that are packed either in packets or in jars. It can be added to any kind of food and is very widely used.

Another trouble area created by cholesterol is in the gall bladder, where cholesterol from the liver bile will sometimes accumulate and form gallstones. There are those who believe that lecithin in the diet may be a treatment for gallstones, but this is not very likely and indeed, we know of no gallstone cases that have been cured by lecithin.

LYSINE

This is one of the essential amino acids, obtainable only from the food that we eat and not synthesized in our own bodies. There has never been any particular reason to feel that people were deficient in their lysine intake and little attention has been paid to it. Recently, however, there has been some experimental work that is not conclusive, but that does indicate that the body well supplied with lysine is able to heal its infections of herpes simplex. Herpes is the scientific name for what we usually know as cold sores and it has recently gained a great deal of attention because it has been found that the same virus infection is becoming widespread as a venereal disease. If you suffer from such an infection, there is no assurance that lysine is going to cure it. The sad fact, though, is that medical science knows of no other cure and so you might as well try the lysine. It is available in tablets and at its worst is probably harmless.

MAPLE SYRUP

Like molasses, maple syrup is considered more natural than sugar because it goes through less refining and still contains some of the minerals that occur in the sap in the maple tree. People who like sweets but feel guilty about eating them use products like maple syrup, because they can pretend that they are better for their health. In actuality, there is little or no difference between maple syrup and sugar except for the flavor. Any nutrients other than sugar that are contained in the maple syrup are in such small quantities that they are of no significance whatsoever.

MARGARINE

The margarines you are able to buy in a health food store differ in no way from those you can get anywhere else, with the exception that those that are more obviously undesirable will not be carried. Margarine is made by a special process that involves taking liquid oils and bubbling hydrogen gas through them. To the extent that the oils are unsaturated, their molecules possess open bonds to which atoms of hydrogen attach. The oils thus become thicker and more solid, gaining the consistency of butter, which is the object.

Known and used for many, many years, margarine became popular with the first medical scares about dietary cholesterol. Butter contains cholesterol and the oils used for making margarine do not. This has led many people to believe they were improving their diet and protecting their hearts by using margarine rather than butter. Not true. Any saturated fat, and the hydrogenation process saturates the oils used, will have the same effect on the liver of stimulating it to produce more cholesterol, which is the actual problem of those with high-cholesterol levels in the blood. However, it is possible to hydrogenate oil only lightly, so that it will become thick enough to remain firm under refrigeration but will melt at room temperature. This process makes the resulting margarine somewhat less saturated than butter and, if you subscribe to the theory, somewhat less dangerous to your arteries and your heart. The margarines you will find in a health food store are all of the type that must be kept refrigerated and the store will not carry those that remain solid at room temperatures.

The ones you will find in your supermarket refrigerator, which are some of the commercial varieties available everywhere, tend to be made of the oils that have the best reputation for health, notably safflower, sunflower, sesame, and corn. Once they have been hydrogenated, of course, they are neither better nor worse than any other oils. These margarines, however, will also be of the kind that contain no preservatives and in some cases, no added coloring matter, so that instead of being the pale yellow of butter they will be white. Inasmuch as they could easily be colored with a perfectly harmless and nutritious coloring such as carotene, which would add vitamin A content, this entire approach is merely promotional. The freedom from chemical preservatives, of course, is another matter. This could be very desirable, but it does exact a price. The margarine that contains no preservatives and is not fully saturated is extremely vulnerable to rancidity. It must be kept refrigerated at all times and should be bought only in quantities small enough to be quickly used up. Do not underestimate the importance of this. It is the ease with which they become rancid that has caused the use of unsaturated oils to become associated statistically with a higher incidence of cancer.

MILK, ACIDOPHILUS

For those who wish a daily intake of the benign and health-promoting acidophilus bacteria, it is possible to get milk to which the culture has already been added. This has been recommended by the medical profession for children with special dietary disorders for at least fifty years. It is still an excellent remedy. See ACIDOPHILUS for a fuller discussion of why this may be desirable.

MILK, NONFAT DRY

Skim milk is not a very pleasant beverage, yet there are many people who wish to obtain the special nutritional advantages of milk with all of its fat eliminated. For such people, there exists nonfat dry milk, which can be bought in cans and can be added by the spoonful to other foods. It consists simply of skim milk that has been dehydrated, leaving a residue of the milk minerals and protein, this being scientifically regarded as one of the two proteins that have an amino acid distribution that is perfect for human consumption. The powder is also especially useful for hikers and campers, since it will not spoil even at outdoor summer temperatures and can easily be reconstituted into milk by the addition of water.

MILK, RAW

It is one of the tenets of health food devotees that all processing of foods is somehow injurious to its nutritional value, and that only raw food is truly good food. This conviction holds particularly for milk. It has been shown several times in experimental studies that animals fed nothing but raw milk can survive in good health for entire normal lifetimes and produce normal offspring. Pasteurized milk, on the other hand, will not sustain life in the same way all by itself. The difference is not necessarily significant in a world where any nutrients missing from milk can be obtained readily from other sources. However, there can be little doubt that raw milk is a more complete food.

There are two major differences. Pasteurization, which is a quick-heating process, slightly cooks the protein content of the milk and makes it a little harder to absorb and digest; and the enzymes that the milk contains are destroyed by the heat. The bacteria in the milk, particularly the lactobacilli that would otherwise quickly sour the milk are also destroyed—the purpose of pasteurization.

Raw milk involves potential problems, however. Although pasteurization was developed and initiated to prevent souring, it was found also to destroy the bacteria that might also cause a number of diseases in people drinking the unpasteurized milk. Undulant fever, now just about eradicated, was once common among people who drank their milk straight from the cow. Tuberculosis, also, has frequently been traced to milk as its source. Therefore, the states that permit raw milk to be sold also require rigid inspection processes that assure the health of the cows from which the milk comes. Most states do not wish to go through the expense of inspection, or perhaps they are influenced by the commercial dairies that routinely pasteurize everything and do not want the competition of raw milk. In any case, you will probably be unable to find raw milk because your state does not permit it. If you live in one of the states that do permit it, the raw milk is a very good food. You will find that it sours much faster than pasteurized milk. However, you may enjoy the flavor of the souring.

MILLET

This is a grain that has no special nutritional virtues but is used by those who desire a wide variety of grains in their diet. Its chief value is to people who are unable to eat wheat, which includes children with celiac disease and adults with gluten malabsorption syndrome. Such people need substitute grain, of course, and millet is one of those that can fill the gap.

MOLASSES

Sugar begins as a liquid that is pressed from the cane or the sugar beet. It is then boiled for dehydration. If the process is stopped midway, before it is boiled down to a solid residue, the resulting syrup is molasses. Its chief virtue is that it possesses a mineral content that is completely stripped away in the processing that produces refined sugar, and also that it has a flavor, aside from being sweet. There is no doubt that molasses is more of a food than is table sugar, although when you get right down to it, it is still not very much of a food. In using it, keep in mind that basically it is still just sugar and will decay your teeth, upset the levels of glucose in your bloodstream, and put weight on you.

MOLASSES, BLACKSTRAP

This is the crudest and least refined form of molasses, and for that reason has long been advocated as a sugar substitute by some of the theoreticians of health foods. It has a strong flavor that some people consider unpleasant. Its chief claim to fame is that, being only slightly refined, it has a high mineral content, particularly of iron, which has caused it to be recommended as a preventive or even a treatment of anemia. Some sixty years ago it was even banned in many places because the medical profession believed that its high iron content would lead to iron storage disease, an excessive accumulation in the liver that is highly toxic. In fact, however, blackstrap molasses does not contain the necessary adjuncts that would promote the actual absorption of its iron content and so no more than 10 percent or so of its iron actually enters the bloodstream. It will not do you any harm if you like it, other than the harm that is done by all forms of sugar. It should be used sparingly if at all.

NUCLEIC ACID

A great advance in the science of genetics has discovered that in an extremely complicated way the instructors that govern the activity and development of the individual cells in our bodies and regulate when the cells will reproduce themselves and when they will stop reproducing are the acids that lie within the nucleus of each cell. From this have grown some important postulates stating that cell malfunction is caused by a blurring or distortion of the instructions that are contained in the nucleic acids. This blurring is believed to be due to metabolic accidents that introduce various toxic materials, including toxic forms of oxygen such as superoxide and hydrogen peroxide, into the cell, and also simply by age. It is also believed that aging itself and its stigmata, such as drying and wrinkling of the skin, and all the degenerative diseases of aging, could be slowed down or even to some extent reversed if a way could be found to revive the vitality of the nucleic acids and restore the sharpness of their instructional patterns.

Some scientists specializing in geriatric biochemistry have come to believe that a number of nutritional measures can have such an effect. One of them is the dietary consumption of nucleic acids from other foods, notably from yeast. Since one could not conceivably eat enough yeast to obtain a sufficient supply of nucleic acids for this purpose, the acids are extracted from the yeast and are offered in tablets or capsules. Since these nucleic acids undergo the digestive process, they do not enter the system as nucleic acids but rather as their components. It is believed that the body will reconstitute its own nucleic acids, given all the necessary components thus supplied. Results will probably vary from one individual to another. The one caution that must be observed is that if you decide to take nucleic acids daily, whether you take yeast RNA alone or in combination with DNA, you must be sure to drink a lot of fluids—two quarts a day or more. That is because some of the amino acid constituents put a burden on the kidneys that could lead to trouble if the kidneys do not receive adequate flushing. Otherwise this product seems to be perfectly safe.

NUT BUTTERS

Peanut butter, of course, is the major nut butter that is obtainable just about everywhere. Most of those you will find in your supermarket contain up to 20 percent of added hydrogenated vegetable oil of some sort, which the makers claim is added to improve the smoothness of the butter. This may well be so, but nutritionally it is disastrous. The nut butters you will find in a health food store will be pure nuts crushed into a butter and packed in a jar. Since salt definitely improves the flavor, they will be available with salt added for those who wish it, but will also be offered with no salt added whatsoever for the sake of those who must or at least wish to follow a low-salt diet. There is little difference nutritionally between the various nut butters. Considerations of flavor and price will dominate. You can obtain, in addition to peanut butter, cashew and almond butter. Since all it takes to make a nut butter is a simple grinder, many stores will make for you any kind of nut butter you wish.

All freshly made nut butters have a good content of nutritive minerals, with appreciable quantities of magnesium and zinc, both of which are desirable in the normal diet. They also contain poly-unsaturated nut oils, which also make a valuable addition to the diet. But, without any preservatives, they will easily become rancid. It therefore makes better sense to avoid the giant economy size and buy your nut butters in small jars which should be kept refrigerated, even before the jars are opened. Once you have opened one, use it up quickly.

Nut butters are not only high in nutrition but also in calories. Unless you are trying to gain weight, use them sparingly.

NUTS, RAW

Among the hard-core health food devotees, it is believed that roasting (which is actually a form of frying) reduces the nutritional value, and raw nuts are preferred, even though the flavor is far inferior to the roasted variety. This is fine so long as the nuts are obtained in the shell and are kept in the shell until they are eaten. Nutshells provide superb protection and the nuts will not go bad for many months. But shelled raw nuts, which are often used in trail mixes and also simply sold by weight, go rancid so easily and so quickly that they are probably best avoided. Nut butters are also sometimes made of raw nuts, and this same caution applies.

Rancidity is not merely a problem of bad flavor. Statistical evidence indicates that the eating of rancid oils is at least associated with a higher than normal incidence of cancer, and may well be a direct cause.

With the development of the dry roasting process, there is really little reason to eat raw shelled nuts. The enzymes destroyed in roasting are of negligible nutritional value and otherwise the dry roasted nuts contain the same nutrients and have a better flavor.

NUTS, UNSALTED

These are now available everywhere and the same nuts may very well cost less in your neighborhood market than they do in a health food store. Salted nuts do contain a great deal of salt in proportion to their weight, and all that salt is not good for anyone. Even though many people can handle that much salt without apparent harm, it is a sensible precaution to prefer the unsalted as long as you enjoy the flavor.

OILS, POLYUNSATURATED

Your health food store will offer you a wider variety of polyunsaturated oils than can be obtained anywhere else. They will tend to be cold-pressed, but not necessarily so. Look for the words "cold-pressed" on the label if that is what you are seeking. Since there is little or no difference among them nutritionally, the various types of oils are not given separate listings. Among the varieties that you will find in a health food store, some are unusual. The kinds include: avocado, corn, cottonseed, peanut, safflower, sunflower seed, sesame oil. You should choose the flavor you prefer.

See COLD-PRESSED OILS for additional information.

PET FOOD

The ordinary pet foods you can get at the market are loaded with preservatives and other chemical additives, which cause many people to consider them undesirable and not to be fed to a loved pet. This has lead to the development of special pet foods, kibbled or canned, that are produced primarily for the health food devotee. They tend to be far more elaborate than is necessary, following the old promotional technique of listing on the label a multitude of ingredients that sound attractive but are nutritionally meaningless to the pet for whom the food is intended. There are inclusions of wheat germ, sunflower seeds, whole wheat, and rice polishings, none of which mean anything in particular to your animal. Some of the vitamins are important to an animal's health and high-vitamin ingredients like yeast and fish-liver oil may well be a nutritional blessing to your pet.

The pet foods you will find in a health food store are certainly more expensive, but if your own pet is in less than excellent health, it could well be worth the difference in price to get the animal what is probably a superior food, even though there is a lot of promotional folderol involved in it. If your pet is doing fine on the 25 pound bags of kibbled food you can get at every market, there is no reason to change.

As several studies have shown, the most important element in the life and health of a pet is raw food. Better than on any prepared pet food, cats will thrive on raw kidneys of all kinds, chicken heads, fish heads and tails, and such. Dogs do better on the prepared foods if you will take the trouble to include some raw meat in their diet a couple of times a week. That seems enough to provide them with the enzymes and perhaps other nutritional elements in meat that are cooked out even in the all-meat dog foods.

PLANKTON

There are hundreds and perhaps thousands of varieties of single-celled plants and animals that live in water. Those varieties that cluster together in colonies and are eaten by fish as a normal food are known as plankton, regardless of the species. Living in the sea, plankton are a protein food that contains all the minerals that are found in seawater. Scientists who worry about the future when the world population, if it keeps growing unchecked, will have outstripped the ability of the earth to produce food, have seriously considered the possibility of breeding plankton in huge quantities to provide additional food for humans. It could be done. Aside from the problem of making the plankton palatable, which will not be easily solved, in nutritional terms these single-celled creatures would be pretty nourishing.

Recently, however, some fast-buck operators within the health food industry have begun packaging dried plankton and offering it as a miracle food to a public they hope will be gullible enough to swallow it. Most often it is being presented as a new element in a reducing diet that claims to speed up the metabolic consumption of fat and by its special properties double or triple the rate at which weight is lost. It won't work. There is nothing all that special or different about plankton. Since those with arthritis suffer intensely and are unable to obtain much relief from medical treatment, arthritics tend to be people who will try anything in the hope of getting rid of their pain. And sure enough, plankton is being offered as a treatment for arthritis. There is no reason to believe that anything about it will do the arthritic any good.

If you could eat plankton in such quantity that it would serve as an actual food, it would make a pretty good food but one that contains far too much sodium and iodine for human health.

All in all, plankton is a fairly nutritious material that possesses the one advantage of a high selenium content, in case you happen to need more selenium. It will do you no harm to take some plankton every day, but do not expect any health miracles from it because you will not receive them.

POLLEN

See BEE POLLEN for a discussion of this product. There is no difference between pollen and bee pollen. Bee pollen is removed from hives and it is theoretically possible for pollen to be harvested by other means that do not involve the bee. This is actually done in Sweden from enormous fields of ragweed, but in the United States all domestic pollen is obtained from beekeepers, who get it from their hives. Any pollen you might buy comes from mixed sources and might contain one or more varieties to which you are allergic. Pollen has killed a few people and caused asthma and hay fever attacks in a great many more. Be very cautious about its use.

POPCORN

Dry popcorn that has not been salted and has had no butter or oil added to it is a food just about as good as a dry cereal that contains no salt or sugar. It is simply kernels of corn that explode to a far greater mass when heated. It is quite filling and a good thing to nibble if you are on a reducing diet, since it provides relatively few calories for the amount of bulk that you put into your stomach. It contains vitamin E and provitamin A and some unimportant mineral content.

A more popular popcorn item is sweetened or candied popcorn, which in a health food store will be sweetened with honey rather than sugar syrup. This is supposed to make the product more nutritious. Actually, it is even less so because honey is sweeter and it contains more sugar per ounce than sugar syrup, and it is more, rather than less, fattening. True, the sugar of honey is fructose, which can be metabolized without insulin and therefore can be eaten to a limited extent by diabetics. In every other way it is just as bad for you, however, and should not be indulged in except very sparingly.

PRETZELS

Pretzels are normally made of fully processed white flour and are heavily salted for flavor. That makes them a forbidden food to the health food devotee. However, many people like pretzels and it was only to be expected that a health food version would be developed and sold. It is not salted, of course, and is made from whole-wheat flour. You might enjoy it at that, and it is probably better for you. Regular pretzels containing no salt are also available in many of the stores.

PRODUCE

Just about any fruit or vegetable that you can obtain in your normal market is also available in the produce bin of your health food store. The plant foods that are considered, factually or mythically, to be of special nutritional value are listed individually in this section. In all cases, the true advantage offered by the fruits and vegetables you can get in a health food store is that they are supposed to be free of pesticides. In the case of those that have thick or tough coverings that are not eaten, this makes no difference at all. Examples are all melons, avocados, and oranges. No pesticide spray is going to penetrate the shells or skins of these foods, and so you are not going to swallow any pesticides in eating them, even if they come from the big commercial growers.

With a wide variety of produce, however, there will be residues on the food if it has been sprayed. There are very good reasons why we all should keep these poisons out of our stomachs if it is possible to do so. Thus, if you trust the store where you shop to make a determined and conscientious effort to secure produce that is truly organic, it is probably worth your while to pay a premium for your lettuce and tomatoes and apples and strawberries and such. The best indication of a trustworthy operation is that the store will at times have very little produce to sell. If the bins are always full and there is always a wide variety of goods offered for sale, you can be pretty sure that the store is getting its produce from the same wholesale markets as any other store and that it has been raised by the same growing methods, which include the liberal use of pesticide sprays.

PROTEIN POWDER

Although there is a great deal of evidence showing an association between a high-protein diet and certain forms of cancer in the lower intestinal tract, kidney problems, and high blood pressure, there are still a great many people who believe that a high-protein diet is all to the good and who look for ways to increase their protein intake. For such people there are bottles of protein powder, which is frequently nothing more than casein, the protein portion of kelp, dried to a solid powder. This product will do exactly what it claims to do—give you added protein with an amino acid distribution that makes it certain the body can use this protein to build or rebuild lean tissues, as well as for the many other purposes to which the body puts its protein intake.

It is widely believed, with no justification, that protein is not fattening and makes a good diet food. Actually, all foods that you eat, including proteins, are skillfully converted by your body into sugar, and if you eat more calories than you are able to use or eliminate, the foods will put weight on you. There is also a strong belief that weight lifters and body builders and people who engage in heavy physical activity require such protein supplements. In actuality, the normal American diet has far more protein than the body can put to constructive use as protein and there is no need for supplementation no matter what your activities are.

If for some unlikely reason you should have an actual need for greater protein intake than your diet provides, protein powder is an efficient way to obtain it.

PROTEIN POWDER, SOY

There is an erroneous but strong belief, particularly among vegetarians, that the soybean contains a complete protein that is the nutritional equal of any meat. This is no more true of the soybean than it is of any other plant. Soy does contain a high proportion of protein, but to be of protein value to the human body such protein must contain all the essential amino acids distributed in the proportions that the body can best use. All plant proteins are deficient in one or more of the essential amino acids. In the case of the soybean, it is methionine. Thus, if you use a soy protein powder, only a small proportion of it can actually be used by the body as protein, while the rest will be either wasted or converted into glucose.

This is bad news for vegetarians, who are among the minority that may actually need a protein supplement. For such people it is suggested that a bread containing both soy and wheat flour, each supplying the deficient amino acid of the other, will give them a good quantity of high-grade protein. Beans mixed with either corn or wheat will work the same nutritional trick. Do not, however, let yourself be taken in by all the propaganda about the superiority of soy protein. It does not exist except in the minds of its promoters.

PUMPKIN SEEDS

Millions of pumpkins are consumed every fall and each one has hundreds of seeds, yet it never occurred to anyone to do anything with those seeds until a German, of no known credentials, sent a letter to an American natural health magazine some twenty years ago. The letter stated, without offering any kind of proof, that the men of Bulgaria live to advanced ages and do not have any trouble with their prostate glands. This was attributed by the letter writer to a steady consumption of pumpkin seeds. The letter was seized upon, and with absolutely no additional evidence, the magazine began advocating that men eat pumpkin seeds for the benefit of their prostate glands. In the years that followed there has still been no evidence produced that pumpkin seeds are of any value to the prostate.

Today pumpkin seeds are a standard item in the health food store and keep selling in substantial quantities. Like all seeds, they have a fairly good mineral content and since zinc is one of the minerals, they are conceivably of some value to the prostate, like any other seed or nut. They have little flavor and are not very pleasant to eat because they are all shell with just a little seed inside.

REDUCING AIDS

It is as true of health food customers as it is of people all over, that they always want to lose weight and are always ready to try something new that promises better results than the previous try. The health food stores are rather limited in their ability to sell reducing aids because they are committed to a policy of avoiding drugs and chemicals generally. Thus they do not carry the drugstore products that may contain chemical stimulants or tranquilizers or drugs that depress the appetite. When some method comes along that relies upon a food product, however, they will seize upon it and give it a heavy sales push, being very reluctant to abandon its sale even if it has been shown to be ineffective or dangerous. The businessmen who run health food stores are, it seems, as human as everybody else. The reducing aids they are currently pushing are:

ALGAE (PLANKTON). These single-celled plants and animals that live in the sea are food for the fish and might someday become food for people as well. They are rich in iodine and if you happen to be deficient in iodine, which slows down thyroid activity, taking algae or any other iodine supplement such as kelp would speed up your metabolic activity and help you lose weight. In no other circumstance is there any reason to believe that the marine organisms are of the slightest use as a reducing aid. For a fuller discussion, see ALGAE in this section.

FRUCTOSE TABLETS. One of the recent reducing diet fads is based on the known physiological fact that when blood sugar goes low, a little sugar going into the bloodstream acts as a wick that starts the body fat burning and breaking down to produce more sugar as required. Fructose is advocated for this use because it can be metabolized without requiring insulin, which is frequently defective in overweight people. For the purpose, fructose tablets, which provide standard small amounts of the sugar, are being sold.

The technique still requires stringent restriction of food intake, of course. Like most diet fads, in practice it will work successfully for some people and not at all for others, and the effect tapers off quickly. It presents the same hazards to the health as any crash diet. If you have to lose ten pounds in two weeks, however, this might be worth a try.

KLVB6. This is a reducing aid that has already lasted for about ten years, which in itself is quite remarkable. The initials stand for kelp, lecithin, vinegar, and vitamin B_6. These four nutrients, each of which is purported to have a metabolic effect that stimulates the loss of weight, were originally advocated in rather substantial quantities. Then promoters began putting out tablets that contain each of the nutrients, true, but in such small quantities that it is hard to believe they can have anything but a psychological effect. Many women who use these tablets say that they do have a diuretic effect and the users find them very helpful in the week preceding their menstrual periods when their tissues have a tendency to accumulate fluid. So far as weight loss goes, however, it is likely that if you cut down your food intake you will lose the same amount of weight, whether or not you take these tablets.

LIQUID PROTEIN. The product itself is harmless, but the claims made for it are extremely dangerous and several people have died as a result of believing them. The product is collagen, a body material that functions something like a cement to hold tissues together and in place. Collagen is pure protein, and it has been reasoned that a crash diet in which the dieter ate nothing but pure protein ought to be successful because of low caloric intake with the body protected against any wasting of its lean tissues. Unfortunately, those who advocated dieting using liquefied collagen as the only food failed to recognize that collagen is not a complete protein. For protein to be complete, all ten essential amino acids must be present in proportions that the body can use efficiently to grow and reconstitute its own protein tissues. Collagen sadly lacks such a distribution of amino acids and as a result, even though it is all protein, it is useless to the human body as a protein food.

The consequence has been that people who thought they were feeding themselves with liquid collagen were actually starving themselves. Several have died, many more have become seriously ill, and the government has tried to ban the sale of this product. It has been unsuccessful because the product itself cannot be said to be at fault. It is the claims and misinterpretations associated with it that induce people to misuse it that have made the real trouble. However, if you are tempted to put yourself on a liquid protein crash diet, don't.

RICE, BROWN

The brown outer covering of a grain of rice contains enough of vitamins B_1 and B_2 to prevent beriberi when rice is the basic food in the diet. When that brown coating is polished away, the rice is practically devoid of any vitamin content. For this reason, and also because brown rice has more flavor, many people prefer it and realistically consider it a better food. The chief virtue of rice, however, is that it contains no sodium and it is therefore a valuable adjunct to the diets of people who must restrict their sodium intake. That is true of course whether the rice is brown or polished. On the whole, however, brown rice is the better choice.

RICE POLISH

When rice is polished, the brown coating that is removed is rich in vitamins B_1 and B_2 and is sometimes eaten by people as a fully natural vitamin source. Rice polish is not bran. It is fully digestible. It has no particular flavor and is not used very much, but it is a perfectly good product.

ROSE HIPS

This is the seed of the rose that forms after the flower withers and which, when freshly harvested, is very rich in vitamin C. Unfortunately, the varieties of rose hips that have the high vitamin C content are imported from Scandinavia. By the time they reach our shores, they have dried out and lost most of their vitamin C content. They are then ground into a powder, a process that destroys the rest of the vitamin C in them, and they are then sold as a natural source of vitamin C, which is wild misrepresentation. The rose hips powder is also claimed to be rich in bioflavonoids, which it is not particularly. In fact, it is one of the most worthless products you can buy, unless you happen to like its flavor when it is brewed as a tea. It is added to vitamin C tablets and to many multivitamin preparations simply because a lot of people have been misled into believing in it. In fact, though, the only kind of rose hips that have nutritional value are the fresh ones that are still whole and moist, and there is no place you can buy them.

ROYAL JELLY

This is a product of the beehive that over the years has found a small but enthusiastic group of steady users. In the hive, when it is desirable to have a new queen bee, a female is segregated and fed with this jelly, which is produced by the bees and does have a remarkably high vitamin and mineral content as well as special enzymes and perhaps other, unidentified nutrients. The result of this special nutrition is a queen bee that is far larger and stronger than any of the other bees and capable of laying thousands of eggs. Those who take royal jelly believe that this same special nutrition has a rejuvenating effect and a therapeutic influence on practically everything that can go wrong with the human body.

There is no convincing proof that royal jelly has any particular effect other than being, for its weight, a highly nutritious food. It is sold in capsules and is very expensive so people do not use very much of it. If you happen to feel flush, it might be interesting to try some royal jelly and see what kind of effect it has on you. But there is no reason to suppose that you cannot get along perfectly well without it.

RUTIN

This is the special bioflavonoid that is derived from buckwheat. It is considered one of the two most valuable of the many types of bioflavonoids. See BIOFLAVONOIDS in this section for full information.

SAFFLOWER OIL

Of the many types of plant oils that are available, safflower oil rates highest as a polyunsaturate. This means that, within the scope of your own physiological functioning, if polyunsaturates will succeed in reducing the levels of cholesterol in your blood, safflower oil will work a little better than any of the others. On the other hand, because its molecule contains more open bonds to which oxygen can attach, it is the most vulnerable to rancidity of any of the edible oils. It also has a relatively unpleasant flavor compared to many of the others. If you use safflower oil, use it in small quantities, keep the lid of the bottle tightly closed, and keep it refrigerated at all times.

SALAD DRESSINGS

There is a wide variety of salad dressings, both liquid and dehydrated, to be found in the health food store as in any other store. Some of them are identical, but you can also find in the health food store dressings that will contain special ingredients not easily matched anywhere else. These include apple cider vinegar, higher grade vegetable oils, like avocado or sesame, and a preponderance of herbal seasonings. Many of them contain no salt and are a valuable addition to the salt-free diet.

SALT SUBSTITUTES

Sad to say, in all the world the only thing that tastes like salt is salt. Food chemists have labored over the decades to produce some other chemical combination that would have the same flavor and the same ability to enhance the flavor of food. There are many such products available everywhere, and none of them is really satisfactory. They tend to contain potassium chloride, which serves to replace some of the potassium that is lost if you are on diuretic therapy. Its flavor is bitter rather than salty and if you use a lot of it, it may irritate your stomach and might even start an ulcer.

More successful salt substitutes are preparations that make no effort to taste like salt but in their own way improve the flavor of the food you eat. In effect they are dehydrated herbal seasonings with their own strong and pleasant flavor. There are a number of them and each one tastes different. The only way to find the one that is most to your taste is to try them.

SEA SALT

If you take seawater and evaporate it completely, the solid residue that is left is sea salt. It will contain some of the minerals that are also in the seawater, though others, like magnesium, are lost in the evaporation process. Although the trace minerals have nutritive value, the salt is still salt and is just as bad for you as table salt. In actuality, there is enough salt naturally present in the foods we eat so that no nutritional purpose is served by adding more. It contributes only flavor at the risk of raising the blood pressure and retaining too much water in your tissues. It should also be noted that all salt is sea salt, for the salt that comes from mines or cliff-sides was deposited by the sea thousands or millions of years ago. There are many sources of mineral nutrition other than sea salt and it seems just plain foolish to pay a premium for this product.

SESAME SEEDS

These small seeds are best known as an adjunct to breads and rolls, usually sprinkled on top. They are a pleasant flavor enhancer and may also be added to salads and cooked vegetables. The individual seeds are too small to be eaten as a snack, but their uses are many and pleasant. They contain polyunsaturated oil, protected from rancidity by the shell of the seed itself, and some trivial vitamin and mineral content. For several thousand years folklore has held that a mixture of sesame seeds and honey has an aphrodisiac effect.

SLIPPERY ELM

This is an ancient Indian remedy for sore throat and it is still one of the best. Available in tablets that are sucked, it produces a thick and somewhat slippery liquid that coats the throat and, while it cures nothing, is temporarily very soothing. It is more effective than far more expensive preparations. It is the inner bark of a variety of elm tree.

SOUPS, CANNED OR DEHYDRATED

You will find no salt in the soups that you can buy in a health food store, which is their only difference from any other commercially prepared soups. In fact, when any of the major soup companies decides to put out a line of salt-free soups, it promptly appears on the health food store shelves. No one has yet mastered the problem of producing an enjoyable soup that contains no salt.

SOYBEANS

The soybean is an excellent, highly nutritious legume. It contains a high quality polyunsaturated oil, lecithin, good mineral values, and a higher proportion of protein than other beans. This having been said, it should hastily be added that the soybean is not as great a food as many people believe it to be. While it contains most of the essential amino acids, it is deficient in methionine and because of that deficiency, soybeans eaten by themselves will not be used as protein by the human body except to a very limited extent. If eaten in large quantity, as for example if one should make an entire meal of soybeans, the effect would be catabolic—

the protein tissues of the body would be broken down to some extent to furnish the lacking methionine.

It should also be noted that raw soybeans contain a chemical that inhibits the body's production of the enzyme trypsin. This is a very important digestive enzyme released by the pancreas into the duodenum. Thus the raw soybeans you toss into your mixed salad in the belief that you are thus building your health may in fact be building nothing but indigestion.

The proper way to use soybeans is to cook them and then eat them as a vegetable dish or add them to stews and such. If you eat some bread with the same meal, the mixture of bread and soy will combine into a truly high-grade protein that will give your body the protein values you expect.

There are several varieties of soybeans and their flavors vary widely. Try them all to find the one you like best.

SOY CHIPS

These have been developed in the quest for alternatives to potato and corn chips that will taste good without salt. Soy flour is used and, because the soybean naturally possesses a faint bitterness, the chips do have a distinctive flavor even though no salt is used in their preparation. What is wrong with them is what is wrong with all chips. They are fried, and frying as a cooking process is in itself suspect, being believed by many to produce cancer-causing substances. And, having a high content of the frying oil, chips are all high-calorie foods that will be fattening as a snack.

SOY FLOUR

Because the nutritive value of the soybeans has been so greatly exaggerated, some people try to use it as a substitute for wheat flour. The effort is never very successful because, simply, soybeans are not a grain and they contain no gluten. If you tried to bake a soy bread it would come out as flat as a pancake. And even as a breading it lacks the proper stickiness and tends to just crumble off the meat or vegetable for which it is being used. The best way to use soy flour is to mix it with your wheat flour in proportions of approximately one part soy to five parts wheat. This is the best ratio to combine the proteins of the two into a single high-grade protein, and the proportion of wheat is high enough so that you do not lose any of the excellent cooking qualities that wheat alone possesses. Soy flour is made from soybeans after the oil has been pressed out. The remaining bean is dried and milled into a flour.

SOY MILK, EVAPORATED

There are many infants who are unable to digest cow's milk, usually because the protein of cow's milk occurs in giant molecules that cannot be handled by some undeveloped digestive systems. For such infants, particularly when they are at the nursing age, substitute milks must be found. And for this purpose, soy milk is a good substitute that is satisfactorily nourishing to an infant. The weakness of its protein values is of no significance in this application because the human infant really does not require much protein. Mother's milk, for example, which is the best of all possible foods for an infant, contains less than half as much protein as cow's milk.

Soy milk is the liquid pressed out of the soybeans, including the oil content. It is dehydrated by evaporation and sold in cans and can be reconstituted to any desired extent by the addition of water. Because it plentifully contains the emulsifier lecithin, there is no problem in mixing the oil content with water. It is a good, nutritious product.

SOY PROTEIN

This product is largely a fake, though it must be said that many of the people who manufacture it believe in it implicitly. It is produced because of the widespread myth, subscribed to especially by the vegetarians, that the soybean is the one plant that contains complete protein equal in quality to meat. It does not. Methionine is what is known as the limiting amino acid, present in such short supply that only a small proportion of the protein in the soybean is usable in our bodies as a complete protein. The rest is either converted into glucose and ends up as mere calories, or it can even have a protein-wasting effect on the body. The legend of soybeans as a high-protein food is so persistent and powerful, though, that it is quite profitable to manufacture protein supplements made exclusively of soybeans. In fact, there are many misguided people who will avoid good protein supplements made from casein and egg whites in favor of soy proteins.

This product is sold in enormous quantities to weight lifters and body builders who believe they need protein supplements in order to build larger muscles. It is used by vegetarians who want to fortify their diets and by many other people as well. All of them are not getting what they think they are getting. It is of little or no value as a protein supplement. However, since in fact even body builders get more good protein than they need in their normal diets, and an excess can in some circumstances be a serious health problem, the soy protein does not do any particular harm and in a perverse way, may even be better for those who use it because it does not give them the protein they are trying to get. They could get the same effect much more cheaply by not using any protein supplements.

SUGAR, BROWN

There is widespread understanding that sugar is an empty food contributing nothing to our well-being but offering too many calories and sometimes causing severe health problems. Dental decay and maturity-onset diabetes are the two best known, but sugar can also damage the liver and lead to the formation of triglycerides, a particularly difficult form of fat in the bloodstream. It is bad for the liver, the pancreas, and the heart and could even affect our mental abilities. Yet the fact remains that sugar is very enjoyable and the goodies that can be made with it are delicious. Not willing to lose the pleasure they get from sugar, people persuade themselves far too easily that some substitute type is better for them. The substitute to which they turn is brown sugar.

Brown sugar is sugar. Because there is a market for it, the sugar producers take some of their ordinary refined granulated sugar and add a little molasses to it to give it a brown color. Nutritionally it is just about indistinguishable from table sugar and it is just as bad for you.

SUGAR, RAW

Raw sugar is not raw. It goes through the same refining process as regular sugar, but it is stopped before all the molasses has been removed. It is sometimes said to contain B vitamins and minerals that facilitate the metabolic handling of sugar, but you would have a hard job finding them. It is simply another type of sugar that is a pale tan in color.

SUGAR, TURBINADO

This is a type of sugar that is produced without boiling off the moisture content, which is removed instead by centrifugal force in machinery especially constructed for the purpose. That, according to the legend, does not destroy the enzymes in the sugar syrup and therefore leaves a less refined and more wholesome product.

It is still sugar, and still bad for you.

SUNFLOWER OIL

See COLD-PRESSED OILS in this section.

SUNFLOWER SEEDS

This is one of the oldest snack foods known to man, and one of the best. Sunflowers, which will grow wild in the poorest of soil, are an easy crop to raise. They need no fertilizers or pesticides. The plant is a single enormous flower that develops hundreds of seeds at its heart. The seeds are eaten raw by birds and humans alike. And even though they are an oily, high-calorie food, if you eat them in the shell they probably will not put any weight on you, because it takes time to remove each shell with your teeth and extract a little seed.

Sunflower seeds taste very good. They contain a polyunsaturated oil and, if they are present in the soil where the flower grows, abundant quantities of zinc and magnesium. They are also believed to have unknown but valuable properties, which possibly reside in their enzyme content. A physician in Los Angeles says that he has used them successfully to help patients stop smoking. Others have believed that sunflower seeds improved their weak eyesight. Whether or not such reports can be believed, sunflower seeds are relished as cattle feed and by all birds that eat seeds and that is usually a good indication of a food's quality.

Sunflower seeds also come with the hulls removed, particularly as a standard item in trail mixes. Once the hull has been removed they are very vulnerable to rancidity. Since the hulls are soft and the seed is easily extracted, it surely makes better sense to buy the seeds in their natural state. They also come roasted and salted and are absolutely delicious that way, but of course, then you face the hazards of too much salt and the added cooked oil.

SUPEROXIDE DISMUTASE

Under the influence of radiation of many types, such as X rays, microwaves, and even cosmic rays, some oxygen is transformed into an aberrant form that is known as superoxide. Superoxide is considered particularly potent as a cause of various body ills, which include aging, some forms of cancer, and one type of cataract. The body protects itself by producing an enzyme called superoxide dismutase that transforms superoxide. But some scientists believe that as the radiation in our environment increases, the body is no longer able to produce enough superoxide dismutase to protect itself, and that it does well to take in more of the enzyme as a dietary supplement. Hence, this enzyme is now being produced and sold.

One problem in its use is that in the first step of its transformation, superoxide becomes hydrogen peroxide, which is every bit as dangerous and inimical to health as superoxide. If the body is well supplied with another enzyme known as catalase, further transformations take place and the superoxide is eventually converted into water. But in order to make sure of that, it is best to eat some dietary catalase at the same time as one takes the superoxide dismutase. If one looks carefully, it is possible to find superoxide dismutase tablets already containing added catalase. Most brands, however, do not.

You can also add catalase to your diet by eating any raw fruits or vegetables. The enzyme is abundant in all of them.

TOFU

Increasingly popular, tofu is the curd of soy milk, which is the coagulated portion of the milk that forms when it is separated by souring. It is kept in the refrigerator and is sold in blocks. Although it has little flavor, tofu is used for a variety of purposes. It is cut into small cubes that are added to soups like noodles. It can be cut into various shapes that are then used with dips just as a stalk of celery or a corn chip might be. Tofu can be seasoned with practically anything and can be baked or fried to provide a meat substitute. In fact, just because it is so bland itself that it takes on the character of the seasonings used with it, tofu is a highly versatile food.

Nutritionally, tofu has about the same qualities as soybeans. It is claimed to be a high-protein food, but actually it is not. See SOYBEANS in this section. It remains a good, nutritious food, however, with a variety of uses and it could occupy a valued place in your larder.

TRITICALE FLOUR

This is a hybrid grain, a cross between wheat and rye, that still contains gluten and produces a tasty bread. Nutritionally it has no special properties except that it has a higher protein content than either wheat or rye. However, it is an incomplete protein and of no special dietary significance. Since triticale is a very hardy grain, it requires little in the way of pesticides and in some years requires none at all, which is certainly desirable. It contains enough gluten to bake a light-textured bread and its chief advantage is its flavor.

TRYPTOPHAN

This is one of the essential amino acids that bears a special relationship to the chemistry of the brain. It contributes to the body's productions of serotonin, a brain chemical that has a calming effect on the nervous system and is believed to participate importantly in inducing sleep. For this reason tryptophan is believed by some to be a natural tranquilizer, and is the major ingredient in various combination products that are purported to help people fall asleep. Many people who have tried such products have found them ineffective. Others use them regularly and swear by them. It would be hard to say whether this is merely a placebo effect or whether they do in fact help at least some people to fall asleep more easily.

VEGETABLE JUICES

If you want a bottle of carrot juice you can get it at your health food store. You can also get just about any other kind of vegetable juice that the human imagination can conceive. You can find tomato juice packed without any salt, which does not taste as good but is better for you. You can also get a variety of mixed vegetable juices and even find some from which celery juice has been excluded, celery having really large amounts of sodium.

As a general rule, the vegetable juices at a health food store tend to be more expensive, of very high quality, and free of any added salt. Nutritionally, all vegetable juices have a good vitamin and mineral content and make a worthwhile addition to any meal.

WEIGHT-GAIN PREPARATIONS

Yes, there are people who need to gain weight and find it difficult to do so. Moreover, they tend to get pretty sick of their doctor's recommendation that they drink lots of malted milks and eggnogs, which they are unable to stomach. Strangely, it seems that only the health food industry has come to grips with the fact that when people need to gain weight, it is more lean tissue they need on their bones and not more fat.

There are some such preparations in every health food store. They are generally high-protein foods such as egg white, which is pure high-grade protein, and casein, which is the high-grade protein of milk. Dried and powdered, they are combined with the B-complex vitamins and perhaps some form of iron to facilitate the weight-building process, and are flavored so that they can be added to whatever liquids you enjoy and make those liquids far more nutritious.

We have pointed out in several places that most people get too much protein in their diets rather than too little and protein supplements are not needed. The big exception is those whose lean tissues are obviously wasted, for whatever reason, and who do need rebuilding. The process of building the lean tissues to normal size and weight requires exercise above all things, but the weight-gain preparations are a second important requirement for those whose appetites are poor.

WHEAT GERM

This is a dietary product that has a bigger reputation than it deserves. It gained it, probably, because it was found to be rich in vitamin E at a time when the virtues of vitamin E were being vigorously explored and promoted. Wheat germ would be everything they say it is except for two important problems it presents. In the first place, it has a high content of phytate, an acid that attaches to calcium and locks it into a form in which calcium will not dissolve. Thus, the more wheat germ you eat, the more problems you are likely to have with your calcium nutrition. Since calcium is important to the regularity of the heartbeat, the strength and solidity of the teeth and bones, and the functioning of the nervous system, you may well want to think twice about eating anything that can interfere with the functioning of the calcium in your body. In addition, wheat germ is oily and once it has been removed from the protective grain of wheat, it easily and quickly becomes rancid.

The wheat germ, which is the tiny seed at the heart of the grain, does have a high nutritional content. Its oil, if not rancid, can be especially valuable and it contains really surprising amounts of vitamin E and most of the B-complex vitamins. It is high in phosphorus, which nobody needs, but also in magnesium and sometimes in zinc, if the soil in which it was grown contained that mineral. It is no wonder that so many people have come to believe that wheat germ is one of the most nutritious of all foods.

But its phytate content does reduce its nutritional appeal considerably, and the ease with which it becomes rancid leaves you unable to know, from one day to the next, whether it is going to do you good or harm.

WHEAT-GERM OIL

This particular oil is taken daily by many athletes on the advice of their coaches and trainers, in the belief that it increases their energy and endurance. It was thought for many years that the oil possessed special properties because of its high vitamin E content. And because of that, many more athletes as well as ordinary citizens have been using wheat-germ oil as an energy booster.

In fact, research at one interested laboratory has found that wheat-germ oil does have such special properties, but that they are contained in a fraction of the oil itself, which is a special lipid called octacosanol. In a famous case before the Federal Trade Commission, this was proven to the satisfaction of the commissioners.

The same cautions about wheat-germ oil apply as to any other oil that contains no preservatives. It will easily become rancid and harmful. Buy it in the smallest obtainable bottle and keep that bottle tightly capped at all times. Store it in the refrigerator.

WHEAT GRASS

Wheat is a type of grass, as are all the other true grains. It grows as a grass, which produces the wheat grains as its seeds. There is one semireligious movement, however, whose followers believe that there is special nutritional value in the grass itself, if it is clipped and eaten before the wheat forms. No credible evidence is presented for this. It is a matter of belief alone.

WHEY TABLETS AND POWDER

When cheese and other dairy products are made, it is the curds—the solid matter produced by souring—that are used. There is left a watery and almost colorless fluid known as whey. Normally the whey is discarded but there are some health food enthusiasts who believe that it has special nutritional value. To satisfy their desires for whey in easily used form, the stores carry it powdered or tableted and available for use. It is supposed to be a general builder of health with no claims for any special therapeutic values.

WHOLE-WHEAT CEREAL

Whole-wheat hot cereals are not popular with the general public and are sometimes unobtainable in a regular market. You can always get them in a health food store, however, where they are in consistent demand. They are of higher nutritional quality than the fractionated farina types, and they are usually of excellent flavor. They contain B vitamins and essential minerals and are a more valuable and nutritious addition to the diet than any dry cereal, including those that are made of whole wheat.

WHOLE-WHEAT FLOUR

You can get whole-wheat flour just about anywhere, even if you want it stone ground and free of preservatives. Recognition of its values has become universal. Add a little soy flour to it for the ultimate in nutritious breads.

YEAST, BREWER'S

Yeast is a true high-nutrition product. What is erroneously claimed for soybeans is true of yeast—it is a plant containing large quantities of high-quality complete protein. It contains all the vitamins of the B complex and a wide variety of minerals, at least one of which is better obtained from yeast than from any other source. That is chromium, which in yeast is bound to a special protein element known as the glucose tolerance factor (GTF). Chromium in very small quantities is needed by the pancreas for the production of insulin. In order to be properly used by the pancreas, however, the chromium is greatly assisted by its combination with GTF, and chromium from yeast has been found far more effective than any other in stimulating the pancreas to produce more insulin of better quality. It has been found that diabetics require less insulin when they have a small daily intake of GTF chromium from yeast. In some cases it has even been possible to eliminate insulin and control the disease by diet alone.

Selenium is a second mineral found in good supply in brewer's and other yeasts that is normally less than adequate in the average diet yet is of strong significance. Where the diet of women contains more selenium they have much less tendency to develop breast cancer. This trace mineral is an antioxidant that scavenges superoxide, protects against the formation of peroxides in the bloodstream, and exerts a strong protective effect in other ways as well. Selenium potentiates and strongly increases the biological activity of vitamin E.

Brewer's yeast does present a couple of problems. Its flavor is bitter, which is why it was the strain chosen for the brewing of beer. Also, in some people it tends to produce an unreasonable amount of gas, which is both embarrassing and uncomfortable. This yeast can sometimes be bought treated to eliminate the bitter flavor, but nobody has yet found a way to degas it. After a few weeks of use, however, the gas producing effect generally wears off. If you can tolerate it for that long, you have found yourself a truly valuable high-nutrition food supplement. It is available in tablets and as a powder.

YEAST, NUTRITIONAL

Strains of yeast that are not bitter like brewer's yeast but otherwise possess the same nutritional advantages are cultured as nutritional yeast. These are perhaps the best of all yeast products to buy, since in the culturing it is possible to fortify the content of unusual nutrients such as selenium and chromium by controlling what is fed to the yeasts. They do taste better and generally have the same or better nutritional values. The nutritional yeasts are widely used in combination products such as energy-promoting supplements and antioxidant combinations.

YEAST, TORULA

This is the one kind of yeast that is not recommended. It is the strain that was originally grown as a by-product of paper manufacture, since it is the only kind of yeast that could thrive in sulfite liquor. More recently, several oil companies have begun culturing this yeast on the wastes of oil refining and selling the resulting products to be processed into imitation meats for mass feeding. There is nothing necessarily objectionable about that, but there is a great deal of suspicion that attaches to any product derived from oil or coal. Time after time, such products have proven to be cancer causing, and while there is no evidence against torula yeast in this respect, one should at least be suspicious and very cautious about the use of this oil-grown yeast.

Torula yeast is also completely devoid of selenium, which is a great lack inasmuch as selenium is an extremely important trace mineral and one that tends to be deficient in the American diet. Since the other nutritional yeasts contain rich supplies of selenium and are grown in perfectly safe culture mediums, why bother with torula?

YOGURT

Yogurt is milk soured to a custard-like thickness. It is a low-fat product that introduces living lactobacilli into the digestive tract with beneficial effect. It is also a form of milk that most people find agreeable, and all in all, it is a pleasant and wholesome product. Most yogurts, however, have fruit preserves added to improve the flavor. The sugar in these preserves adds a negative element to what would be a better food without it.

In your health food store you can obtain yogurt that has not been flavored in any way and also yogurt that has been flavored with natural fruits and no sugar added. In the states where raw milk is permitted, you can also get it made of raw milk. Try some of the yogurt in the health food store. It is nutritionally superior.

There are also yogurt products that are not so good for you. Among them are yogurt chips, which are fried and therefore as high calorie and undesirable as any other type of chips. There are also the yogurt freezes, which resemble ice cream and are heavily loaded with sugar, but prey on the good name of yogurt for public sale.

Real yogurt without sugar is a terrific food. Forget the rest.

YOGURT STARTER

Many people like to make their own yogurt at home so they can know exactly what has gone into it and also eat it at just the stage of development they like best.

For such people there are tablets of yogurt starter, which is simply *Lactobacillus acidophilus* or some similar strain of milk-souring bacteria. When you make it yourself, you do not have to pasteurize the finished product and so will be getting the full supply of lactobacilli into your system. They protect you against several types of intestinal infection and also provide increased bulk and moisture for easier bowel movements.

The longevity that used to be characteristic of Bulgarians is attributed to yogurt, but it was strictly homemade yogurt. If you believe in the legend and want to do as the Bulgarians did, you will also have to make your own at home.

SECTION 4:

COSMETICS, EXERCISE EQUIPMENT, AND THERAPEUTIC PRODUCTS

COSMETICS

Just about any kind of cosmetic that you can buy in a drugstore or a department store cosmetic section is duplicated in the health food store. There are only a few exceptions. One of them is hair dyes, which tend to be very strong chemical preparations that can injure the hair and scalp unless applied by an experienced operator. You will find little in the way of hair coloring in the health food store. No bleaches. No black or brown dyes. You can obtain henna preparations to redden the hair, because henna is a natural and apparently nonirritating product.

As with hair dyes, so it tends to be with all cosmetic products. You can find lipsticks and mascara, shampoos, and a wide variety of creams and lotions, but they will tend to be confined to those that are considered hypoallergenic. They will not contain those particular ingredients, which, in many cosmetic preparations, can and do activate allergic reactions ranging from skin blotches, blisters, and pimples to sneezing and asthma attacks. This does not mean that the hypoallergenic cosmetics do not also stir up allergic reactions. There are precious few substances in all of the world to which an allergy-prone person cannot become allergic, especially if exposed to it day by day. But you have a far better chance of being able to use the hypoallergenic cosmetic in comfort and safety. Usually the manufacturer has eliminated the known allergens and that creates a considerable reduction in the hazards.

There is a price that must be paid for this relative freedom from allergic reactions. In fact, there are two prices. The hypoallergenic cosmetics are more expensive, in department stores and drugstores as well as in health food stores, and they are not as fully satisfactory as their regular counterparts. The lipstick may be less vivid because it does not use an allergenic color, or may be less creamy and with a greater tendency to cake. The shampoo may not be as strong a cleanser, and the moisturizing cream may not moisturize quite as effectively. The simple fact is that the cosmetic ingredients that sometimes provoke allergic reactions are included in the cosmetics not because their makers want to stir up trouble for you. They are included because they are the most effective ingredients the maker can find for the strictly cosmetic purposes of making you look and feel more attractive. But within the limits of omitting ingredients that sensitive people cannot tolerate, the maker of the hypoallergenics is also putting out as good a product as he can and you may well find it perfectly satisfactory.

You will also find in health food store cosmetics, as in all others, the same strange ingredients that are added essentially to appeal to the faddist in you. There are cosmetics containing animal placenta, royal jelly, collagen, and other strange materials and a variety of vitamins, all of which seem to increase the sales appeal of the preparations, if not their cosmetic effectiveness.

And lastly, if you are a natural-living purist, do not expect to find the cosmetics in the health food store to be free of chemicals. In most cases it is just not possible to make an effective cosmetic preparation without the use of chemical preservatives, emulsifiers, stabilizers, and such. If you really don't want chemicals even to touch your skin, then you had better concentrate on your natural beauty without using cosmetics at all.

The cosmetic section of your health food store will contain some or all of the following:

ALOE VERA GEL

Aloe vera is a tropical plant whose sap has a great reputation, mostly deserved, for soothing and moisturizing the skin and for promoting the healing of minor burns and skin blemishes. It is widely used in cosmetic lotions and creams, in which it is frequently the only active ingredient. If it is the action of the aloe vera that you want, you might as well save yourself some money and buy just aloe vera. The gel comes in small plastic bottles that you can use to try the product, and in much larger bottles that you will find handy if you decide to use some every day.

ALOE VERA OINTMENT

To soothe chapped skin and lips, cool and relieve minor burns, and moisturize skin that might have been dried by sun or wind, you will find this ointment quite effective. Aloe vera is the active ingredient and you can get the same effect at lower cost by using the gel.

ASTRINGENTS, FACIAL

These preparations are essentially alcohol, cut to an acceptable strength with water. Alcohol will dissolve most oils, which is the true purpose of an astringent. It is good to use in the morning after removing a night cream, to eliminate the last traces of the cream and induce the pores to close. Astringents sometimes sting slightly and pleasantly when applied to the skin and they certainly leave it cleaner. Unlike most astringent preparations, those you can get in the health food store will usually not be perfumed, although they may be. Most of them will leave a faint alcoholic aroma on your skin as though you had been drinking vodka.

ASTRINGENTS WITH ALOE VERA

This combination does not seem entirely rational. Astringents are used to close pores after a hot wash or sweating and to dry skin that is too oily. The aloe vera would at least partially neutralize this effect by moisturizing the skin. It is probably added only because the name has sales appeal. The main ingredient, as in all astringents, is alcohol.

BATH SALTS, MINERAL

You will not find ordinary bath salts or bubble bath in a health food store, probably because these preparations have been reported occasionally to cause vaginal infections in small girls. Instead you will find bottles of some of the minerals that are known to be essential in nutrition, prepared to facilitate their dissolving in your bath water. The theory is that some of the minerals penetrate the skin and benefit health, but there is no evidence that this ever actually happens. Mineral baths, however, have long been popular at spas and many people find them invigorating and bracing. If you do, you can certainly use mineral bath salts to have your own mineral bath at home.

BLUSHERS

Most of the red dyes that are approved by the FDA are regarded with suspicion by the health food enthusiast and will not be contained in products of the health food store. Instead, to give your face a pink tinge, blushers will contain hematics, which are fundamentally the red coloring material of the hemoglobin of the red blood cells. They may also contain silicates to absorb moisture for your skin for longer effective use of the cosmetic. Blushers come in a dry patty, a pressed cake of tinted power, that is applied to the skin.

BLUSH CREAM

If you prefer cream blushers, they can also be obtained in that form. The creams will contain sesame oil or some other light vegetable oil that has a good nutritional reputation. They contain preservatives to protect the oil against rancidity. There is no known advantage to using a nutritional oil for this purpose, but neither is there anything wrong with it, and it sounds good.

BODY LOTION

Lotions are all thick liquids intended to be rubbed into the skin to smooth and soften it and to soothe it when it needs soothing. They are particularly useful on the legs after shaving but may be used anywhere. The latest development in cosmetics everywhere, including the health food store, is to add elastin to such lotions. Elastin is supposed to soften the skin and make it more flexible, which would theoretically have an antiwrinkling effect. Such lotions also frequently contain vitamin E simply because its legend holds it to be a wonder vitamin with sexual connotations. It has no particular value in a body lotion.

BRUSHES

Natural bristle brushes are very likely the only kind that you will find in your health food store. They are the best hair brushes, as they have always been, and also the most expensive. For body brushes, you might well prefer nylon bristles, which are made with rounded tips and are often softer, so that they will have less tendency to scratch you. But you will probably have to go elsewhere to get anything but natural bristle. Many health food products, including vitamins, are packaged in plastic containers, yet there is still a bias against the use of plastics in the manufacture of brushes.

CALLUS REMOVER

Any callus remover is basically an acid that eats away the dead skin of the callus. This cannot be avoided, but in the product intended for sale in a health food store it is glossed over by the addition of aloe vera or some other natural cosmetic product, which is featured more prominently on the label. The aloe vera will do nothing for the callus but it may well persuade you that you are using a more natural product.

CLEANSER, DEEP PORE

This is merely a disguised form of astringent. It is a diluted solution of alcohol, which will certainly do the job of dissolving cosmetic oils in the pores so that a wipe will clear them away. Don't pay a fancy price for what should be a very inexpensive product, even though it is quite effective for its intended purpose.

CLEANSING CREAM

An ordinary cleansing cream will contain one or more chemicals employed to dissolve oil, just as the alcohol does in a liquid cleanser, so that when the cream is rubbed in and wiped away, any dirt or old cosmetics on the skin will come away with it. The cleansing cream sold in a health food store, however, will instead feature papaya as an ingredient. This tropical fruit contains a protein-dissolving enzyme, papain, which if left on the skin for five or ten minutes will actually dissolve the outer layer of dead skin, so that it can then be wiped away with whatever foreign matter has been clinging to it. It will clean effectively without using water, which is the true purpose of cleansing cream. The method is rather harsh, though it will leave the face with a nice glow to it.

CLEANSING LOTION WITH CUCUMBER AND WITCH HAZEL

Witch hazel is an alcoholic decoction of the herb. It has a pleasant fragrance that is not sweet and it is a good cleanser and astringent. In this particular lotion it is the witch hazel that is the active ingredient, replacing the common chemical solvents of skin oil. The addition of cucumber has no particular value but makes the lotion seem more natural. In female folklore the cucumber is considered a skin improver and it is often an ingredient in homemade natural cosmetics.

CLEANSING LOTION WITH MILK AND HONEY

Milk and honey, of course, has been a symbol of luxury since Moses told the Israelites that he would bring them to a land of milk and honey. That does not mean that the combination has any cleansing values, and indeed it is hard to see how it could have. The honey, especially, is a high-sugar food which, if left on your face, will probably attract more flies than men. Milk, on the other hand, has an ancient, though probably unwarranted, reputation as a skin improver and was, in fact, bathed in regularly by none other than Cleopatra. Such products can be fun to use if you don't take them too seriously. As a cleansing lotion, this would be no better than any other and perhaps not quite as good.

CLEANSING AND SOFTENING LOTION

In order to have a softening as well as a cleansing effect, this type of lotion is based on fluid oils, which are rubbed into the skin and then removed. As cleansers they are about as effective as cleansing creams. They will deposit more oily residue than the creams do, which has a temporarily softening effect but will also give the face a tendency to get dirty faster.

COLOGNE

The perfume industry has at its command an enormous variety of synthetic fragrances which, combined with essential oils from flowers, can provide endless sophisticated combinations of scents. Those that are marketed through the health food store, though, shun all synthetics and are therefore far more limited in variety. Their fragrances are either floral or herbal and they are not offered in combination. The pure fragrance of a single flower or herb can be delightful and will usually have a clean, fresh quality that you may well prefer. Whether you use these or a more sophisticated fragrance is entirely a matter of preference. Some people can be allergic to the synthetics, but is just as easy to be allergic to a floral or herbal essence.

CUTICLE CREAM

The purpose of a cuticle cream is to soften the cuticles of the fingernails so that they can easily be pushed back or trimmed. Soap and water will serve the purpose and is the usual method. It cannot be sold as a cosmetic product, however, and therefore an oil cream is offered. Jojoba oil, obtained from a desert plant, has received a great deal of publicity and is a new fad. Because of the current sale value of the name jojoba, it is the oil that is generally being used today in cuticle creams as well as many other products. Its only actual advantage is that it is cheaper than the food oils.

DEODORANTS

The deodorants that are featured in all those TV commercials employ various highly effective chemical combinations that will do what they are supposed to do, at the cost of surprisingly frequent skin irritations. Health food stores will not sell them. The only natural deodorizing material available is chlorophyll, the green fluid that acts like blood in plants. It is also possible to react badly to chlorophyll, but the instances of its occurrence are far less frequent. You will find a chlorophyll deodorizer effective.

EYE MAKEUP REMOVER CREAM

In any cosmetic that is used around the eyes, the most important consideration is to avoid using any material that could injure the eyes. This cream, which uses jojoba oil as its cleansing agent, may require a little too much rubbing for complete removal of the makeup, but on the whole it will work and cannot harm the eye. It will leave a bright oily residue but will not dry the skin of the eyelid as soap and water might do.

EYE SHADOW

All eye shadows employ a light oil with which the coloring matter will mix well, so that they can be applied easily and will cling to the skin without having to be rubbed in. The oil that does the job and also sounds attractive to health food enthusiasts is rice-bran oil, which is what you will find employed in the very limited selection of eye shadows in these stores.

EYEBROW PENCIL

The eyebrow pencils you will find in a health food store are the same as you will find anywhere else. They are sometimes labeled a little differently to reassure you that they are made with natural oils. We know of no unnatural oils.

FACE MASKS

Though efforts are sometimes made to disguise the fact, all face masks are basically clay. The clay is softened and liquefied in water and applied all over the face, except the eyes and nostrils. As it dries out, it shrinks and solidifies. When it is removed, it carries along with it dirt and oil that were on the surface of the skin and blackheads and other blemishes that have become fastened to the clay. There is a very pleasant feeling of relief when the mask is removed, and following it up with an astringent or a good wash will leave the face immaculately clean and with a reduced number of blemishes. It is also believed to make the skin more taut and smoother, but whether it will have this effect on you can only be verified by your own experience.

Those materials that are mixed into face masks in order to increase their sales appeal and presumably their effectiveness as complexion treatments are:

GINSENG AND GINGER. The two Oriental products are found together in masks. The ginseng is probably added for the sexual connotations of the herb and the ginger because it is very slightly irritating and will bring more blood to the surface of the skin. If any other claims are made with regard to these ingredients, ignore them.

MINERALS. There are minerals such as zinc and magnesium that play a role in the health of the skin, but they are not absorbed through the surface of the skin and their presence in a mask cannot be expected to have any effect.

MINT. The oils of the various varieties of mint are all slightly irritating when applied to the surface of the skin. Mixed with the clay of a mask, they lend it a pleasant fragrance and will draw more blood to the skin's surface. When the mask is removed you will look nice and pink for a while and your face may have a pleasant tingle.

PLACENTA. This membranous tissue, which is associated with reproduction in the wombs of animals, has become a major fad in the cosmetic industry. It is used in practically everything and is believed to have rejuvenating qualities. There is, as yet, no way to prove or disprove the belief.

FACE POWDER

Known and used for hundreds of years, cornstarch is still the softest and silkiest-feeling material that can be utilized as a face powder, and it is the one that is used for the nicest powders, including those you will find in the health food store. Since a lady must be able to carry it in her purse without spilling, it is pressed into a cake, for which purpose a little oil is added to hold it all together. Rice-bran oil, which is very light in texture, is the one that is favored and featured to make the powder seem somehow more natural than the other guy's.

FACIAL CREAMS

Many women find it a sheer sensuous pleasure to sit before a mirror and rub a cream into the face and then remove it again. We would not wish to deprive anyone of this hedonistic occupation. But we do believe a separation should be made between facial creams as instruments of pleasure and facial creams that claim to have some other effect on the face. When used with some practical purpose, such creams are employed by people—not always women by any means—who are troubled by dryness, roughness, and/or wrinkling of their faces. These oils are thickened to a consistency that gives the user control over how much is applied and where it goes and are easier to remove entirely than a lotion or liquid oil would be. Using such a cream automatically involves massaging the face, which is beneficial, and it will ordinarily leave the face feeling smoother and refreshed.

To the basic cream there are frequently added other "magic" ingredients that in folklore, legend, and advertising promotions are supposed to have wrinkle-removing moisturizing and perhaps rejuvenating qualities. Such ingredients are often strange, but that seems to be what sells cosmetics. They are found not only in health food stores, but everywhere. Those that are currently being used in facial creams are:

COLLAGEN. This is a protein material of all animal bodies that has the special function of acting as a kind of cement that holds the cells of an organ together. With age, the quantity and efficiency of collagen diminishes and one result is wrinkling. If one could increase the amount of healthy collagen within the face, it would reduce the wrinkles. There is absolutely no reason to believe, though, that applying collagen to the surface of the skin can accomplish this or anything. It will not penetrate the skin.

PABA (Para-aminobenzoic acid). This is one of the B-complex vitamins and Adelle Davis claimed in one of her books that it would restore color to gray hair. It didn't work when she tried it herself, but since then PABA has been known and used as a cosmetic vitamin. There is no known reason to include it in a face cream.

PANTHENOL. This is the oily form of one of the lesser vitamins of the B complex. It has been found of definite value as a hair treatment, giving the hair more body and improving its luster as well. Because of this panthenol has gained a cosmetic reputation, which is probably why it is included in face creams. It would not be of any value unless you have a beard.

PLACENTA. This is the membranous tissue that protects unborn animals and through which they receive their nourishment and excrete their wastes. A strong legend has grown up around placenta as a rejuvenating agent. It is liquefied and injected into patients at rejuvenation clinics and spas and lately it has become a popular additive to cosmetics. It is conceivable, though not likely, that placenta applied to the skin could have some rejuvenating effect.

POLLEN. This is the fertilizing material—one might almost say the sperm—of flowers. It seems inevitable that all materials connected with reproduction will develop a legend of rejuvenating qualities, and pollen is no exception. It was first used in Swedish facial creams, which users found to be not rejuvenating but of excellent quality as skin improvers. There is no way of telling whether this was because of the pollen or in spite of it. It is now included as an ingredient in many American facial creams.

VITAMINS A AND D. Vitamin A, taken internally, plays a role in the maintenance of healthy skin, which is connected with the ability of the sebaceous glands to maintain a proper acidity of the natural skin oils, which protects against bacterial infections. Retinoic acid, a form of vitamin A that is available only on prescription, peels the skin and is effective against acne. These facts give vitamin A a reputation as a skin vitamin, which is why it is added to facial creams. There is no evidence that vitamin A applied to the surface of the skin has any effect whatever. Vitamin D is frequently added with it simply because they occur together in the fish-liver oils that are used as a source of vitamin A.

VITAMIN E. A few years back there was quite a vogue for adding vitamin E to practically all cosmetics. That was when it was still believed that vitamin E was an enhancer of sexual abilities and the legend added to the sales appeal of the cosmetic. Since then the legend has been well exploded. People who have used vitamin E creams have been for the most part disappointed in them. Nevertheless they continue to be made and presumably people buy them. There is no reason to suppose that vitamin E applied to the skin will have any effect on it.

MISCELLANEOUS. Truly strange materials such as wheat germ and apricot-seed flour are sometimes added to facial creams because the materials have a generally good reputation among health food devotees. All they can add to a facial cream is a slight grittiness that may bring added blood to the skin as the cream is rubbed in and thus may temporarily leave the skin with a healthier appearance when the cream is removed.

FACIAL SCRUB WITH APRICOT KERNELS

Because apricot kernels are used as food by the long-lived people of Hunza, they have gained a legendary value as a health food. Reduced to a flour, they are used as the grit in some facial scrubs. The flour makes as good a grit as any but used in this way, it has neither positive nor negative health values. It will help to loosen and free the skin of old cosmetics and scrubbing with it will induce just enough irritation to make the skin look pink and feel refreshed after the lotion is removed.

FACIAL SCRUB WITH WILD OATS AND HONEY

A scrub is a lotion that contains a little grit to give it a more positive effect in freeing and removing old makeup from the skin. Wild oats is as good a material as any to provide the grit and it sounds nice and natural. The honey might serve to make the lotion a little stickier and thus, perhaps, remove more dirt.

FIRMING CREAM

A firming cream is simply a facial cream containing additional ingredients that are supposed to tighten the skin and thus reduce wrinkling and any tendency to sag. To serve this purpose the currently used ingredients are elastin and collagen. Collagen, internally, holds the cells together and thus makes organs firm and keeps them where they ought to be. It is doubtful whether it can do the same on the surface of the skin. Elastin is reputed to improve the elasticity of the skin so that when it is creased by a smile or a frown it will not form wrinkles but return to its normal place. It is being widely used today, which proves nothing except that it is fashionable.

FIRMING LOTION

See FIRMING CREAM above. The lotion is just the same, except that it is prepared as a liquid.

FOUNDATIONS

A foundation is a quick-drying fluid applied all over the face that forms a film of a uniform pale color over which more vivid makeup is then applied. Since foundations have a tendency to clog the pores, there have been complaints in the past that they irritated the skin.

In the attempt to solve this problem, they now have a soothing ingredient, aloe vera, included in the formula and are also made to form a thinner film than was previously the case. During the summer months or in the Sun Belt they will also contain a standard sunscreen that protects the skin against damage from sunlight.

GLYCERINE

This is an old, old pharmaceutical product that by virtue of having been around for so long is now accepted as natural in health food stores. Old as it is, it is still the best product around to relieve chapping and/or dryness of the skin. It is widely used for chapped lips and has a pleasant, sweet taste. In the old chapped-lip remedy of glycerine and rose water, the rose water merely added a pleasant fragrance, while the glycerine did the job. Glycerine is also good used simply to soften the skin.

HAIR COLOR

In the world of cosmetics there are many preparations designed not to dye the hair, but to give it a slight tint that it will keep only until the next time it is shampooed, when the tint will wash off. Some of the colors used, however, have been found dangerous when taken internally and others are under suspicion. A preparation you will find in a health food store that is aimed at temporarily adding color to your hair is one in which the coloring matter is beet juice. This is nice and red and perfectly safe. If you don't want to give your hair a red tint, however, you will have to look elsewhere for your hair color.

HAIR CONDITIONER

The stated purpose of a hair conditioner is to treat ordinary or nondescript hair and make it look beautiful. For this purpose, hair conditioners are supposed to soften hairs that may be dry and brittle and thus make them more manageable; to make the hair be or seem to be thicker and more luxuriant; and to give the hair an attractive luster that makes its color more vivid without actually changing it. Needless to say, the cosmetic industry has labored long and expensively in its laboratories to develop ingredients that will serve these purposes. They tend to be synthetic substances to which natural hair treatment materials are added to enhance the appeal of the product. This is true in all cosmetic lines and is no different in the health food store, except that the store's wares will be limited to those that feature natural materials on the label. The natural substances that are used are:

BALSAM. This is a resin from an evergreen tree with a particularly pleasing, fresh fragrance. Diluted, it has a slightly sticky quality and will deposit a microscopic film on each hair that can literally be said to thicken the hair, but not so that your eye can actually see any difference. It adds some luster and helps the hair to stay in place.

ELASTIN. It is included because it is enjoying a big cosmetic fad at the present time and is being put into just about everything in order to stimulate sales. Elastin is claimed to improve the elasticity of the skin but there is no reason to suppose it has any effect on the hair.

HERBS. There are a number of herbs that are sometimes included in hair conditioners in order to make the cosmetics seem more natural. For the most part, what they really add is a pleasant natural fragrance. Lavender is particularly pleasant and is often used. Myrrh is another fragrant ingredient. Nettle, sometimes added, will make the scalp tingle when the conditioner is added so that you feel it is actually doing something. Other herbs that are often used are chamomile, comfrey, burdock, and cherry bark. They all combine into a very pleasant herbal fragrance.

PANTHENOL. This is a form of pantothenic acid, one of the B-complex vitamins, which makes panthenol acceptable as a natural ingredient even though it is compounded in the laboratory. It is a water-soluble oil that is claimed to actually enter the hair shaft and make it thicker and more flexible. However it does it, panthenol does manage to give your head of hair more body and luster and truly improves the appearance. It is very popular and is used in many cosmetic preparations, whether it is appropriate or not.

YUCCA. This is a desert plant whose sap is being recommended by a few physicians to be taken internally for relief of the pain of arthritis. It has gained a big reputation in health food lore and it is probably for this reason that it is sometimes included in hair conditioners. No special claims are made for it.

HAIR REJUVENATOR

We know of only one product that takes advantage of the freedom permitted in cosmetic claims to contend that it actually makes the hair younger. Of course you will take such a claim with many grains of salt. There are products that can make the hair look younger temporarily, but only one material has ever been found that would actually increase the vitality of the hair follicles, and that material caused cancer and may not be used. This particular product uses arnica, aloe vera, and placenta as its active ingredients. Arnica is an herb that irritates the skin and has long been used in liniments. Except in extremely mild diluted solution, it would be too strong and irritating for the delicate skin of the scalp. It would, however, attract more blood to the scalp, an effect that can easily be accomplished with simple massage without irritating the skin. Aloe vera, which soothes the skin and promotes healing, is a worthwhile cosmetic but would seem to have no function in relation to the hair and scalp. Placenta is believed by many to be a good skin rejuvenator, but there has never been any indication that its supposed rejuvenating effect would apply to the hair follicles and the scalp.

Cosmetic products generally claim to do far more than they can actually deliver. This is part of the game and many of us actually like to be fooled, particularly with these feminine toys that are so delightful to use. To claim rejuvenation of the hair, however, is just going too far.

HAIR RESTORER

This is a panthenol product that makes an excessively exaggerated claim. Panthenol, at least in the belief of many, actually thickens the hair shaft and thus makes the entire head of hair look thicker and more luxuriant. It makes a good hair conditioner but it will not induce any new hair to grow.

HAIR-RESTORER VITAMINS

This is a combination of vitamins and minerals taken internally. It will always include pantothenic acid, PABA, and zinc and can also include any other vitamins and minerals that strike the fancy of the maker. It makes no difference because the product will not stop hair loss and definitely will not grow new hair. Many people who are losing their hair become so desperate they will try anything and, sad to say, hair-restorer vitamins have been sold to the tune of hundreds of millions of dollars. They may be fine nutritionally but will do nothing for the hair.

HAIR RINSE

The soaps in shampoos tend to leave a slight film on the hair after rinsing with water. And since even the detergent shampoos do contain soap, which provides the lather, the soap film that slightly dulls the color of the hair is a universal problem. You can remove the film with a vinegar solution or use something better smelling that comes in a bottle. There are many effective rinses, but your health food store will tend to sell only those to which panthenol or some other more "natural" ingredient has been added.

HAIR SPRAY

Something sticky that causes hairs to cling to one another is needed to keep the hair in place after setting or cutting. There are a hundred such sprays but your health food store will sell only those that add to the chemical formula some "natural" ingredient. Panthenol and liquid protein are favored. If the liquid protein happens to be egg white, it will contribute to the action of the spray. In a spray, which is applied only to the top of the hair, panthenol would seem to serve no purpose.

HAIR STRENGTHENER

This is simply capsules of gelatine, which has been known for a hundred years or so to soften and strengthen brittle fingernails and hair. You can save some money by getting a package of unflavored gelatine and making your own at home. There is nothing wrong with these capsules, though, and they will do what is claimed.

HAND CREAM WITH GLYCERINE

See GLYCERINE above for the uses of this old remedy. In the cream it is the glycerine that is the active ingredient. You can save a little money by buying simple glycerine and using that.

LIP GLOSS

This is essentially the same cosmetic product that can be bought anywhere, with the exception that it will contain no scent or flavor additives to make your lips sweeter to the people you kiss. This avoids some of the chemicals that would be contained in an ordinary lip gloss, but it still tints your lips with vivid shades of red that would be frowned upon in other applications.

LIPSTICK

Ordinarily, lipsticks are based on mineral oil, which is about the thickest oil you can get and which does not become rancid. These are distinct advantages which are, however, avoided in lipsticks that are sold in the health food store, because mineral oil taken internally has a bad reputation for carrying vitamins out of the body and causing intestinal irritations. Lipsticks found in the health food store will employ some substitute lipid such as lanolin or coconut oil and will not contain any fragrance. They may flake off your lips faster than other lipsticks.

LOTIONS, HAND AND BODY

In its composition a skin lotion is very similar to a skin cream, except that it is a thick liquid rather than a thin solid. It is meant to smooth the skin and to soothe any sensitive or rough spots. It will add surface moisture to skin that may be dry or chapped, say, from washing dishes. Lotions are very pleasant to use and a favorite of all women. Their basic ingredient will be either a light oil or glycerine, no matter where you may buy them. Those obtainable at a health food store will be only those that can make a special claim to being natural, either because they contain a vegetable oil or some special ingredient that appeals to health food devotees. They may or may not contain a fragrance and which type you buy is your own choice.

Some of the popular though not terribly meaningful lotion ingredients are: avocado oil, a perfectly good oil whose chief virtue in a lotion is that it has little or no odor and is thus better for a cosmetic than, say, peanut or sesame oil; various herbs that have their own pleasant, natural fragrance; strawberry oil, just a smidgen of which is added to the lotion for fragrance; and various vitamins, particularly vitamin E, which may actually speed the healing of scraped or chapped skin surfaces.

MASCARA

This is the same mascara you can buy in any drugstore, a product of modern chemistry. All they can find to say to make it seem more attractive in a health food store is that it is made with natural protein. That means nothing. No one has bothered to make anything with unnatural protein.

MOISTURIZERS

These may be either creams or lotions whose claimed purpose is to penetrate the skin, depositing moisture beneath the skin to smooth out wrinkles, alleviate dryness, and generally improve the skin's texture and appearance. It is one of the cosmetic facts of life that oils do not penetrate the skin and that the only thing that will actually moisturize in this manner is water, which has only a brief effect. Nevertheless, moisturizing cosmetics continue to be based on various oils and to claim that they do get inside the skin. Though they do not live up to their claims, moisturizers are designed to leave the skin feeling pleasantly soft and to alleviate any surface dryness. All moisturizers sold everywhere contain special ingredients employed to make them seem more natural, and these are the kinds that you will find in your health food store. Ingredients added for this purpose are:

ALOE VERA. Effective for soothing skin irritations and skin generally, aloe vera is a valuable ingredient in any cosmetic that is supposed to make the skin feel better.

APRICOT-KERNEL OIL. Apricot kernels are popular among health food devotees because they are considered a protection against cancer and because they are eaten by the frugal and long-lived people of Hunza, a principality in the Himalayas. The myth of magical efficacy that surrounds apricot kernels is the only plausible reason for inclusion of this oil in a moisturizer. It is no better or worse than any other thin food oil.

AVOCADO. The avocado is such a soft fruit that it can be used whole as a thickener in a moisturizing cream or lotion, or only its oil may be employed. The avocado has a very high nutritional value as a food, but it has no particular value as a cosmetic.

COLLAGEN. Sometimes known as "intercellular cement," this animal protein does hold body organs and tissues firmly together. It is widely used cosmetically in many products, including moisturizers. It will not penetrate the skin and it is doubtful that it serves any purpose on the surface.

CUCUMBER. This vegetable with its high water content and very soft seeds has long been used cosmetically and folklore attributes magical properties to it that have never been borne out in practice. It is liquefied and then added to lotions where it is pleasant enough to use, having only a faint, herbal odor and little tendency to spoil.

HERBAL FRAGRANCES. For people who consider the synthetic essences used in perfumes as undesirable, herbal fragrances are an opportunity to use a moisturizer that is pleasantly scented yet can be considered natural. Rosemary, mint, and cloves are commonly used and sometimes the more resinous fragrances like eucalyptus and balsam. None of these fragrances is claimed to have any cosmetic virtue other than its scent.

JOJOBA OIL. This oil of a wild desert plant may someday be used as a substitute for petroleum. Meanwhile it is a new oil that has recently gained attention and it is of plant origin and completely natural. That is enough for it to be seized upon as a cosmetic ingredient. Indeed, it has lately become something of a fad and the oil is included in a wide variety of cosmetics, including moisturizers. It has a definite odor that adds fragrance to the moisturizer. Otherwise it works just like any other oil. It will not penetrate the skin.

NUCLEIC ACIDS. Some twenty years ago a medical researcher discovered that he could design a nucleic acid facial cream that, to a limited extent, would actually get some ribonucleic acid (RNA) under the skin and be able, again to a limited extent, to rejuvenate the cells of the living skin. Later he abandoned this approach to employ, instead, the chemicals that are precursors of nucleic acids, which penetrated the skin better and seemed to be more effective.

His later formulation is so expensive to manufacture that no one has ever attempted to do it. A moisturizer containing nucleic acids might have some success at getting RNA through the pores, and then again it might not. It would all depend on how the moisturizer is made and what other materials accompany the nucleic acids. Ideally, they would not only moisturize themselves but would revitalize the glands that produce natural skin oils.

ROYAL.JELLY. Very high in selected vitamins and minerals, royal jelly is the special food manufactured by bees and fed to an embryo that they wish to grow into a queen. The queen bee it produces is larger and stronger than ordinary bees and fully fertile, able to produce thousands of offspring. Royal jelly has been used as a food supplement for many years and has developed a legend that endows it with magical properties. Since the most persistent belief is that it is a rejuvenator, it is only natural that cosmetic makers would use royal jelly in their products, since rejuvenation is the true motivation of many of the people who use the cosmetics. A moisturizer that contains both royal jelly and nucleic acids might be worth a try if rejuvenation is your purpose.

VITAMIN F. This is simply a somewhat deceptive way of stating that the moisturizer contains oil. What is called vitamin F, although it is not recognized as a vitamin, is a small group of fatty acids that are abundant in the food oils. Since oil is an ingredient of practically all moisturizers, one that features vitamin F on its label will turn out to be exactly the same product that you can buy everywhere with no mention of vitamin F. That does not make it bad. Moist moisturizers are pleasant to use, and, at least temporarily, produce pleasant effects.

MOUTHWASH

The purpose of a mouthwash is to suppress any unpleasant odor in the mouth and substitute one that is enjoyable. The so-called antiseptic mouthwashes may in fact destroy bacteria as claimed, but within half an hour after using the bacteria in the mouth will replenish themselves and the net effect of the antiseptic is zero. The mouthwashes you will find in a health food store neither claim nor possess any antiseptic properties but simply put a strong natural fragrance in your mouth. Most commonly they are flavored and scented with cloves, cinnamon, or spearmint. Some brands also contain some vitamin C, but that is merely for sales appeal. It does nothing for you unless you swallow it.

NAIL CARE PRODUCTS

You will find a full range of nail care products that differ only slightly from those sold everywhere else. They include conditioners, base polishes, frosts, and finishing polishes, in just as wide a range of colors. The only difference is that the health food store products contain no formaldehyde. Formaldehyde is a very useful chemical that is a powerful solvent, an antiseptic, and an embalming fluid. Unfortunately, as it dries and for weeks thereafter it releases fumes that can irritate the eyes and nose and even produce toxic internal reactions. Giving up its use means giving up a very effective solvent, but it is certainly safer, particularly for sensitive people. Because they contain no formaldehyde you will find that the nail cosmetics in the health food store are a little more difficult to apply, and do not go on quite as smoothly. Nevertheless, they are quite satisfactory and will not make your nose run or your eyes burn.

NAIL POLISH REMOVER

The most common nail polish remover uses a solvent, acetone, to dissolve the polish so it can be wiped away. Unfortunately, acetone, like formaldehyde, gives off toxic fumes and it is banned from the products in the health food store. Instead, what is known as a cutting oil, usually old-fashioned banana oil, is employed. It takes a little longer to do the job but it works and will not stir up any of your sensitivities. A little jojoba oil is added because otherwise the banana oil would be excessively drying. In its total effect such a polish remover is somewhat of an improvement over the standard product.

OIL, BATH

These products are intended to be floated on the surface of your bath water, presumably to counter the drying out of your skin that results from cleaning it with soap and water. No bath oil serves this purpose very well, since in actuality little of it gets on your skin. However, the oils are fragrant and the heat of the bath intensifies the fragrances, giving you a very pleasant feeling of luxury and femininity that may actually serve to make the bath more relaxing and pleasurable. These bath oils will employ natural floral fragrances and sometimes additional material meant to make them seem more like a health food, such as apricot-kernel oil or a combination of honey and lemon. Such additives possess no special virtue.

OIL, BODY

Also called skin oils at times, these products are intended to be applied to the skin and rubbed in with only the excess being removed. The normal condition of the skin is very slightly oily, the skin's natural oil being gently acidic in nature and furnishing what is known as the acid mantle, such acidity being sufficient to destroy some types of bacteria that might otherwise cause skin infections. The preceding is the justification for using body oil to restore the natural oily condition of the skin after it has been dried out by washing or has just become drier than it ought to be. Normally the skin quickly restores its own oils and a body oil is hardly a necessity for most people. Rubbing it into the skin is a sensuous pleasure, however, and it can have a soothing and smoothing effect where that is needed. It is fundamentally just an enjoyable way of fussing with yourself. The oil used is usually coconut, which has the advantages of being almost devoid of odor and having little tendency to turn rancid. Where a curative action such as the alleviation of chapping is intended, jojoba is sometimes added or substituted. Some of these oils are packaged without any fragrance, which is a shame since smelling pleasantly sweet is part of the fun. Normally, skin oils are scented with herbal or flower fragrances.

PERFUME

See COLOGNE in this section. Perfumes are exactly the same except that they are stronger, containing a higher proportion of the fragrant essential oils.

SCALP TREATMENTS

These products are intended for use after shampooing, to deposit a little clean oil on the surface of the scalp. This makes sense, since dryness of the scalp promotes scaling and itching, and, if it is habitually dry, the scalp will not be able to supply the light film of oil that gives hair its luster. It could be almost any light-bodied oil, but since these are health food products, they employ oils that have a big reputation among health food devotees, notably panthenol and jojoba. The oils are thinned sufficiently to lend themselves to brisk rubbing, which is part of the treatment, and to add only a very light film to the scalp, which is as it should be.

SHAMPOO

The purpose of a shampoo, of course, is to clean the hair and scalp. Inasmuch as few people shampoo daily, enough time elapses for oil and grime to accumulate along with hair cosmetics, so that a shampoo is usually considerably stronger than a soap or detergent used for the rest of the body, in order to do a thorough cleaning job. The ideal shampoo would be a pure detergent which, by its chemical nature, attaches itself to the water rinsing the head and departs without leaving any film. People have never been willing to believe that anything that does not lather cleans, however, and so all shampoos contain enough soap to produce a thick lather that will deposit a light film on the hair. Regardless of whether they are all soap or a detergent-type of soap mixture, claims for perfect results are nothing but ballyhoo.

A good strong shampoo will leave the hair and scalp very clean but very dry, so many shampoos contain conditioners that are supposed to leave a slight residue of oil, even while the hair is being cleaned. This should and does leave the hair in more manageable condition and with a gloss, hence more vivid in color. There is a price, however. A shampoo by its nature dissolves and removes oil, so in a shampoo containing a conditioner the shampoo itself must be weaker if the oil is to be effective. In other words, it will condition but it will not clean as well and it might perhaps be more effective to shampoo first and then employ a separate conditioner.

The shampoos available in health food stores are a selection of those you can find everywhere, selected for their additives that are popular among health food devotees in other uses and hence exert sales appeal in the highly competitive shampoo market. They will tend to contain less detergent or none at all to avoid sensitivity reactions to detergents, which are common, and they will not be very strong cleansers for the same reason.

The different ingredients you will find featured on the shampoo labels are:

ALOE VERA. This sap of a tropical plant has genuine soothing qualities and might well be helpful for a scalp that feels sore or itchy. It is dubious, though, how much of it will actually be deposited by a shampoo. If your scalp needs aloe vera, a separate application might be more effective.

ASCORBIC ACID. This is vitamin C, and though it plays many beneficial roles in the human body, it is not known to be of any value applied to the hair and scalp.

BANANA OIL. This appealingly natural-sounding oil has mostly mechanical applications. It is used to strengthen lightweight paper structures on model airplanes, among other uses, and perhaps might also strengthen hair that tends to be brittle and break off.

BIOTIN. This is one of the lesser-known vitamins of the B complex about which there is some suggestive but far from conclusive evidence that it might stimulate hair growth. If that is your problem, it might be worth a try.

COCONUT OIL. This oil has very little scent of its own and what it has is pleasant. In a shampoo that contains no fragrance, it is preferable to other oils that have a stronger scent.

ELASTIN. This protein material has developed a powerful though not necessarily true legend about its ability to restore more useful flexibility to the skin. Presumably in a shampoo it is intended to do the same for the more brittle hair.

HERBS. The fragrances of herbs are preferred to those of flowers in shampoos because their scent can be characterized as clean rather than sweet. This seems somehow more natural. Such shampoos can also contain one or more of the endless variety of herbs that are claimed, with little or no substance, to have endless curative qualities, including control of dandruff. Do not look for any health benefits from herbal shampoos, but you will probably find their fragrances very pleasant to use.

JOJOBA. This oil has been promoted for so many cosmetic applications that it has become a kind of universal ingredient in all types of cosmetics. The claims made for it are certainly exaggerated but it is a perfectly good oil, as good as any as a conditioner in a shampoo. However, it has a definite odor and if you want to try shampoo with jojoba, you will do well to select one that contains a pleasanter fragrance to mask the jojoba.

KELP. Hair does have a mineral content, which it obtains from the blood that nourishes the hair follicle. These minerals seem to play a role in the life and health of the hair shaft, and perhaps it is for this reason that occasionally shampoos will be found containing kelp, which is used nutritionally as a source of minerals. There is no reason to suppose, however, that the minerals can penetrate the hair shaft directly from the outside. It is doubtful that the kelp actually contributes anything but a selling point to the shampoo.

KERATIN. This is the particular type of protein tissue that makes up hair and fingernails. There have been some experiments to determine whether keratin as a nutrient would stimulate the growth and/or health of hair and fingernails, but the results were completely negative. Any claim that keratin in a shampoo will improve the hair should be regarded with skepticism.

LANOLIN. There was once a famed pitch man who rented a store on 50th Street in New York City, erected a speaking platform, and proceeded to charm millions of people into believing that the lanolin he was selling was a hair restorer and dandruff remedy. Eventually he was put out of business by the police, but since then this mutton fat has had an unjustified reputation as a miraculous hair treatment. Some lanolin is contained in most of the shampoos you will find in a health food store and it must be admitted that it is as good as any other lipid as a conditioner. It will do you no harm and there is no reason to shy away from it.

NUCLEIC ACIDS. It has been found that in a carefully prepared cream that is rubbed into the skin, the nucleic acids RNA and DNA can to a limited extent penetrate the skin and stimulate the regeneration process. It is perhaps because it is hoped that they will do the same through the skin of the scalp that these genetic materials are included as an ingredient in at least one shampoo. There is little reason to suppose it will work, though, and in all probability the nucleic acids add nothing to the virtues of the shampoo.

PANTHENOL. This oily form of the vitamin pantothenic acid has a demonstrated value as a hair improver. It is included in practically all types of preparations for the hair and will probably be of some value as a conditioner even in a shampoo. Regular use of panthenol in this and other hair cosmetics may well improve the appearance of your hair.

PERFUMES. These are limited to the natural floral fragrances, which is no hardship since the lighter fragrances of the florals is more appropriate in a shampoo than the heavier synthetic essences.

PROTEIN. Although the source of the protein is anonymous, you can be sure the effect will be just about the same as that of keratin, elastin, etc. That is, the protein will do nothing to your hair although the shampoo itself may be perfectly fine.

SAFFLOWER OIL. Known as the most unsaturated of the polyunsaturated oils, safflower oil is often used dietarily on a cholesterol-reducing program. Neither its odor nor its flavor is pleasant and there is no particular purpose for substituting it in a shampoo for some other oil like coconut that is much nicer to use.

VITAMINS A, D, AND E. These are the vitamins that are soluble in oil and which, therefore, are easily added to the conditioner portion of a shampoo. They will not penetrate the hair or scalp and serve no purpose other than to offer an additional selling point to those who are susceptible to the idea of vitamins for everything.

SHAMPOO, BABY

A baby shampoo must, of course, be very gentle. Its acidity index (pH) will be neutral or close to it. In addition, there is usually a content of glycerine, which is soothing to anyone's skin and will be equally soothing to the skin of a baby's scalp. It contains no perfume or any other ingredient that could irritate the most delicate of skins. It is a good product.

SHAMPOO, DANDRUFF

This product poses a real problem for the makers of health food cosmetics. True dandruff, as distinguished from the tendency of a dry scalp to flake, is a low-grade bacterial infection. There are highly effective trade shampoos that control dandruff and prevent its recurrence as long as the shampoo continues to be used, though none of them actually cure the infection. The ingredients that keep the bacteria under control are all pharmaceutical in nature, however, and cannot be disguised as natural in any way, and a health food store will not sell them. What is offered as a dandruff shampoo contains oat flour, which acts as an abrasive when rubbed into the scalp and will loosen much of the scale so it can be washed away. For undetermined reasons, it also contains the minerals magnesium and aluminum, though neither one has any antiseptic properties, and witch hazel, an herb that is both fragrant and astringent. It will temporarily remove dandruff but will in no way prevent its recurrence.

SHAMPOO, HYPOALLERGENIC

Since some people react allergically to detergents, soaps, and/or perfumes, they require a shampoo that will not stir up their sensitivities. The trick is to put in as few ingredients as possible and keep the acidity index at or very close to neutral. This is no guarantee against allergic reactions but it does reduce the chances considerably.

SHAMPOO, ORIENTAL

Oriental women, for the most part, are blessed with a genetic inheritance of thick, lustrous hair. It was, therefore, only a matter of time until someone would produce a shampoo containing the "secret" of Oriental hair beauty. There are several such now available containing silk protein, which presumably is expected to impart the beauty of silk, and ginseng, an herb treasured in the Orient (and grown mostly in West Virginia) for supposed aphrodisiac properties. Ginseng contains estrogen, which has truly been found to stimulate hair growth. Unfortunately, it was also found to stimulate skin cancer on the scalp in the tests that were made. There is so little estrogen in an Oriental shampoo that there is no reason to be afraid of it. But by the same token, however, there is too little to bring about any regeneration of the hair and, in fact, it cannot be expected to have any effect. These shampoos are sometimes perfumed with the fragrance of incense and perhaps can make you smell and feel Oriental, even if they do nothing for your hair but wash it clean.

SHAMPOO, SUNSCREEN

This is something new containing the same sunscreen elements that you will find in a protective skin lotion. The purpose is to protect your hair against bleaching by the sun's rays, and it will give your hair some protection, though most of it is rinsed out with the shampoo.

SHAMPOO, TINTING

The world is full of shampoos containing just enough hair dye to temporarily lend your hair a slight added tint or deeper color. Practically all of these dyes can irritate sensitive skin and they are not used in products sold in health food stores. The one exception is henna, which is natural coloring matter and nonirritating. If you want to add a touch of red to the color of your hair, a shampoo containing henna will do the trick effectively.

SKIN FRESHENER

This product is not much in demand and you will generally find only one brand in a store. It contains papaya and alcohol. The alcohol removes the oils on the skin making it more accessible to the protein-dissolving action of the papaya enzyme. The outer layer of dead skin is partially removed by this action, leaving the skin a little pinker and with a temporary feeling of freshness.

SKIN PEEL

This is a lotion containing a mild acid that is strong enough, when applied to the skin, to dissolve away the outer layer of dead skin. In so doing, it gives the skin a thorough cleaning and the slight irritation it induces brings a good amount of blood to the surface to leave the skin looking youthfully pink for a few hours. It will remove some blackheads and whiteheads. It should not be used often, however. Read the instructions on the bottle carefully and follow them.

SOAP

Everybody uses soap numerous times during the day, which makes it a prime cosmetic product. All soaps are basically the same. The essential fatty acids are oil or meat fat combined with lye to form material that cleans by dissolving oils and then floating them away along with whatever dirt has clung to them. Since meat fats are considered undesirable in the lore of health foods, you will not find the less-expensive soaps based on meat fat in a health food store.

Soaps made from oils tend to be less harsh and are considered more desirable. They cost more. They also, in the health food store, will contain one or more special ingredients to give them an aura of the natural, although, actually, all soaps meet the requirements of a natural product. The added ingredients soaps may contain singly or in combination are:

ALMONDS. Crushed into small fragments, almonds add a pleasant fragrance to the soap and a soft abrasive that helps remove old cosmetics.

ALOE VERA. This tropical plant juice is notably soothing and pleasant to use and is included in just about all types of cosmetics. You might find it enjoyable even in a soap.

APRICOT KERNELS. Added as a flour or in small fragments, apricot kernels provide a soft grit that can help to thoroughly loosen old makeup so it can be washed away. Their legendary reputation as a food has no meaning in a soap.

AVOCADO OIL. It is a common practice to add a little oil to the finished soap so that it will have less drying effect on the skin. Avocado oil is as good as any other for this purpose.

BUTTERMILK. In folklore, buttermilk is recommended to improve the complexion and those who believe that it works will presumably choose buttermilk soap.

CLAY. Used for facial masks that do temporarily make the face look younger, clay has a good cosmetic reputation that is being traded upon when it is added to soap. In a soap it would serve merely as a finer yet tougher abrasive than the food particles that are more commonly used.

COCOA BUTTER. Long used as a skin softener, cocoa butter will presumably serve this purpose as an ingredient of soap. Its chocolaty odor, however, is not to everybody's liking.

COCONUT OIL. A little coconut oil added to a soap will serve, like other oils, to keep the skin from becoming too dry in washing. A soap made entirely from coconut oil is good when it must be used with salt water, but it will not lather in fresh water and therefore will not clean well.

CUCUMBER. Folklore endorses the cucumber as a moisturizer and complexion improver, which is why it is sometimes added to soaps.

GOAT'S MILK. Legend has it that goat's milk was the complexion aid of famed beauties of the past and perhaps it did have some such effect, being a very rich milk with a lot of fat in it. In our judgment, it is less desirable than one of the thinner food oils.

LANOLIN. This fatty material is a standard ingredient in virtually all complexion soaps. It is a bit thicker and heavier than food oils and has a more positive effect in leaving a film of fresh oil on the face to replace what has been washed away.

LECITHIN. This lipid is an emulsifier and as such can sometimes play an important role nutritionally. As an additive to soaps it really adds nothing in particular.

MUSK OIL. This oil has a very strong, very sweet odor which has long been used as one ingredient in perfumes and has recently enjoyed a vogue as a recognizable fragrance. Not enough of it could possibly be used for any purpose other than fragrance. It is one of the few fragrances that can be found in this group of soaps, whose users tend to regard perfume in a soap as sinful.

OATMEAL. Cooked oatmeal was used by ladies as a face mask and many think it a complexion improver. At the least, it will add a softly abrasive quality to the soap that will help to remove old cosmetics.

SESAME OIL AND SEEDS. The oil is as good as any other to gentle the action of a soap and inhibit drying of the skin. The seeds have the soft firmness that can scrub away old makeup yet not feel harsh.

VITAMINS A AND E. In a soap, these perfectly fine vitamins are nothing more than a gimmick to make the soap seem something more than it actually is. They will not penetrate the skin and play no role on the surface of the skin.

WHEAT GERM. Famed as a health food, wheat germ is undoubtedly included in soaps for its aura of wholesomeness, which is meaningless in this application. Yet it can provide a perfectly effective soft grit to scrub away old cosmetics.

YOGURT. It is difficult to see why soured skim milk should ever be included in a soap except that it is generally popular. Yet, like buttermilk, it may be developing its own legend as a complexion improver and there is a remote possibility that it could turn out to be one.

SOAP, ACNE

There are, today, some fairly effective acne preparations consisting basically of an antibiotic in combination with lauryl sulfate. To be of value, they must be left to dry on the skin for an appreciable time. No acne soap can be expected to have much effect and no effect at all is a more likely prognosis. Nevertheless, there are such soaps that carefully omit any antibiotic ingredients because of the prejudice against them, but do contain lauryl sulfate. They also list as an ingredient sodium hydroxide, which is lye and is actually an ingredient of all soaps. Tea, which contains tannic acid, may also be included as an ingredient because it acts as an irritant and will draw more blood to the skin. It may also have a slight peeling effect which could be helpful.

SOAP, BABY

To provide increased gentleness, baby soaps contain a high proportion of glycerine, which is itself a form of soap that has a soothing effect on the skin. It may also contain vitamins A and/or E for no particular reason but sales appeal.

SOAP, CASTILE

This is a high-quality soap in which olive oil is the only fat employed. It is very gentle and has a deservedly good reputation.

SOAP FOR DRY SKIN

Such soaps are just like any others but have a higher oil content, which makes them less drying to the skin but also somewhat less effective as cleansers.

SOAP, HERBAL

There is a widespread conviction that perfumed soaps are bad for the skin and to be avoided. Consequently, few of the soaps you will find in a health food store contain any fragrance and will simply leave your skin smelling like skin. There are some people, however, who stubbornly prefer a fragrant soap and for them there are provided soaps with various clean-smelling herbal fragrances. Any of the dozens of aromatic herbs may be used in varied combinations and you simply pick the one you like the best. Not strictly herbal but similar in nature are other occasional natural scents such as strawberry, almond, and peppermint.

SOAPLESS CLEANSERS

Every woman knows that a bit of cotton containing oil or cold cream will remove a good bit of dirt from the face, without drying the skin. That is all that soapless cleansers are. Whether they are liquids or bars, they simply furnish you with a light-bodied oil with which you can rub off dirt.

SPLASH TONER

This is an alcohol solution that is inexpensive enough to be splashed on your skin with abandon. It is astringent in nature and will give your skin a nice brisk, clean feeling. If it contains aloe vera, as they usually do, it will also make your skin feel smoother and softer.

SUNBURN RELIEF

Not for the health food stores are the sunburn lotions that contain anesthetic preparations to numb the skin to its pain. Shunning such effective lotions on principle, the health food store can offer only ointments containing aloe vera, which is soothing, but not soothing enough to be of much help with a painful sunburn.

SUNTAN LOTION

There is nothing unusual about these lotions, which can be obtained just about anywhere. They are acceptable in the health food store because the chief active ingredient, PABA, is not only an effective preventer of sunburn but is a vitamin. Jojoba oil and cocoa butter serve to prevent drying out of the skin, which is in itself a preventive of severe burning. Aloe vera is also included because it is generally good for the skin and pleasant to use.

TOOTHBRUSHES

The all-natural bristle toothbrushes you will find in a health food store are hard to get elsewhere. Most dentists will tell you they are superior in performance.

TOOTHPASTE

There is only one type of toothpaste you will find in a health food store. It uses chalk as its abrasive agents, chalk being considerably softer than the abrasives in the brands you get at the drugstore or market. It will not scratch the tooth enamel and is as abrasive as most people need. To remove definite staining, however, it will not work as well as the trade brands. The toothpaste will never have a sweet taste, since both sugar and saccharine are shunned. It will be flavored with clove or cinnamon. And since some health food enthusiasts are violently opposed to the use of fluoride, while others like it, the toothpaste comes both with and without. It is really a very good toothpaste for most people.

WRINKLE-CONCEALING STICK

Similar to a foundation cream, this is basically a heavy oil (jojoba) that can be used to fill in deep wrinkles, after which cosmetics are applied and the skin looks smooth and younger. It is thick enough to stay in place yet soft enough not to crack. It may not be worth the bother at most times but will certainly be useful if you are about to appear before the TV cameras.

EXERCISE EQUIPMENT

You will not find much in the way of paraphernalia for exercising in a health food store and frequently will find nothing at all. The health food movement believes enthusiastically in sports and exercise, but the store is in no position to compete with sporting goods stores, and it does not try. The one exception is in body building equipment, perhaps because it is a line that does not interest the general public and which, therefore, the sporting goods stores frequently ignore. In any case, those health food stores that cater to athletes will often sell the specialized devices that are dear to the muscle men, as well as vitamin and mineral combinations that are just like all the others but labeled to suggest that they promote athletic ability.

The store you patronize may well carry the following gizmos for grunters and groaners.

BARBELLS

These are the standard equipment of weight lifters, consisting of an iron rod to which can be affixed one or more iron plates at both ends to provide variable weights mounting up to the hundreds of pounds. Better get some instruction before you attempt it. You can easily rupture yourself.

BENCH, ADJUSTABLE

For dedicated body builders, the best way to put the finishing touches on particular groups of muscles is to keep the body in a slanted position while exercising with weights. These benches make it possible.

BICYCLE, EXERCISE

These are stationary devices that permit you to get the same exercise in the privacy of your own home that you would riding a bike. It is a good exercise for anyone. If you buy an exercise bicycle, however, make sure that is is one on which you can adjust the tension. If it is too easy to pump, you get no exercise at all. The idea is to adjust it to a point where it is difficult to turn the wheels but will not be so hard that you give up. As your leg strength increases, you gradually increase the tension.

BOOTS, CAST-IRON

Putting these on your feet will give you a weight from 6 to 10 pounds that your legs carry around during a timed walking period. It is intended to firm and strengthen the calf and thigh muscles and perhaps work off some flab as well.

CHINNING BAR

Chinning is about the first body-building exercise you had to perform as a schoolchild and it will still strengthen and firm your arms and shoulders. Portable chinning bars hook onto a door jamb so you can chin yourself in any doorway.

DUMBBELLS

These fairly light weights held in the hands add to the effectiveness of calisthenics designed to build the arms, shoulders, and chest.

GIRDLE, SWEATING

Made in sizes for men as well as women, this is a panty girdle of heavy rubber that is intended to fit tightly. As long as you have it on, and you can wear it all day long if you like, it will keep the enclosed section of your body hot and unventilated and will promote profuse sweating. This is supposed to take off fat from the buttocks, hips, upper thighs, and abdomen. It will certainly provide a temporary reduction in girth because of sheer water loss, but it is not certain that the loss will have any permanency.

GRIPPERS

There are a number of devices for strengthening the hands by frequent squeezing of something offering resistance. A sponge ball will serve the purpose perfectly well. However, most grippers are metal coil spring, either with or without handles that must be pushed together and then released.

JOGGING MACHINE

This is fundamentally a treadmill with a meter attached and a rough moving surface that is set into motion by jogging (or walking or running) on it, turning rollers to register an approximation of the distance traveled. You can, of course, jog in your home without a machine but some people like this gadget.

PULL EXERCISER

Especially intended for development of the pectoral muscles and building the breasts, the pull exerciser is fundamentally a piece of elastic that is either a rope or a band and offers enough resistance so that it is difficult to stretch out.

SKIPPING ROPE

Not for today's exercise devotees is the old length of clothesline that was used for skipping for a hundred years. Today it has fancy handles and is both strong and elasticized, which makes it possible to achieve faster rotation than possible with an ordinary rope. It is inexpensive and if you are able to do it, rope skipping is an excellent exercise.

WORKOUT BELT

It used to be called a truss. It is actually a support garment rather than a belt, made of leather or a tough and heavy alternative material. When worn it provides good support to the lower back, the abdominal area, and the male genitals to help you guard against disabling yourself while doing heavy exercise.

THERAPEUTIC PRODUCTS

Theoretically, a health food store does not sell anything intended for the treatment or cure of any illness. That is the province of the licensed pharmacist. In fact, if you were to ask an employee of a health food store what you should take for your bladder infection, diabetes, or headache, and he recommended anything in his store, that product would immediately be considered misbranded by the Food and Drug Administration, and his entire stock of it might well be seized and condemned. So store personnel are instructed never to suggest or recommend anything for the treatment of any illness, and the labels on the products themselves do not contain such suggestions either. They simply state the contents of the bottle or the package.

Yet, in a very real sense, nearly everything you buy in a health food store is a sort of therapeutic product, considered as such by many customers and used by them to treat health problems. They believe in the therapeutic efficacy of particular products because they have read about them in books or magazines or have heard a popular lecturer speak about them. For an obvious example, people will take vitamin C to treat a cold though there is nothing on the label of the bottle that suggests in any way that vitamin C is a cold remedy.

There is thus a duality in many vitamin and mineral products, and food products as well, which can be used either as simple diet supplements to insure the taker against deficiencies or as treatments for health problems. There are some products, however, that nobody would ever use for anything except treatment of health problems, even though the store personnel will insist that they are food supplements for the prevention or correction of deficiencies. You would not, for example, take tablets of freeze-dried thyroid gland for their food value, but only for the value you believe they possess to correct a problem of basal metabolism or the thyroid gland itself. Such products with unmistakable and unambiguous therapeutic purposes are the ones listed in this section. In a few cases the listings duplicate and carry cross-references to the listings in other sections. This is simply for the convenience of those who, buying the product for therapeutic purposes, may consult this section first. It is to be expected, though, that your own conception of which section should be consulted for information about a product will not always be correctly anticipated. If you think it should be in the therapeutic section and it is not, try one of the earlier sections before you give up.

ADRENAL GLAND CONCENTRATE

Physicians who practice nutritional treatments for many years favored the use of adrenal cortical extracts (ACE) for some forms of low blood sugar (hypoglycemia). More recently this pharmaceutical preparation has been banned for reasons best known to the FDA. Doctors who are free to write prescriptions for any one of the adrenal hormones may no longer prescribe this combination of them. But if they really believe in this treatment, while they will give you nothing in writing they may well recommend that you go to a health food store and buy some adrenal gland concentrate for yourself. This is powerful stuff and you would be foolish indeed to try to use except under medical supervision.

AGAR FLAKES

Agar is a seaweed derivative that has long been used as a shortening in kosher kitchens for pies and other baked products that are to be eaten at a meal containing no dairy products. It works well and now has been discovered to be noncaloric, which makes it highly desirable for the making of low-calorie baked goods.

ALGAE

See ALGAE under Section 3: Foods and Food Products. This is being touted as a perfect food, which it is not. If you ate it in any quantity, the iodine and sodium content would both be far too high. It is being used as a reducing aid but great care is required. Too much reliance on algae could lead to severe deficiency diseases.

ALGIN

Extracted from one variety of Pacific Ocean kelp, algin is a non-nutritive material that has the remarkable property of being able to remove heavy metals from the body. So strong is the affinity for heavy metals that algin literally pulls lead, strontium, and other toxic heavy metals right out of the blood as it courses through the walls of the intestines. Being nonnutritive, the algin is then excreted, taking the metals out of the body with it. If we are ever menaced by fallout of radioactive strontium 90, algin will be the official method used by the authorities to remove it from the body.

ANTACID TABLETS

Although the thinking of the natural living nutritionists is that most digestive disturbances are caused by too little acids rather than too much, it is still recognized that some hyperacidity does exist. The aluminum salts that are used in most antacid tablets are shunned by the health food stores, which consider aluminum a hazardous metal. What is left is calcium carbonate, a perfectly good product that will usually ease your discomfort quickly.

APPETITE DEPRESSANTS

There is no natural product that will actually depress the appetite, but sometimes pharmaceutical chemicals do sneak into a health food store to meet a demand. The one that the stores seem to consider more acceptable than others is benzocaine, which is the active ingredient in any appetite depressant you find in a health food store.

ASPIRIN

Although aspirin might come within the definition of a natural product, it does cause a little bleeding in the stomach and habitual use can cause ulcers. Nevertheless, it is the most reliable of pain-killers and there is no completely harmless natural product that can take its place. If you buy any type of analgesic or headache remedy in a health food store, it will probably contain aspirin as its active ingredient, although you will find this out only by reading the small type on the label. Any other herbs and vitamins that these tablets may contain are there only to disguise the fact that what is really being sold is aspirin.

BED WEDGES

These wedge-shaped chunks of foam latex or plastic are sometimes very good to give your head and neck firm support while you are lying in bed. They help if breathing in a horizontal position is difficult and are sometimes good if you have a tendency to develop a stiff neck while you are sleeping.

BLOOD PRESSURE KIT

The types of kits sold in health food stores have various devices that permit them to be operated at home without requiring the use of a stethoscope. They are far from being perfectly accurate, but that is also true of the medical assistant who takes your pressure at a doctor's office. If you want or need frequent blood pressure readings, these kits can be useful and cost far less than running to the doctor twice a week.

BRAIN, DEHYDRATED

Brain tissue is a rather fatty protein in structure, rich in a variety of enzymes and the hormones of several glands that the brain contains. There are some physicians who believe that like cures like, or to be more explicit, that if you have a brain problem such as senility, the eating of brain will encourage improvement of your own brain. It is for such a use that tablets of brain tissue freeze-dried or dehydrated at low temperature are manufactured.

BRAN TABLETS

There are a few health problems that are not considered diseases and for which, therefore, the health food store may frankly offer products designed to treat them. They are problems like headache, fatigue, and in this case, constipation. It is as a constipation remedy that bran tablets are sold. They are not very effective for this purpose.

BROMELAIN

The stem of the pineapple is the source of this enzyme that is protein dissolving (proteolytic) in nature. It is used here chiefly because a German physician who is well respected among the devotees of health foods has proclaimed that he used bromelain in his practice as a kind of pipe cleaner for the coronary arteries. If this enzyme can truly dissolve and clear out the debris that clogs the coronary arteries and narrows their lumen, then it would certainly be of value to many people. This use has been neither proved nor disproved. Bromelain, however, has been shown to be of value in reducing inflammations of arthritic joints and was originally introduced for that purpose. It may also function as a digestive enzyme.

CALLUS REMOVER

This can be any of half a dozen or so mild acid solutions that are applied to a callus to slowly dissolve the dead skin. For those who don't like to fool with acids, there is an electric device that is gently abrasive yet quickly wears the callus down.

CELL SALTS

Homeopathic medicine was very popular in America in the late nineteenth and early twentieth centuries, and since the homeopathic physicians apparently practiced quite as successfully as others, it is not to be sneered at. The basis of the practice in America was the use, in extremely small doses, of the twelve cell salts, which, administered singly or in combination, were considered to be able to treat any illness. They are still being manufactured by a pharmaceutical company in St. Louis that seems to be the sole supplier to health food stores. Naturopaths, of whom there are perhaps a thousand in various parts of the country and who have their own college to train new naturopaths, practice homeopathic medicine to a limited extent and also employ herbal and nutritional treatments. They recommend cell salts to their patients. There are also numerous others who continue to use the cell salts even though they are opposed to the use of drugs, since these salts come in such minute doses that they are somehow considered not drugs at all.

If you wish to know what cell salts are considered to be good for, you can probably buy an inexpensive pamphlet published by the manufacturer and sold in health food stores. The salts are fondly and commonly known by various abbreviations of Latin names with not even the users knowing the full names. To avoid confusion, check the labels on which the modern and recognizable chemical name of the salt is always stated.

The twelve cell salts, or tissue salts, as they are frequently called, are: calcium fluoride, calcium phosphate, calcium sulfate, ferric phosphate, magnesium phosphate, potassium chloride, potassium phosphate, potassium sulfate, silica oxide, sodium chloride, sodium phosphate, and sodium sulfate.

CHARCOAL

These tablets are sold as a remedy for internal gas and are pretty good for the purpose. Charcoal does have a remarkable ability to absorb gases, which is why it used to be used as the air-filtering element in gas masks. Much internal gas is merely swallowed air, however, and charcoal will not absorb that.

CHROMIUM (GTF)

It has been shown that nutritional yeasts improve the quality and efficiency of the insulin we produce and thus are of value to diabetics and, in fact, all who have any tendency to elevated levels of blood sugar. This activity has been traced to the chromium content of the yeast, since it comes bound to a protein element that has been called the Glucose Tolerance Factor. GTF chromium is extracted from yeast and is intended for use by anyone with a high blood-sugar problem. It will not cure diabetes but it will often reduce the insulin requirement. For further information, see CHROMIUM in Section 1: Vitamins and Minerals.

COUGH MIXTURE

There is not much value to be expected or derived from the syrup of rose hips that is offered as a cough mixture. The drugs that effectively anesthetize the nerves that induce coughing when irritated are all shunned in the health food store. No one has yet found any drugless mixture that will work.

DIURETIC, HERBAL

Anything that acidifies the blood will promote increased urination, inasmuch as the kidneys will keep drawing water from the blood in order to maintain the slight alkalinity that is normal. In this sense, herbal diuretics are effective. They will not, though, draw sodium out of the tissues to be eliminated with the water, which is the true purpose of most diuretics. If the sodium content of the body is not reduced, any water loss through increased urination is quickly replaced.

DMSO

This by-product of the manufacture of paper is derived from wood pulp and therefore is accepted as a natural product, even though a hundred other drugs derived from natural plants are shunned as unnatural. What gives DMSO its special status is probably just the fact that its medical use has been banned by the FDA, pending further investigation. In the health food movement it is frequently assumed that the government authorities are always wrong and conspire against the public health, and that whatever the government opposes must be good.

DMSO may not be sold for medical purposes, but there is no

restriction on its commercial use as a solvent. If your health food store sells it, it will be as a solvent preparation, or perhaps it will be sold under the counter for medical purposes. If you buy it at all, it is probably better to buy it illicitly, buying the product that is manufactured by pharmaceutical companies in Mexico. This assures you that it has been made to pharmaceutical standards of purity and is not contaminated by any of the toxins that can easily creep into a commercial solvent that is not regulated as to impurities.

Such caution is particularly important in the case of DMSO, because it has the very special property of penetrating the skin and entering the blood in a few seconds. Thus, even though you only rub it on your skin, its impurities will immediately enter your body. The drug itself has been found to alleviate the pain of arthritis and back pains, both of which are very hard for people to bear. It has also been found to reduce swelling and, in fact, promises to be a very useful and very important drug, if and when it is determined to be safe enough for human use. But use of a commercial grade is far too risky for any sensible person, and for all we can be sure of now, even use of the pharmaceutical preparation may carry dangers as yet unknown. If you suffer agonies of lower back pain or arthritis, the temptation is great. But you'd better resist for now.

DUODENUM

The second chamber of the digestive tract is a frequent site of ulcers and the place where much digestive disturbance occurs. If you happen to have a problem in your own duodenum, and if you hold the strange belief that the way to treat it is to eat the duodenum of cattle, then you can obtain tablets of dehydrated duodenum in many health food stores. They are either freeze-dried or dried at temperatures below 140 degrees to preserve any enzyme content they may possess.

EAR WAX CONTROL

If you have a tendency to form hard plugs of wax in your ears, it becomes uncomfortable and sometimes painful. A mild solvent to soften the wax can be helpful and reduce the number of times you have to go to the doctor to have your ears cleaned. It is the same product you can get in any drugstore.

ENERGY CAPSULES

Ambiguously named in order to stay out of trouble, these are actually supposed to increase sexual energy. They contain pumpkin-seed oil, the pumpkin seed having been vigorously publicized as an improver of the health of the prostate gland on the basis of no evidence at all. Don't be a sucker.

ENZYMES, DIGESTIVE

More often than you would think, the indigestion and heartburn you experience are caused not by an excess of acid in your stomach, but by too little. Doctors, for reasons best known to themselves, keep prescribing antacids for all sorts of vague stomach pains, but their patients all too often find them ineffective. If you are in that boat, digestive enzymes might very well be the right answer to your problem. The product, available in many brands, is invariably a good one that has been carefully designed to give your digestive tract the boost it may require in enzyme production.

There are two types available. One will provide only stomach enzymes—chiefly betaine hydrochloride, which is a form of hydrochloric acid, the principal digestive juice of the stomach. It will also contain pepsin and other stomach acids. Many digestive disturbances, though, actually occur in the duodenum, which obtains alkaline digestive juices from the pancreas as well as synthesizing its own. The most complete preparations of digestive enzymes contain, as well as the stomach enzymes, such duodenal enzymes as pancreatin, ox bile, and trypsin. For greatest efficiency, look for those that are prepared for timed release that do not actually release the duodenal enzymes until they reach the duodenum, some two to three hours after swallowing.

FLAX SEED

Contained in many constipation remedies, flax seed is also sold by itself for the same purpose. It works by inducing intestinal irritation which attracts more fluid. If you have a constipation problem, this product will relieve it but will not solve it.

FOOT MASSAGER

You place your foot on top of this nifty electrical device and it vibrates, giving the sole of the foot a stimulating massage. It induces relaxation of the muscles of the foot and thereby relieves aches and pains. Often it is enough to restore your feet after a day's work so that you can go out dancing at night.

GARLIC CAPSULES

See GARLIC in Section 3: Foods and Food Products.

GEROVITAL

This is one of the best known of the preparations claiming to restore youthfulness to the aged and infirm. Based on the anesthetic procaine, it was designed and is still used by Dr. Anna Aslan of Rumania, whose own clinic has a big reputation in the field of rejuvenation. Duplications of the Gerovital formula in the U.S. proved ineffective when tested and it has been banned by the FDA.

The authority of that agency is limited to interstate commerce, however, and Gerovital may be obtained openly in those states that permits its manufacture and sale. Las Vegas is the big center in the United States and the trade in Gerovital flourishes in Mexico. It is also sold under the counter in many health food stores.

Since there is no government supervision of its manufacture, if you buy Gerovital you have no assurance at all that it is Dr. Aslan's formula you are getting. Nor have you any assurance that what you buy does not contain ingredients that will harm you. Even if, by chance, the Gerovital you buy should be Dr. Aslan's exact formula, it is still a drug product with nothing natural about it, which makes it hard to see why a health food store committed to the avoidance of drugs and chemicals of all kinds should bother with it. Nevertheless, there is an illicit traffic in this drug, whose value is questionable at best.

GLUTAMINE

Found to have improved the intelligence of retarded children, glutamine has now been overpromoted as a food for the brain. It is an amino acid which is synthesized by our own bodies and also found in many foods. Despite the reputation it has been given, it is doubtful whether glutamine tablets will have any effect whatsoever on your intelligence.

GRAPEFRUIT DIET PILLS

The Grapefruit Diet, like all crash diets, is dangerous to follow. It becomes even more dangerous if you use these pills of concentrated grapefruit rather than the whole fruit. Even though they have vitamins C and E added, they in no way fulfill your nutritional requirements to stay alive and healthy.

HAIR-BUILDING VITAMINS AND MINERALS

See the listings under COSMETICS in this section.

HEALING LOTIONS FOR THE SKIN

These preparations are based on allantoin, which does speed the healing of abrasions and chapping. They also contain an oil to make the skin feel smoother. See the lotions listings under COSMETICS in this section for fuller information.

HEART, DEHYDRATED

If you are one of those few who believe that eating the heart of an animal will improve the condition of your own heart, it is available in tablets, carefully dehydrated to preserve all its nutrients. But don't rely on it. The heart and other organ meats are excellent foods, but a few tablets a day will not give you enough of them to make any difference.

HEATING PADS

These are the same heating pads you can get just about everywhere, and a great comfort if you have sore muscles or vague pains. The heat induces greater activity of the blood in the affected area. The pads can be used either moist or dry.

HEME

A treatment for iron deficiency anemia, heme is the iron-transporting fraction of the red blood cells, and heme iron is the best absorbed and utilized of all forms of iron supplements. Peculiarly, it has never been popular nor is it much recommended by doctors.

But it is very good for the purpose. If you need supplemental iron, heme is the way to take it. For additional information, see IRON in Section 1: Vitamins and Minerals.

HERNIA SUPPORTS

There is no difference between the ones in health food stores and those you can buy in any drugstore. If you need one, get it where it costs the least.

HOT WATER BOTTLES

It probably makes no difference at all, but having a choice, your health food store will carry only those hot water bottles that are made of natural rubber. It costs a bit more than synthetic rubber or plastics and that makes it a poor buy.

IRON

See IRON in Section 1: Vitamins and Minerals.

KIDNEY, DEHYDRATED

Kidneys are an excellent food and, properly prepared, can be delicious. But in tablets of the desiccated kidney substance you can hardly obtain enough of the food value to make any difference in your diet. Actually, this product is made for those who believe that by eating a small amount of kidney every day, they will improve the health and function of their own kidneys. Not many people believe this.

LACTASE

Newly arrived on the market, lactase is the enzyme that splits milk sugar into simpler forms that can be digested. Dark-skinned races tend to lose their ability to produce this enzyme early in child-hood, while many Caucasians also lose it with advancing age. If you drink milk and can't produce lactase, the milk will cause intestinal pains, gas, and diarrhea. Adding lactase directly to the milk solves the problem.

LAETRILE

This is the best known of today's unapproved and officially banned cancer treatments. Within the health food movement there is an extensive and enthusiastic subdivision of people who believe fully in Laetrile and consider its banning a conspiracy of wealthy cancer specialists in the medical profession. It is freely obtainable in Mexico and in several states that permit its internal manufacture and sale, and it is sold under the counter in many health food stores.

Laetrile is extracted from apricot kernels and is administered both intravenously and through tablets taken by mouth. It has a high cyanide content, which those who believe in the treatment say is poisonous only to cancer cells, leaving normal cells unharmed. Most authorities disagree. However, chemotherapeutic agents generally are materials that are poisonous but are more poisonous to cancer cells than to the rest of the body, and as such can sometimes destroy or reduce the tumor while the patient manages to survive. If Laetrile should ultimately be found to have this much value, it might well ultimately be generally employed as a cancer treatment. It is also claimed to have a palliative effect, reducing the pain and suffering of patients it cannot cure.

Because Laetrile contains cyanide, which is a poison, it should not be taken by anyone without close medical supervision.

LAXATIVES

The natural laxative carried in a health food store contains flax seed and psyllium, both of which provide effective temporary relief from constipation. They are not quite as gentle as might be desired, however. A more lasting and much more pleasant way of improving the condition is to increase the proportion of foods containing indigestible fiber in your daily diet.

LOOFA SPONGE

This is a natural sponge with a rough texture that makes it a good massaging material to make the skin tingle and bring the blood to the surface. There is a widespread belief, considered baloney by most authorities, that female bodies accumulate on their hips and thighs a special type of fat that has been labeled cellulite, and that it takes vigorous massage to break it down and get rid of it. If you consider yourself afflicted with the possibly nonexistent cellulite, the Loofa sponge is what is recommended for massaging. You can buy it as a sponge or shaped into a mitt that you slip on your hand.

LYSINE

This essential amino acid has had some success in helping people to overcome infections by the herpes virus. Such infections occur chiefly around the mouth where they are known as cold sores, but they have also affected enough women in the vaginal region to create a marked problem. The infections are both painful and remarkably persistent, resisting all the treatments that have been found able to eliminate other types of viruses. If you have a herpes infection, there is no guarantee that lysine will cure you, but it is certainly worth a try. Use the high-potency 500 milligram tablets that are made for this purpose.

MAGNESIUM OROTATE

Magnesium is one of the minerals required by the heart, and it is chiefly for protection against a second heart attack that a prominent German physician gives his patients magnesium orotate. As with all minerals, it is a problem to get the body to absorb as much as it may need. Orotic acid is believed to be an excellent transporter that somehow gets more of the magnesium absorbed directly into the heart muscle than does any other of several dozen different transporters.

MASSAGE MITT

To give yourself a vigorous massage that will give your skin something of a beating, yet not scratch or tear it, some kind of special rough material is required. It might well be a terry washcloth, but if you prefer, you can buy a mitt that has its palm covered with hundreds of rubber pimples. It will do the job. See also LOOFA SPONGE in this section.

NEGATIVE IONIZER

This is an electronic device that adds electrons to molecules of air, giving them a temporary negative charge. Air pollutants such as pollen and smoke particles are usually carried through the air by molecules with a positive charge. When these molecules are neutralized or made negative, the pollutants leave them and drop to the ground. This principle makes the negative ionizer an effective air cleaner that has been of help to asthmatics. It is especially useful in smoggy areas.

Some negative ionizers produce ozone, which is the main toxic ingredient of smog. In buying one, be sure to check the technical information which will tell you whether or not ozone is produced. If it is, get a different make.

OVARIES AND UTERUS, DEHYDRATED

With desiccation processes that retain the active enzymes and hormones in tissues, these tablets of female organ tissues are used by women during or after the menopause. Synthetic estrogen, which has proven hazardous in replacement therapy, is best avoided, yet some women feel they do need the replacement therapy. Whole ovarian and uterine tissue will provide small doses of the dwindling hormones in as natural a condition as can be achieved, so that no adverse reactions should be stimulated. These hormones are very powerful and should be taken only under medical supervision.

OXYGEN

With many people requiring frequent emergency supplies of oxygen, kits for breathing the pure gas are sold in drugstores and also in health food stores. There is no difference between them.

PANCREAS, DEHYDRATED

This organ produces both the insulin that controls the level of sugar in the blood and most of the digestive enzymes that operate in the duodenum. When pancreatic function becomes inefficient, serious health problems result. In theory, these tablets of pancreatic tissue contain the food elements that a pancreas requires for regeneration and full function. There is no evidence as to how well it works, if at all.

PAPAIN

The enzyme of the papaya fruit has the faculty of dissolving protein. It is widely used as a commercial meat tenderizer and is sometimes used as a digestive enzyme as well. It has been found medically that papain injected into a slipped vertebral disk will dissolve some of the disk and sometimes relieve the back pain that a slipped disk causes. People are now taking papain dietarily in the hope that it will have the same effect on an aching back. There is no reason to suppose that it does.

PECTIN CAPSULES

Pectin, the thickening ingredient of jams and jellies, is a nonnutritive fruit product. It has been well established that in passing through the digestive tract pectin removes some of the cholesterol from the bloodstream and promotes regularity of the bowels. It is of confirmed value in the diet and if you don't eat enough fruits to get your pectin in that manner, it's a pretty good idea to take some capsules of pure pectin daily.

PILLOW, SUPPORT

Shaped to keep your head firmly raised while you sleep, these foam support pillows are very useful for people who get stiff necks while sleeping or whose noses get stuffed during the night. Those in the health food store are made of natural rubber, the lighter-weight plastic foams being frowned upon for no good reason.

PITUITARY GLAND, DEHYDRATED

The pituitary is considered by endocrinologists to be the master gland of the body, controlling the functions of all the other glands. Any type of glandular malfunction might have its cause in the pituitary. It is tempting to believe that the eating of desiccated pituitary tissue could preserve or regenerate one's own pituitary function, but there are not many scientists who believe it. The tablets are available if you want to give them a try.

POTASSIUM OROTATE

Potassium is a vital mineral required by the heart muscle and by all body cells for the maintenance of fluid balance. It tends to become depleted as a result of diuretic therapy or whenever the weather or heavy exercise induces heavy sweating. Potassium depletion has a serious effect on the heart, and for its replacement there are some physicians who prefer potassium orotate to any of the dozens of other potassium salts that might be used. If potassium orotate is as efficient as claimed, you would want very low potencies. Too much can be as bad as too little.

PROPOLIS

This product of the beehive works quickly to relieve a sore throat and is otherwise of antiseptic value in the digestive tract. See BEE PROPOLIS in Section III: Foods and Food Products.

PROSTATE GLAND, DEHYDRATED

A healthy young prostate produces and stores hormonal substances that are of value to men. A steady intake of carefully dehydrated prostatic tissue would possibly provide a man whose own prostate is deteriorating with a supplemental supply of these hormonal substances. These materials are both powerful and dangerous, however, and should not be taken except under careful medical supervision.

PROSTATE REMEDIES

With advancing age, the prostate gland enlarges in more than 30 percent of all men. The enlargement creates a pressure that prevents complete emptying of the urinary bladder and leads to bladder and kidney infections and backaches, as well as such minor discomforts as dribbling after urination and having to get up during the night. There has never been a satisfactory medical treatment for the problem, which leaves the field open to all sorts of products claiming to be remedies. Such supposed remedies based entirely on natural ingredients are to be found in health food stores.

The ingredients, which are used in various combinations, include three amino acids—glycine, allanine, and glutamic acid—and pollen, zinc, and magnesium. Although it may be nothing but placebo effect, they do seem to work for some people, and one of them might be worth a try.

SANDALS, MASSAGE

If your feet ache when they get tired, massage helps. These sandals, which have hundreds of small rubber bumps set into their insoles, are supposed to keep massaging your feet while you walk in them. It is less effective than a hand massage but it does have some effect and you can use it anywhere.

SILICON

There is a well-read book by a French author that claims that minerals are transmuted within the body, and that the best way to increase one's calcium supplies is to eat not calcium, but silicon. Horsetail, an herb with a high silicon content, is offered for this purpose. No scientific study has ever seen any evidence of actual transmutation of minerals within the body.

SITZ BATH

If you have hemorrhoids, you can temporarily relieve pain and itching with an anesthetic ointment. Many people have found, though, that the very best treatment is to keep the anal area immaculately clean. That is probably the reason for the success of the sitz bath, which has been employed for hundreds of years. The modern sitz bath is small in size and attached to a toilet seat. You can fill it with a special mineral solution if you like, but just plain warm water will work as well.

SPLEEN

The spleen is a part of the lymphatic system, which is important in protecting against infections yet which deteriorates rapidly in practically everyone. Since its function relates to filtering the blood rather than putting anything into it, it is hard to see what anyone expects to gain from tablets of dehydrated spleen tissue. They are available, however, for anyone who wants them.

STOMACH, DEHYDRATED

The stomach produces but does not store digestive enzymes. There is no particular therapy for which it is recommended, but in case you think you will benefit by consuming tablets of desiccated tissue of all the body organs, stomach is one of them and you can get stomach, too.

SUPEROXIDE DISMUTASE

This enzyme is synthesized within the body in order to neutralize superoxide, a highly toxic form of oxygen that results from many types of radiation, including ultraviolet from the sun and gamma radiation from space. The recent development of many new forms of radiation, such as microwave, radiowave, X ray, and others, is believed by some to create a greater burden of superoxide than the body's own production of dismutase can handle. Supplements of the enzyme are therefore offered and used. Be careful, though. It actually converts superoxide into hydrogen peroxide, which is equally dangerous unless it is further converted by another enzyme, catalase, into water. To increase your supply of catalase, you must eat raw fruits and vegetables. Any cooking will destroy it.

TESTICLES, DEHYDRATED

The testicles produce and store not only sperm cells but also testosterone, an incredibly powerful hormone that stimulates masculine development but is very dangerous in excess. Tablets of dehydrated testicle tissue are offered for sale, but should not be used except on the advice and with the supervision of a doctor.

THERMOMETER TAPE

For those who find the old-fashioned thermometer hard to use, this tape will record the skin temperature in numerals that are easy to read. Since it cannot be used internally, it is not as accurate as a mercury column thermometer.

THYROID, DEHYDRATED

Thyroxin, the thyroid hormone, regulates the rate at which oxygen combines with glucose to produce energy. It is extremely powerful and in excess can produce heart palpitations, tremors, and other unpleasant symptoms. It is therefore available by prescription only, a restriction that apparently does not apply to the whole thyroid gland. These tablets of desiccated thyroid tissues will contain some thyroxin and should only be used with medical supervision. They are considered by some doctors to be a good treatment for atherosclerosis and a good weight-reducing aid.

TISSUE SALTS

See CELL SALTS in this section.

TOOTH POLISHER, ELECTRIC

When your dentist polishes your teeth he uses an electrically rotated brush, and now there is a less powerful home model with which you can polish your own teeth any time you feel like it. It isn't a good idea to polish your teeth very often. It removes some of the surface enamel, which is replaced in time, but the enamel can wear very thin and your teeth become quite sensitive as a result of frequent polishing.

TRYPTOPHAN

This amino acid has been found to help some people fall asleep faster and is widely used as an ingredient in natural substitutes for sleeping pills. It is also available by itself and might as well be used that way, since it is the active ingredient in the compounds. It actually works for relatively few people.

WATER FILTERS

Avoiding more effective chemical elements, these filters are claimed to remove from tap water any added fluorides, chlorine, and particulate polluting elements. They contain charcoal and frequently bone meal to absorb the fluorides. The type that fastens to the water faucet and through which the water pours rapidly is inefficient for the purpose. Those that are more cumbersome but through which the water drips slowly are far more effective. Filtering elements must be changed frequently because once they become saturated they add pollutants to the water, rather than removing them.

WATER PILLS

Nonpharmaceutical in nature, the water pills you will find in a health food store are made up of herbs that are known to increase urination, such as the common dandelion, which in France is called piss-en-lit. They cannot replace the pharmaceutical diuretics that draw sodium out of the tissues to be eliminated from the body with increased urination. Herbal water pills do not eliminate sodium in the same way, and, therefore, the water that is drawn off will be regained by the tissues as soon as additional fluid is imbibed. However, these water pills can be useful in reducing temporary edema, such as occurs in the week before menstruation.

YUCCA

See YUCCA in Section 4: Cosmetics.

INDEX